History of
LATINOS

History of
LATINOS
Exploring Diverse Roots

Pablo R. Mitchell

 GREENWOOD

AN IMPRINT OF ABC-CLIO, LLC
Santa Barbara, California • Denver, Colorado • Oxford, England

Library of Congress Cataloging-in-Publication Data

Mitchell, Pablo.
  History of Latinos : exploring diverse roots / Pablo R. Mitchell.
    pages cm.
  Includes bibliographical references and index.
    ISBN 978–0–313–39349–5 (hard copy : alk. paper) — ISBN 978–0–313–39350–1 (ebook)
    1. Hispanic Americans—History. I. Title.
E184.S75M595   2014
973′.0468—dc23   2014013584

ISBN: 978–0–313–39349–5
EISBN: 978–0–313–39350–1

18 17 16   2 3 4 5

This book is also available on the World Wide Web as an eBook.
Visit www.abc-clio.com for details.

Greenwood
An Imprint of ABC-CLIO, LLC

ABC-CLIO, LLC
130 Cremona Drive, P.O. Box 1911
Santa Barbara, California 93116-1911

This book is printed on acid-free paper ∞

Manufactured in the United States of America

Contents

Preface

Latinas and Latinos have lived, worked, struggled, organized, and thrived in the United States for hundreds of years. Members of separate and distinct communities of Mexicans, Puerto Ricans, Cubans, Dominicans, and Central and South Americans, Latina/os also have a shared and common history. The term "Latina/o" recognizes this shared Latina/o past as well as the primary place of Latinas (women of Latina/o descent) in Latina/o history.

I have taught a Latina/o history course for more than a decade at Oberlin College, and my students have contributed a great deal to this book with their questions and critiques of the class. I have also been fortunate to work with Kim Kennedy-White, Wendi Schnaufer, Subaramya Nambiaruran, Allison Nadeau, and Vanessa Naranjo at ABC-CLIO. Lilia Fernández and Adrian Burgos Jr. generously gave of their precious time and wisdom at a critical spot in this project, and the book has been greatly improved with their help. The Nord Professorship at Oberlin College also provided important financial support to this project, and I am grateful for the continued encouragement of my colleagues and friends at Oberlin College, in northeast Ohio, and throughout the country.

Thanks as well to my brother, Ben Mitchell, my niece, Estella, and my parents, Beatriz and Philip Mitchell, as well as the McLaughlin, Orr, and Lozier families. We are all still grieving the terrible loss of my sister-in-law, Jennifer Orr. She was an incomparable aunt, a wonderful baker, a fierce fan of Pittsburgh and WVU sports (her car's license plate was Jaromir!), and a loyal friend and relative. Her death has left an absence in our lives that is still hard to reckon.

I am most grateful to Beth McLaughlin and our children, Tayo McLaughlin and Ruby Mitchell. They were my constant, much-loved companions throughout the writing of this book. I would be adrift without them.

Introduction

The beginning of the twenty-first century is a period unparalleled in the long history of Latina/os in the United States. Latina/os (people of Latin American descent such as Mexicans, Puerto Ricans, Cubans, Dominicans, and Central and South Americans) have lived in the United States, or parts of North America that would eventually become the United States, for centuries. In fact, the story of Latina/os begins 500 years ago, when the Spanish began to cut their disastrous path through the Caribbean and large swaths of the Americas, decades before other European colonists would begin (in a similar manner) to devastate the northeastern regions of Native North America. Spanish explorers entered New Mexico and what is now the U.S. Southwest in the mid-1500s, and towns like Santa Fe were established at roughly the same time (the early 1600s) as English and French settlements in Jamestown, Virginia, and Quebec, Canada.

Since then, Latina/os have called North America home. In recent years, the Latina/o population of the United States has risen rapidly, from 14.6 million in 1980 to 22.4 million in 1990 to 35.3 million in 2000. In 2010, there were 50.5 million Latina/os in the United States. Included in this U.S. Latina/o population are 32 million ethnic Mexicans, 4 million Central Americans, and 1.5 million Dominicans, with an additional 1.8 million Cuban Americans and 4.6 million Puerto Ricans in the country's mainland. Los Angeles (5.7 million), New York City (4.2 million), and Houston (2 million) are the cities with the country's largest Latina/o populations.

History of Latinos: Exploring Diverse Roots takes a new approach to the history of Latina/os in the United States. In the past, textbooks have divided the histories of Mexicans, Puerto Ricans, Cubans, Dominicans, and Central and South Americans into separate chapters, concentrating on the arrival and settlement of each group in the United States. This book, while paying careful attention to the unique historical trajectory of diverse Latina/o communities, takes a different path, drawing the various groups into a single narrative and highlighting the interactions and shared communities formed by Latinas and Latinos. This shared Latina/o history framework also allows us to see some broader trends in U.S. history such as the unevenness of citizenship and belonging, the middle area that so many people in the past, and in the present, have occupied between exclusion on the one hand and full inclusion and membership in the nation on the other. Each of the following chapters will cover a critical period in Latina/o history, beginning in the 1500s and ending in the first decade of the twenty-first century. Chapters will also include short profiles of important Latinas and Latinos.

History of Latinos is organized around several prominent themes. First, the book points to the deep links that exist between different Latina/o groups. Whether subject to Spanish colonialism in the Americas, forming merchant communities in East Coast cities in the 1800s, or leading contemporary Latina/o civil rights organizations, Latina/os have shared neighborhoods, shared food and culture (including, of course, the Spanish language and the Catholic religion), and shared political battles, creating bonds and intimate connections across communities.

Second, the book will pay close attention to the experiences of women in Latina/o history. Latinas have played a pivotal, though at times unacknowledged, role in all aspects of life in the Latina/o past, from joining in Spanish colonizing efforts in Native American lands, to forging bonds, intimate and business alike, with Anglo-American newcomers, to challenging U.S. and Spanish imperialism, to building new communities across the nation, to leading labor unions and strikes, to taking charge of social justice organizations and serving on the U.S. Supreme Court. Many of the chapter profiles will also be devoted to prominent Latina individuals in U.S. history.

Finally, the book bears witness to the endurance and resilience of Latina/o communities in the United States. Latina/os have faced persistent rhetorical attacks that questioned and ridiculed their ability to become proper U.S. citizens. These attacks in both mainstream and right-wing media outlets have often portrayed Latina/os as sexually deviant, prone to violence, and intellectually and culturally inferior. Latina/os have also suffered acts of violence on individual and community levels. Despite these continued physical and rhetorical attacks, Latina/os have refused to concede their rights as citizens and full members of the United States. Their struggles and triumphs are at the heart of this book.

Chronology of Key Dates
in Latino History

1493   The Spanish arrive on the Caribbean island that will become known as Puerto Rico. Native groups had been living on the island that they named Borinquen for well over 3,000 years when the Spanish arrive.

1510   A major Taino uprising in Puerto Rico kills 200 Spanish colonists. A Spanish counterattack kills a prominent Taino leader, Chief Agüeybaná, and forces the surrender of Taino forces. Many Tainos manage to escape to the interior of the island, where they continue to resist Spanish colonialism and enslavement.

1527   The journey of Álvaro Nuñez Cabeza de Vaca, one of the most famous and important Spanish explorations of North America, sets sail from Spain. After nearly a decade of wandering through Native American lands, Cabeza de Vaca and three other survivors arrive in Mexico City to a hero's welcome in 1536.

1540   Francisco Vásquez de Coronado leads an expedition to the Rio Grande River in central New Mexico. The expedition eventually reaches what is now the state of Kansas before returning to Mexico City.

1610   Santa Fe, New Mexico, is founded.

1680   In a coordinated uprising involving more than two dozen settlements separated by hundreds of miles and six different languages, Pueblo Indians revolt against the Spanish in New Mexico. More than 400 Spaniards are killed, including 21 of the province's 33 Franciscan missionaries.

1731   San Antonio is founded in Texas. Compared to New Mexico, the Spanish population of Texas is relatively small throughout the

1700s. When San Antonio is founded, officials count about 500 members of the Spanish community in the entire province of Texas.

1781   The town of Los Angeles is founded near El Río de la Porciúncula (now the Los Angeles River).

1806   *El Misisipí*, the first U.S. Spanish-language newspaper, is published in New Orleans.

1810   Miguel Hidalgo y Costilla, a priest in the Mexican town of Dolores, organizes mass protests against the Spanish. His September 16th proclamation, the "Grito de Dolores," rallies tens of thousands of Mexicans to join the revolt. Though Hidalgo's rebellion is eventually defeated by forces loyal to the Spanish crown and the priest executed for treason, independence movements persist throughout the decade in Mexico.

1821   Augustín de Iturbide, a wealthy military officer, issues a statement—the Plan de Iguala—that declares Mexico independent of Spain. The Plan de Iguala, which protects the property rights of large landowners and the Church, and institutes a constitutional monarchy to rule Mexico, also grants citizenship to Indians and to Mexicans of African descent.

1821   Two months after formal Mexican independence, an Anglo trader makes the overland journey to Santa Fe. Santa Fe becomes an important stop in an east–west trade artery that comes to be known as the Santa Fe Trail. The growth of trade along the Santa Fe Trail shifts the orientation of many Mexicans in the region from focusing southward to central Mexico to looking eastward to the United States.

1836   Tensions over slavery and the consolidation of political, economic, and military power in Mexico City lead to war in Texas. The Texas revolt, which began in 1835, continues through the winter and into the spring of 1836, including the Mexican victory at the Alamo in San Antonio. After several severe Mexican defeats, Texas wins its independence in late spring 1836.

1830s   Merchants from Puerto Rico and Cuba in New York City form the Sociedad Benéfica Cubana y Puertorriqueña (Cuban and Puerto Rican Benevolent Society).

1844   The Dominican Republic achieves its independence from Haiti. In the immediate postindependence period, leaders of the Dominican Republic and the United States establish diplomatic relations and increasingly discuss the annexation of the newly independent nation to its larger neighbor to the north.

1846   The Mexican-American War begins between the United States and Mexico. The war ends two years later, in 1848, with the Treaty of Guadalupe Hidalgo.

1847   A year after U.S. troops invaded northern New Mexico and established a military government, an armed rebellion of 2,000 Mexicans and Pueblo Indians kill more than two dozen Anglos and Mexicans, including the governor of New Mexico. The final battle leaves 150 insurgents dead and is followed by mass trials for treason. U.S. officials ultimately execute more than a dozen Northern New Mexicans for their participation in the uprising.

1848   A peace treaty between Mexico and the United States, the Treaty of Guadalupe Hidalgo, ends the Mexican-American War. According to the provisions of the treaty, the Rio Grande, not the Nueces River, becomes the new border between the two countries. In addition, large portions of the Mexican North are placed under U.S. rule and Mexico receives $15 million from the United States. The treaty also includes a provision stating that Mexicans who decide to stay in formerly Mexican, now U.S., territories will be guaranteed protection of their property rights. A critical provision of the Treaty of Guadalupe Hidalgo is the promise that Mexicans remaining in the United States will receive the rights of U.S. citizenship.

1854   The newspaper *El Mulato* is published by Cuban exiles in New York City. While many exile leaders seek the support of the United States, including slave-owning sections of the United States, *El Mulato* strongly opposes slavery and calls for a recognition of the important role of Afro-Cubans in the country's history and culture.

1858   A group of exiled Cuban poets in New Orleans publishes *El laúd del destierro* (*The Exile's Lute*). The first Spanish-language collection of poetry in the United States, the anthology attempts to fuse artistic production with calls for revolution and Cuban independence.

1867   Ramón Betances, a Puerto Rican physician of mixed African and European descent, and members of the Sociedad Republicana de Cuba and Puerto Rico issue from New York City Betances's "Ten Commandments of Free Men" ("Los Diez Mandamientos de Hombres Libres"). The proclamation will become one of the key documents of the Puerto Rican independence movement. The first of the 10 demands calls for the abolition of slavery, and the list includes claims of freedom of speech, of worship, of the press, of the right to bear arms, and of the right to elect one's own government officials.

1868   Puerto Rican rebels, based in the mountain town of Lares, take up arms against both slavery and continued Spanish rule on the island in the Lares Revolt.

1868   Cuban independence leaders lead an armed rebellion against Spanish authorities. The ensuing war (the Ten Years War) will last until 1878.

1876   The Southern Pacific Railroad links Los Angeles with San Francisco, and the city's population soon begins to rise, especially its Anglo population. The 1870 population of LA of 5,700 almost doubles in 1880 to 11,000 and is more than 100,000 in 1900.

1885   María Ruiz de Burton publishes her most famous novel, *The Squatter and the Don*. In the book, a romance between a Mexican woman and an Anglo man, Ruiz de Burton criticizes U.S. politics and big business, pointedly attacking the displacement and forced land loss of Mexican communities in the U.S. West.

1891   José Martí's essay "Our America" describes the link between the descendants of Spanish colonialism, bringing together Mexicans, Puerto Ricans, Cubans, Dominicans, and other Latin Americans under one group. He describes this group as fundamentally different from those inhabitants of places influenced by the history of English, French, or other forms of European colonialism. In this way, Martí is one of the earliest writers to speak of a shared Latino history. Martí also identifies the imperialist tendencies of the United States and argues that the annexation of Mexican land in 1848 was just the first step in U.S. imperialist ambitions.

1895   Poet and political organizer Jose Martí helps lead an uprising against Spanish rule in Cuba. The revolt, a multiracial movement that includes peasants, elites, and middle-class Cubans, will eventually help lead to the Spanish-American War in 1898.

1898   After decades of anti-Spanish organizing and military uprisings by Cuban and Puerto Rican independence leaders, the United States declares war on Spain after the USS *Maine* explodes in the Havana harbor. By July 1898, Spain surrenders and the war ends. After the war, the United States proceeds to occupy Cuba and Puerto Rico with a military government.

1898   In the aftermath of the war between Spain and the United States, U.S. troops install a military government in Puerto Rico. The ensuing U.S. occupation dramatically alters Puerto Rico's economy. The country's agricultural sector is increasingly based on exports, rather than on subsistence farming and addressing the daily living needs of Puerto Ricans.

1903   The Platt Amendment states that the United States will end the military occupation of Cuba if Cuba provides land for U.S. military installations (land that eventually becomes the U.S.-controlled Guantánamo Bay military base). The Platt Amendment is incorporated into the Cuban-American Treaty. The Platt Amendment and the Cuban-American Treaty are instrumental in North American businesses' eventual domination of the Cuban sugar industry and contribute to decades of anti-U.S. sentiment among Cuban nationalists.

1910   The dislocation and violence of the Mexican Revolution, as well as the promise of jobs and higher wages in the United States, lead to thousands of Mexicans immigrating to the United States. By 1920, there are nearly 500,000 Mexican-born people in the United States.

1916   The U.S. military invades the Dominican Republic. The military occupation lasts until 1924, and during this period, the United States helps train the Dominican military, including the man who will come to dominate the Dominican Republic for the next 30 years, the eventual president Rafael Trujillo.

1917   The Jones Act imposes U.S. citizenship on Puerto Ricans. The Jones Act also requires military service for Puerto Rican men. Young men are sent to the mainland with their army groups and are introduced to U.S. customs and culture. For many, this introduction offers a chance to become more familiar with the United States and nurtures the idea of possibly moving to the mainland after their military service is completed.

1922   A strong supporter of women's right to vote, Adelina Otero Warren decides to run for Congress in New Mexico in 1922. Though revelations of her divorce, which previously had not been widely publicized, hurt her campaign, she nonetheless loses by only a slim margin in the general election.

1923   The Puerto Rican Brotherhood is founded in New York City. The Brotherhood's activities include defending Puerto Rican men incorrectly charged with being non-U.S. citizens, providing aid to impoverished Puerto Rican families, and covering the burial expenses of poor Puerto Ricans.

1924   The National Origins Act severely restricts immigration to the United States and sets a quota for immigrants from particular countries. As a result, a major source of workers from Europe and Asia is cut off, leaving many more entry-level, manual labor jobs available for Puerto Ricans, who are newly designated as U.S. citizens.

1925   Puerto Rico's first birth control group, Liga para el control de natalidad de Puerto Rico (Birth Control League of Puerto Rico), is founded by a socialist activist.

1928   The Imperial Valley Cantaloupe Strike is organized by La Union Trabajadores del Valle Imperial (the Imperial Valley Workers Union).

1929   The League of United Latin American Citizens (LULAC) is founded in Corpus Christi, Texas. LULAC leaders are typically attorneys, restaurant owners, teachers, and small-business people. Unlike some groups, which base their organizations on mutual co-operation between Mexican immigrants and Mexican Americans, LULAC excludes all non-U.S. citizens from membership. Members also campaign for voter registration, desegregation of public facilities ("No blacks or Mexicans" is sadly a common sign in Texas well into the twentieth century), and more representation of Mexican Americans on Texas juries.

1929   When the U.S. economy collapses and the Great Depression begins, Mexicans, regardless of their citizenship status, are blamed for supposedly taking "American" jobs and straining government efforts to support needy families. Local repatriation efforts seek to deport Mexicans from large cities throughout the West and Midwest. Hundreds of thousands of people of Mexican descent return to Mexico during the 1930s. Those Mexicans who manage to endure the attacks and remain in their homes and communities in the United States, however, form a new and lasting commitment to their rights as U.S. citizens.

1930   Mexican parents of children in Lemon Grove, California, take the school district to court to force it to halt its practice of segregating Mexican girls and boys from Anglo children. The parents, in alliance with government officials from Mexico and Anglo allies, win their suit.

1930   A lawsuit seeking to ban segregation of Mexican schoolchildren from their Anglo counterparts by the Del Rio, Texas, school district is filed by parents of Mexican students.

1932   The children's story "Pérez and Martina" by Pura Bélpre is published. The main characters of the story, Pérez the Mouse and

Martina the Cockroach, pursue an ill-fated romance. The tale touches on themes that Bélpre, a New York City librarian, will follow throughout her long literary career, such as animal fables, the use of trickster figures, and concern with poverty and unhealthy living conditions.

1933   The *Revista de Artes y Letras*, one of the most prominent Spanish-language periodicals, is founded by a Puertorriqueña, Josefina Silva de Cintron, in New York City.

1934   Historian Jovita González publishes *Dew on the Thorn*, exploring the lives of Mexicans in South Texas at the turn of the twentieth century. *Dew on the Thorn* balances an appreciation of Mexican folklore and culture along the border with a sharp critique of U.S. imperialism and the dispossession and denigration of Mexican communities at the hands of Anglo newcomers.

1938   Labor activist and union organizer Emma Tenayuca leads a major strike of pecan shellers, most of them Mexican women, in San Antonio.

1939   Labor activist Luisa Moreno helps lead the planning of *El Congreso de Pueblos de Hablan Española* in Los Angeles. *El Congreso* is a major civil rights conference addressing important issues like employment, housing, and education for Latina/os.

1940   With her characteristic headdress filled with tropical fruit (the "tutti-frutti" hat), Carmen Miranda stars in a series of hit films in the early 1940s. By 1945, Miranda has an income of $200,000 and is the highest-paid woman in the United States.

1942   Mexico and the United States agree to a system to allow labor contracts for Mexican farmworkers to come to the Southwest to work. Under the program, hundreds of thousands of impoverished Mexican men will eventually abandon their rural communities and head north to work as contract laborers, also known as "braceros." Abuses in the Bracero Program, especially in terms of the poor work and living conditions provided by employers, are widespread.

1942   Los Angeles police round up more than 500 mostly Mexican young people and indict nearly two dozen for the murder of José Diaz, a Mexican immigrant, at the Sleepy Lagoon reservoir near Los Angeles, California. The trial, riddled with legal errors, captures the city's attention for several months, and the young men are eventually convicted and sentenced to long prison terms. Determined family and community members help organize appeals of the convictions, however, and the case is finally overturned by a California higher court.

1943   Anglo sailors and other servicemen on leave rampage through downtown Los Angeles, targeting young men wearing "zoot suits," a fashion style associated with Mexican youth culture. LA police officials refuse to intervene, and the rioting continues for days, often with the support of Anglo residents of the city, before officers finally step in to halt the violence and the terrorizing of Mexican young men and women.

1946   In a landmark civil rights case from Southern California (*Méndez v. Westminster*), Mexican parents and civil rights attorneys force the local school district to abandon its policy of requiring separate schools for Anglo and Mexican children.

1947   Operation Bootstrap, or Operación Manos a La Obra, is initiated in Puerto Rico. The program, a broad, dual-focused plan, seeks both to lure North American industries to relocate to the island and to stimulate migration out of Puerto Rico to the U.S. mainland (an aim justified by supposed "overpopulation" on the island). Under the plan, U.S. businesses are encouraged to recruit Puerto Rican contract laborers to supply their employment needs.

1947   The Puerto Rican government establishes the Migration Division, with offices in the U.S. Midwest and Northeast, which seeks to place workers both in agricultural jobs, where they harvest fruits, vegetables, and tobacco, and in heavy industry like railroads and steel factories. Puerto Rican women are also actively recruited as domestic workers.

1948   *Perez v. Sharp* is decided by the California Supreme Court. Andrea Perez, of Mexican descent but labeled "White" according to the government, and Sylvester Davis, an African American, had applied for a marriage license in Los Angeles but were denied the right to marry on the grounds that their marriage would violate California's law against intermarriage. Perez and Davis successfully challenge the constitutionality of the law. *Perez v. Sharp* foreshadows a point when American courts will abandon their reliance on racial categories in marriage law. Twenty years later, in the case *Loving v. Virginia* (1967), the U.S. Supreme Court rules that laws banning intermarriage are unconstitutional across the nation.

1951   More than 1,000 ethnic Mexican miners lead a strike at the Empire Zinc mine in southwestern New Mexico. An alliance between the New Mexico state militia and the Empire Zinc mine owners does not end the strike and subsequent negotiations lead to gains for workers. The Empire Zinc strike subsequently becomes the subject of the movie *Salt of the Earth* (1954).

1951   Cuban musician Desi Arnaz and his wife, Lucille Ball, star together in the sitcom *I Love Lucy*. The show is a major hit, becoming one of the most popular television shows of the 1950s, and lasts six seasons, until 1957.

1952   Puerto Rico becomes a commonwealth of the United States.

1954   In *Hernandez v. Texas*, Pete Hernandez, who was convicted of murder by an all-Anglo jury in Jackson County, Texas, challenges his conviction on the grounds that Mexicans had been intentionally excluded from juries in the county for decades. The U.S. Supreme Court eventually rules in favor of Hernandez and orders a new trial.

1954   Four Puerto Rican activists, including their leader, Lolita Lebron, fire weapons at members of the U.S. Congress. As they display the Puerto Rican flag, Lebron shouts, "Free Puerto Rico now!" Five members of Congress are hurt, some severely, but no one is killed. The four Puerto Ricans, including Lebron, are captured and receive long prison sentences.

1959   Fidel Castro leads the overthrow of U.S.-backed Cuban president Fulgencio Batista. Diplomatic, commercial, and cultural ties are broken between the two countries and the once vibrant transnational exchange dissolves. In the next three years, nearly a quarter million Cubans leave the island for the United States.

1961   President Rafael Trujillo is assassinated and his tyrannical grip on the Dominican Republic, often with the support of the U.S. government, comes to an end.

1961   Community organizer Antonia Pantoja founds ASPIRA, which focuses on improving educational opportunities for Puerto Rican youth.

1961   The film *West Side Story* wins 10 Oscars, including Best Picture, and showcases the talents of Puerto Rican singer and dancer Rita Moreno. Moreno wins an Oscar for *West Side Story* (she portrays the character "Anita") and goes on to be the only Latina, and one of very few women or men, to win an Oscar, an Emmy, a Grammy, and a Tony award.

1965   The U.S. government sends 40,000 troops to the Dominican Republic during antigovernment protests. The U.S. invasion helps ensure the rule of conservative forces led by Joaquín Balaguer, a former aide of Rafael Trujillo.

1965   The Hart-Celler Act abolishes national origins quotas, which had
        been established 40 years earlier in the National Origins Act of
        1924, and dramatically revises the visa system to give preference
        in admissions to families and relatives. After the Hart-Celler Act,
        immigration to the United States begins to rise steadily, and Latin
        Americans and Asians form the large majority of new, post-1965
        immigrants.

1965   Mexican farmworkers join Filipino workers in a strike against
        grape growers in Delano, California. The strike, which Cesar
        Chavez and Dolores Huerta help lead, lasts for several years and
        results in important victories for Mexican farm laborers.

1967   Rodolfo "Corky" Gonzales, a political activist and community
        organizer from Denver, Colorado, writes the poem "Yo Soy
        Joaquín," which celebrates the endurance of Mexican people under
        U.S. colonial rule.

1967   The Brown Berets are founded in Los Angeles, California. The
        Brown Berets lead protests against the inferior state of public
        schools for Mexican children, the lack of political response among
        civic leaders, and more national concerns such as the Vietnam War.

1968   The Young Lords Organization, which eventually is renamed the
        Young Lords Party (YLP), is founded in Chicago. The multiracial
        organization soon establishes branches in other major midwestern
        and eastern cities. The New York City chapter becomes one of the
        most prominent YLP groups and is characterized by its commit-
        ment to Puerto Rican civil rights on the mainland, by its support
        of reproductive rights, and for championing the Puerto Rican
        independence movement on the island.

1970   Dissatisfied with the traditional party structure in South Texas, La
        Raza Unida Party (LRUP) is formed. Focusing on immediate
        results, LRUP begins to register voters in several counties and
        within a few months manages to win all the seats on the Crystal
        City, Texas, school board and to elect two of the five members of
        the city council. LRUP candidates are also elected mayors in two
        other Texas towns.

1974   Latina/o organizers in San Francisco found the Spanish-language
        newspaper *Gaceta Sandinista*, which is the only newspaper in the
        United States specifically supporting the Sandinista movement.
        The Sandinistas are a Nicaraguan rebel movement that eventually
        succeeds in overthrowing the country's U.S.-backed regime in
        1979.

1975   GALA, the Gay Latino Alliance, is founded in the San Francisco
        Bay Area and becomes one of the first Latina/o gay organizations
        to gain national visibility. In addition to political activism, the
        group sponsors social events like dances and parades.

1975   The Voting Rights Act of 1965 is extended to cover Latina/os as
        well as Asian Americans and Native Americans. The extension of
        the Voting Rights Act also provides for the distribution of bilingual
        voting materials and helps ensure the existence of majority Latina/o
        voting districts.

1980   After Cuban president Fidel Castro announces that all those inter-
        ested in leaving the island can depart from the port city of Mariel,
        tens of thousands of Cubans soon race to the coast, eager to leave
        the island and make a new home outside of Cuba. As a result,
        between April and October 1980, 125,000 Cubans, mostly in boats
        and rafts, migrate to the United States, mainly to South Florida and
        the city of Miami.

1981   Mujeres Latinas en Acción (MLEA) joins with another women's
        organization to establish the first battered women's shelter in
        Chicago to serve primarily Spanish-speaking women. Formed in
        the 1970s, the group also provides services such as day care, health
        care, and legal assistance.

1984   The group Mothers of East Los Angeles (MELA) form to protest
        the construction of a prison in their neighborhood in East Los
        Angeles. MELA also focuses on a range of environmental justice
        issues, including plans to construct an incinerator in East LA, graf-
        fiti cleanup, and raising financial aid support for college-bound
        local young people.

1986   The Immigration and Reform Control Act provides new funding
        for the Border Patrol and requires that employers ensure that their
        workers have entered the country with proper documentation.
        The law also contains an amnesty program that offers permanent
        residency status in the United States to undocumented immigrants
        who can prove that they have lived in the country continuously
        since 1982 and have taken required English-language and civics
        classes.

1987   Gloria Anzaldúa's book *Borderlands/La Frontera: The New
        Mestiza* is published and becomes a classic in the fields of Chicana/o
        Studies, Queer Studies, Ethnic Studies, and Women's Studies.

2008   Dominican American Junot Díaz receives the Pulitzer Prize for his
        novel *The Brief Wondrous Life of Oscar Wao*.

2009   Sonia Sotomayor, a Puerto Rican from New York City, becomes the first Latina/o to serve on the U.S. Supreme Court.

2010   The Latina/o population of the United States grows from 35 million in 2000 to reach 50 million. In 2010, Latina/os represent 16 percent of the U.S. population.

_____ *Chapter 1* _____

Latina/o Beginnings, 1500–1800

American history is filled with tales of great explorers and daring journeys through distant and wondrous lands. While European explorers hailed from many nations and spoke many languages, most of the earliest explorers of what has become the United States were Spanish. In fact, Spanish expeditions traversed the American Southwest (now the states of Texas, New Mexico, Arizona, and California) decades before the appearance of English settlers on the eastern shores of North America. Spanish-speaking communities were also well established in the Southwest and in Florida by the time the Pilgrims arrived in Plymouth in the 1620s. For three centuries—from the mid-1500s to the mid-1800s—the primary European language spoken over a major portion of North America was not English or French, but Spanish.

The first major island occupied by the Spanish after the arrival of Columbus in 1492 was Española (now the countries of the Dominican Republic and Haiti). Military expeditions, led by Spanish soldiers and bolstered by hundreds of Indians, the vast majority undoubtedly coerced or enslaved into service, soon overwhelmed Puerto Rico, Cuba, and other Caribbean islands. From Cuba, Spanish expeditions journeyed westward in the early 1500s, to Mexico under Hernán Cortés, and northward with the Pánfilo de Narváez expedition, which began Cabeza de Vaca's long sojourn through the region (see below), and Hernando de Soto's military campaign throughout many of the present-day states of the American South.

One of the most famous and important Spanish explorations of North America was the journey of Álvaro Nuñez Cabeza de Vaca. Cabeza de Vaca, a prominent Spanish government official, was appointed in 1527 to help establish a colony in "la Florida," which stretched from the southern tip of modern-day Florida along the Gulf Coast to the Río de las Palmas, north

The Spanish invasion of the Caribbean led by Christopher Columbus was one of the founding events of Latina/o history. (National Archives)

of the Mexican coastal city of Vera Cruz. The expedition planned to settle the region, and on board the ships that sailed from Spain were Spanish soldiers, sailors, merchants, farmers, physicians, carpenters, priests, and a handful of women, many of them traveling alongside their husbands. There were also African slaves, including a man named Esteban who was enslaved by Captain Andrés Dorantes, another passenger on the voyage. Esteban was from Morocco in northwest Africa and probably had been first enslaved by the Portuguese and then sold into Spanish slavery.

On June 17, 1527, the expedition, led by a Spanish official, Pánfilo de Narváez, left Spain with five ships and 600 passengers. In September, the ships landed on the island of Española, where 140 men promptly deserted. The expedition was then nearly wiped out by a hurricane in Cuba before embarking in spring 1528 toward the north coast of Mexico. Bad luck struck again, however, and a major navigational error led the ships to the west coast of Florida, near present-day Tampa Bay, rather than to the Mexican mainland.

In Florida, the expedition split in two. One group of about 300 men explored the region on foot, and the rest, numbering about a hundred, including the crew of the ships and the 10 women, navigated the coast by ship. The two groups never reunited, though the ships searched for the men for a year before returning to Cuba. The crew on land wandered for six months in Florida, fighting hostile Indians, and diseases like malaria and dysentery, before building five 30-foot rafts and heading west along the Gulf Coast toward Mexico. In November 1528, two rafts and 80 men landed on a string of islands near what is now Galveston, Texas. The rafts were soon lost and all but 15 of the men died, perishing of cold, hunger, disease, drowning, or violence at the hands of nearby Indians.

After six years of living with both hostile and friendly Native peoples, Cabeza de Vaca and three other survivors (Andrés Dorantes, Alonso del Castillo Maldonado, and Esteban) resolved to try again to reach Spanish territory in Mexico. They headed south toward Mexico, then turned inland, living with several Native communities and gaining reputations as medical healers. As they crossed east to west through northern Mexico, they were often accompanied by hundreds of Indian guides and supporters. In January 1536, the four men finally stumbled upon a group of Spanish soldiers on a slaving expedition, and their eight-year journey through major sections of North America was at last over. By July 1536, the four had arrived in Mexico City to a hero's welcome.

The four survivors' tales thrilled their Spanish audiences in the capital city. In hopes of fabulous riches to the north that would rival Spanish conquests in Mexico City and Peru, Spanish officials in 1539 sent a small expedition northward to investigate rumors of cities of gold. Pointing to the critical role of Catholicism in the Spanish exploration and settlement of the Southwest, at the head of the expedition was a Franciscan priest, Fray Marcos de Niza. Also helping to guide the journey was Esteban, one of the four survivors of the Cabeza de Vaca journey. African-born Esteban, too, was a harbinger of the future as Afro-Spanish women and men formed a significant part of Spanish communities throughout the colonial era. The de Niza expedition, during which Esteban died under mysterious circumstances, proved encouraging after de Niza, upon his return, reported (erroneously as later explorers would discover to their deep disappointment and regret) that cities of gold in fact existed and that he himself had seen them with his own eyes.

Another, far larger expedition was soon organized under the leadership of Francisco Vásquez de Coronado, a wealthy, 30-year-old provincial governor. Coronado's force numbered more than 1,000 and, like so many European explorations before and since, depended on the labor and military support of hundreds of indigenous people (by some accounts, the number of indigenous people was 800). The expedition followed de Niza and Esteban's path into present-day Arizona and then to the Rio Grande River in central New Mexico, where they met and at times fought with Pueblo Indians. The Pueblo communities, stretching hundreds of miles, numbered

40,000 in dozens of towns. Increasingly frustrated by the absence of gold, the Coronado expedition moved north and then east, compelling provisions (often by force) from Pueblo town after town, until finally reaching what is now the state of Kansas. Conceding defeat, Coronado returned to Mexico City in failure.

Meanwhile, Spanish ships began sailing along the Pacific coast of Mexico in the 1530s. By the end of the decade, explorers had charted the 800-mile-long Baja California peninsula, including the head of the Gulf of California, which was named the Sea of Cortés. In 1542, Juan Rodríguez Cabrillo accepted an offer to lead an expedition up the Pacific coast and then, if possible, attempt to reach China. In September 1542, while anchored in the bay of San Diego, a team of Ipai Indians attacked a group of Spaniards who had gone ashore to fish. The Ipai had apparently heard, through extensive Native communication networks, tales of bearded men marauding through the coastal interior killing and enslaving Native people (much like the Spanish slaving expedition that first encountered Cabeza de Vaca and his fellow castaways) and launched their arrows in a preemptive strike against the Spanish. Cabrillo wisely moved his ships quickly up the coast. The expedition visited Catalina Island, off the bay of San Pedro on the coast of what is now Los Angeles, and reached as far as present-day Santa Barbara, before storms forced them to spend the winter on Catalina. Cabrillo died that winter of 1542, after falling on slippery rocks and shattering his shinbone, leading to a fatal infection. In the spring, the expedition continued north up the California coast, eventually reaching the present-day Oregon border before turning back, unable to reach China and with little in the way of new treasure for the Spanish crown.

To the east, Spanish expeditions explored other regions of North America that would eventually become part of the United States. In 1513, Juan Ponce de León and his crew landed on Florida's Atlantic coast, near present-day Cape Canaveral, Florida. Ponce de León named the region "la Florida" for the Easter celebration that was occurring when he first sighted land. The expedition continued south along the Atlantic seaboard of Florida, reaching what is now Miami and the Florida Keys. Though he and his crew mapped the area, Ponce de León did not manage to establish permanent settlement or military bases in Florida.

In all, despite some promising explorations, the Spanish were discouraged by the apparent lack of riches to the north. Spanish officials, therefore, for several decades offered little support to plans to explore or settle the region. By the end of the sixteenth century, however, the increasing presence of English and other Europeans in North America persuaded Spanish officials to attempt to settle what is now the southwestern United States and establish a barrier to further European intrusion in the region. Juan de Oñate, born of substantial wealth and with years of military experience, was selected to lead the settler colony, and the initial company of 130 soldiers and their families departed for New Mexico in 1598. The expedition moved steadily northward and eventually established several small settlements in central and northern New Mexico. Their path would, in time, become the famous Camino de Real, also known as the Chihuahua Trail, an overland trade route covering nearly 2,000 miles and for centuries linking New Mexico southward to the interior of Mexico. Like English settlers in Virginia, who founded Jamestown in 1607, the presence of Spanish settlers and Spanish-speaking towns like Santa Fe (founded in 1610), in what is now the United States, thus dates back more than 400 years.

As in so many colonial endeavors (including those of the United States), the Spanish colonization of New Mexico was filled with violence and the exploitation of Native communities. One of the lowest points of the Oñate expedition was an attack on the Pueblo Indian community of Acoma in western New Mexico in 1598. Located atop an imposing mesa, Acoma villagers refused to concede fully to Oñate's demands and a pitched battle ensued. After a three-day siege and the deaths of 800 villagers, the Acoma surrendered to the Spanish. Enraged and hoping to send a signal to other Pueblo communities that may have been determined to resist Spanish advances, Oñate condemned hundreds of Acoma residents to slavery, including children, who were awarded to Spanish priests and soldiers as household slaves. Men over 25 were further sentenced to the severing of one foot.

The violence of Spanish colonization extended to religious matters as well. A driving force motivating Spanish settlement of New Mexico was the potential conversion of Native peoples to Catholicism. Recall that Fray Marcos de Niza, a Franciscan priest, had led an earlier expedition into the region, and Franciscan missionaries were among the first Spanish settlers in the early 1600s in the Southwest. Eager to convert Pueblo Indians, but no less disdainful of their culture and customs than Spanish soldiers, townspeople, or government officials, Franciscans set themselves to the task of transforming Indian communities.

These attempts to insinuate themselves into Pueblo culture occurred on multiple levels. Like many Native American cultures, Pueblo society was organized around notions of reciprocity and gift giving. Those individuals who were positioned atop social hierarchies achieved their status, and maintained it, through their ability to provide gifts and support to others in the community. Critical to the authority of older Pueblo men over younger men, for instance, was this capacity to distribute resources. Franciscans inserted themselves into this social structure in New Mexico, attempting to usurp the power of Pueblo men by lavishing gifts and attention on Pueblo children and young adults. Since Pueblo masculinity was based in part on the ability to provide gifts and material support to family members, driving a wedge between Pueblo men and younger Pueblos also helped Franciscans weaken the position of Pueblo men in relation to Pueblo women. Franciscans presented themselves, in contrast to Pueblo men, as the best providers and supporters of Pueblo communities. Like many colonial enterprises, Spanish and otherwise, Franciscans thus focused special attention on Native family relations, especially the relationships between Pueblo men and women and Pueblo adults and children, in their attempts to control Pueblo communities and convert them to Christianity.

Such aggressive attempts to transform Pueblo societies at times converged with periods of poor rainfall and the constant presence of fatal disease in New Mexico in the 1600s. In 1636, for instance, smallpox wreaked terrible havoc on the Pueblos, killing 20,000, or about one-third of the total Pueblo population. Four years later, in 1640, 3,000 Pueblos died in another epidemic. Physical violence and persistent Spanish efforts to undermine and transform Pueblo cultures proved especially disastrous when combined with the diseases and epidemics that would burn through Pueblo communities with terrifying frequency.

The Spanish presence in New Mexico in the 1600s was thus placing mounting pressure on Pueblo communities. In 1675, at the request of missionaries in the territory, New Mexican governor Juan Francisco Treviño escalated the ongoing campaign against Pueblo religious practices. Treviño ordered the execution of 4 Pueblos in the plaza at Santa Fe on accusations of witchcraft and the public whipping of 43 others. Among those whipped was Popé, a Pueblo man who had long resisted Spanish authority. After his release, Popé began encouraging and organizing rebellion against Spanish rule. The hardships of a near-decade-long drought, coupled with the increasing demands of the Spanish, helped Popé win a receptive audience in the Pueblo communities.

In 1680, from his headquarters at Taos, Popé led a revolt against the Spanish in New Mexico. In a coordinated uprising at more than two dozen Pueblo settlements, separated by hundreds of miles and six different languages, the Pueblos killed more than 400 Spaniards, including 21 of the province's 33 Franciscan missionaries, and sacked or destroyed every building and church. Those Spanish who survived the initial attacks fled to Santa Fe, where they were surrounded by a combined force of 2,500 warriors who burned the town and mocked their persecutors, now barricaded in the Governor's Palace, by chanting phrases from the Latin Mass. After a skirmish that temporarily drove the Pueblos back, the Spanish retreated hundreds of miles south, to El Paso, now an important United States-Mexico border crossing, along the Rio Grande River. In El Paso, the Spanish survivors established a community around a mission founded there in 1659. The

Popé (Popay) helped lead the successful Pueblo Revolt against Spanish rule in New Mexico in 1680. (Architect of the Capitol)

Pueblo people watched this retreat from the hills overlooking Santa Fe, triumphant in their attempt to have their homeland back again.

In 1692, on an expedition to reclaim New Mexico for Spain after more than a decade, Diego de Vargas led a contingent of 200 soldiers from El Paso north to Santa Fe. De Vargas surrounded Santa Fe and forced its surrender, pledging mercy if the Pueblos would swear allegiance to Spain and return to the Christian faith. By year's end, de Vargas had reimposed Spanish rule over New Mexico. One of the lasting impacts of the Pueblo Revolt was a profound reorientation of Spanish rule in New Mexico. No longer would Franciscan missionaries seek to insinuate themselves so forcefully into Pueblo villages. In fact, Spanish officials began around 1700 to focus far more attention on fortifying and enlarging Spanish towns and villages than on converting Pueblo Indians to Christianity. In this respect, the Pueblo Revolt succeeded in restoring an important degree of autonomy for Pueblo communities in New Mexico.

After 1700, Spanish settlements expanded in New Mexico, and a vibrant trade network developed between Spanish New Mexicans and a range of Native peoples, including Pueblo, Navajo, Comanche, Ute, and Apache communities. This trade included agricultural products, livestock, buffalo hides, and domestic items like cookware and blankets. The Spanish population in New Mexico grew to nearly 20,000 by the end of the 1700s, with most people living in or near the towns of Albuquerque and Santa Fe. Albuquerque's population was 6,100 in 1790, and Santa Fe had 3,600 inhabitants. While agriculture remained the focus of the economy, some New Mexicans raised sheep and other townspeople worked as carpenters, blacksmiths, or weavers of wool blankets. In Albuquerque in 1790, about 400 of the 600 individuals who were listed with occupations were farmers, while 150 were "craftsmen" and 60 were "day laborers." The tilt toward agriculture was even more pronounced in Santa Fe, where there were 350 farmers, 28 craftsmen, and 34 day laborers.

Though officially discouraged by Spanish authorities, the traffic of humans (as in the developing British colonies to the east) was also an integral part of New Mexico's economy in the 1700s. The Spanish society of New Mexico was divided into four main groups. The most powerful group was the nobility—one to two dozen families who owned large tracts of land and controlled much of the wealth in the region. Like the nobility, the second group claimed Spanish, as opposed to Indian, heritage and owned some land. Both groups defined themselves in opposition to a third group, enslaved Apache or Navajo Indians, also known as genízaros, who had been captured or purchased in the ongoing Indian slave trade. The final group, Pueblo Indians, at times worked or lived in Spanish communities but managed to maintain a certain level of autonomy in separate communities at a distance from Spanish towns or villages.

Indian slaves in fact formed a significant portion of New Mexico's population in the 1700s. One count listed 1,300 slaves in a Spanish population of 4,300 (and a total New Mexico population of 16,000). In 1793, one historian estimates that a third of New Mexico's population (9,600 of 29,000) were Indian slaves. This reliance on slavery was not unique to Spanish colonies in the Americas. English colonies on the Atlantic coast of the continent were founded in the early 1600s in regions like New England and Virginia. As in Spanish regions, slavery—largely African slavery—played a critical role in British North America. So too was sexual violence against slaves an entrenched feature of both English and Spanish colonial enterprises. In another shared feature, the children of interracial rapes, as well as the children of other less coercive sexual liaisons, including at times intermarriages, contributed to the creation of deeply multicultural communities throughout North America, from New England and Virginia to Nuevo México.

At the same time, though both societies depended on slavery, race relations differed considerably in the two regions. Racial hierarchies in Spanish colonies tended to be somewhat more fluid than in British colonies. British America was racially divided into three main groups, white, black, and

Indian, in the colonial era. There was little flexibility in this racial hierarchy and few allowances were made for people of mixed racial heritage. This racial order would eventually transform into the "one drop rule" in the United States, where any trace of African heritage would prohibit an individual from identifying as white.

In Spanish America, on the other hand, social categories were more nuanced, with multiple classifications for a range of racial mixtures. These categories included *mestizo* for a person of Native American and European heritage and *mulato* for mixed African and European heritage. Racial inequality, of course, and the horrors of slavery were nonetheless also profound in Spanish America, and historians disagree about the severity of one slave system over another. For Latina/o historians, this difference between English, and then U.S., rigid racial divides and more fluid racial hierarchies in Spanish and formerly Spanish colonies like Mexico, Puerto Rico, Cuba, and the Dominican Republic has become a critical feature of Latina/os' experiences in the United States.

Other regions of North America also drew the attention of Spanish officials and explorers in the 1600s and 1700s. The exploration and colonization of California, for instance, which had stalled in the mid-1500s, resumed in the late 1700s. Spanish officials sought settlements in California that would provide revenue, facilitate increasing trade with Asia, and, most importantly, discourage other European, especially Russian and English, expansion in the region. The military presence was therefore pronounced in California, with the establishment of four forts—at San Diego, Santa Barbara, Monterrey, and San Francisco—that housed 400 men. Religious goals also motivated Spanish settlement, and a Franciscan missionary, Junípero Serra, was appointed to lead the new missions to be founded in California. Eventually these missions, which depended on the often coerced labor of Indian women and men, would control significant portions of land and wealth. The late 1700s in California also featured the founding of towns that, in the coming centuries, would become the home of millions of Spanish-speaking Americans. In addition to the towns of San José, near the fort of San Francisco in Northern California, and Santa Bárbara, the town of Los Angeles was founded in the early 1700s near the San Gabriel mission and el Río de la Porciúncula (now the Los Angeles River).

For Spanish officials, settling entire Spanish families, not just Spanish men, in California was a priority of the colonization plan in the late 1700s. Pedro Fages, governor of California, stated bluntly, "The Indians were hostile to men without women, believing them to have been outcasts from their own societies who had come to take away the Native women" (Pubols 2010, 20). Serafina Lugo, for example, had initially remained at her home in Sinaloa, Mexico, with her children while her soldier husband, José Joaquin

Cayetano Espinoza, joined an all-male military exploration to San Diego in 1769. Five years later, however, Lugo resettled with her husband and children in California. She was joined on the journey to the new colony by the families of her brother and two sisters, including several children.

Similar Spanish colonial aspirations fueled attempts to establish settlements in the region of Texas in the 1700s. Though Spanish trading expeditions into Texas exchanging Spanish goods for pearls, deerskins, and bison hides had begun in the 1650s, news of French exploration and settlement along the Mississippi River in the 1680s encouraged more extensive colonization plans. Between 1685 and 1690, nearly a dozen expeditions were sent to Texas. The reports of such expeditions convinced Spanish officials and religious leaders to field larger campaigns with the broader goals of military fortification against French (and other European) expansion and Christian conversion of Native Americans.

Due to the numerical and military superiority of Native communities in Texas, however, the growing Spanish presence in Texas over the course of the 1700s depended on the Spaniards' ability to accommodate to Native interests, rather than large-scale Native assimilation to Spanish demands. For instance, Spanish expeditions were exclusively male and, despite the occasional presence of missionaries, largely military in nature. According to one historian, the 1689 Alonso de León expedition included "a military leader, about ten officers, eighty-five soldiers, two missionaries, one guide, one interpreter, and twenty-five muleteers, craftsmen, and laborers in charge of supplies, food stores, and manual chores" (Barr 2007, 28). Native communities in Texas tended to interpret this absence of women among the Spanish forces as a sign that the Spanish were not committed to peaceful settlement in the region. Sexual violence, in fact, plagued the first Spanish attempts to establish colonies in the early 1690s. In response, the Caddo Indians, the most prominent Native group in the area, expelled the Spanish from their lands and forced them to abandon their forts and missions in that region of Texas. When the Spanish finally returned to Texas two decades later, they did so on Caddo terms and were far more committed to curbing sexual violence against Native women by Spanish men and including Spanish women among the new colonizers.

Improved Spanish ability to negotiate with and accommodate to superior Native forces in Texas opened the path to new settlements in the region in the 1710s and 1720s. Civilian settlers and towns, such as La Bahía in 1721, San Antonio in 1731, and Laredo in 1755, soon followed. Compared to New Mexico, the Spanish population of Texas was relatively small throughout the 1700s. In 1731, when San Antonio was founded, officials counted about 500 members of the Spanish community in the entire province of Texas. Fifty years later, the community had grown to nearly 4,000, including more than 700 in Laredo. Though some Tejana/os (members of Texas's Spanish communities) worked in agriculture, ranching was the basis of the Tejana/o economy in the 1700s. Ranchers sold their livestock, which included cattle and sheep, in local markets and also participated in regional trade networks stretching toward central Mexico.

Relations with a variety of Native groups continued to shape Spanish society in Texas throughout the 1700s. Like the rest of the Southwest, Texas Indians suffered profound losses over the century, with epidemics proving especially devastating to Native communities. A smallpox epidemic killed several hundred Caddo Indians in 1691, and shockingly high rates of disease and death would persist through the next century. One historian has estimated that recurring epidemics contributed significantly to a 90 percent drop in Caddo population between 1691 and 1810. Another report from Comanche territory in eastern Texas in the 1780s described a smallpox outbreak that killed two-thirds of the population. Epidemics threatened Indians living in Spanish villages and missions as well. According to one count from San Antonio, outbreaks of disease occurred in nearly every decade between the 1720s and 1780s. Despite such horrific losses, Indian groups in Texas continued to exert considerable power in the region.

Similar dynamics occurred during the Spanish colonization of Arizona. In 1591, Jesuit missionaries were granted permission by Spanish authorities to establish missions in the northern provinces of Sinaloa and Sonora, parts of which are now southern Arizona. By 1620, more than 50 Jesuit missionaries had been assigned to the region. One of the best-known Jesuit missionaries was Eusebio Francisco Kino, who traveled extensively in the region and helped found numerous missions in the late 1600s and early 1700s. As in New Mexico, indigenous communities resisted, at times violently, Spanish attempts to replace Indian religious practices with Christianity, and for much of the period before 1800, Indian groups like the Tohono O'odham in Arizona managed to hold off Spanish colonial incursions.

Spain, of course, sent military forces, explorers, and settlers throughout the Americas beginning in the 1500s, establishing Spanish strongholds in what would become, centuries later, the native lands of future Latina/o immigrants to the United States. The Caribbean island that eventually became known as Puerto Rico was first visited by the Spanish in 1493. Native groups had been living on the island for well over 3,000 years by the time the Spanish arrived. Beginning in 1200, the Taino Indian culture rose to prominence on the island that they named Borinquen. Taino communities were established throughout the Caribbean, including on the islands that would be renamed Cuba, Española, and Jamaica by European invaders.

Christopher Columbus led an expedition that landed on Borinquen in fall 1493 and Columbus promptly christened the island San Juan Bautista (it was eventually renamed Puerto Rico). Taino communities were soon besieged by Spanish military forces and forced to work in mining operations, principally gold mining. Across the Caribbean, coercive labor practices devastated Native, including Taino, communities. By one account, only a tiny percentage of Taino workers (10% at most) survived even a few months of Spanish forced labor.

In addition to deaths by forced labor, and the constant presence of deadly diseases, Tainos also suffered through repeated attacks by Spanish soldiers. In 1508, Juan Ponce de León led a military expedition through the island. His forces established the towns of San Germán and Caparra, which would later become the city of San Juan. Two years later, in 1510, a major Taino uprising killed some 200 Spanish colonists. Ponce de León led a counterattack that killed a prominent Taino leader, Chief Agüeybaná, and forced the surrender of Taino forces. Many Tainos managed to escape to the interior of the island, where they continued to resist Spanish colonialism and enslavement. Others were captured by Spanish soldiers, and Ponce de León ordered some to be branded on the forehead with the letter "F" in honor of the Spanish ruler Ferdinand. While some Spanish-Taino encounters were less marked by violence and death (some Taino women married Spanish men, and according to one census, 40% of Spanish men were married to Taino women in 1514), the Taino population was almost completely destroyed in Puerto Rico by the 1540s.

Puerto Rico's economy and population would grow slowly over the next several centuries. Agriculture, ranching, and sugar and tobacco production were the major sectors of the economy. In the 1600s, Puerto Rico became a center of the trade in leather and by 1620, there were approximately 100,000 cattle on the island. In the 1700s, coffee cultivation was introduced and coffee production eventually outpaced all other forms of agricultural production. Much of this growth, limited though it was, depended on African slavery. As occurred throughout the Caribbean, Spanish colonists came to rely on slave labor in Puerto Rico, and Afro-Puerto Ricans constituted a major portion of the island's population by 1800.

Like Puerto Rico and Española, the island of Cuba was occupied by the Spanish early in the 1500s. It was a major trading center in the Spanish Caribbean, a strategic location for military operations, and a critical base for further exploration of the region (Cabeza de Vaca's journey through North America, remember, began from Cuba). As a colony of Spain, Cuba's population and economy grew unevenly, with periods of rapid growth punctuated by years of stagnation and halting development. In the 1700s, for instance, Cuba's economy expanded, driven especially by the rapid growth of tobacco and sugar production. Cuba's annual output of sugar increased from 2,000 tons per year in the 1730s to 5,500 tons annually by the end of the 1750s. In the second half of the 1700s, the production jumped even higher, from 10,000 annual tons in the 1770s, to 12,000 tons in the 1780s, to 26,000 tons in the late 1790s. The number of acres devoted to sugar cultivation also increased, from 10,000 acres in 1762 to 160,000 acres in 1792. Accompanying this growth in the 1700s, however, were periods of contraction, when Spanish colonial economic policy stifled Cuban producers' profits and imposed strict limits on trade.

The 1700s in Cuba were notable in two other respects. First, the expansion of the Cuban economy, especially in terms of sugar production, depended on a massive rise in African slavery on the island. Between 1512 (the beginning of the African slave trade in Cuba) and 1763, a total of about 60,000 enslaved men and women had arrived in Cuba. This number, while substantial, was dwarfed by the 100,000 slaves who arrived in the next four decades alone. By 1792, there were 85,000 slaves in Cuba, and 54,000 free people of color, in a total population of 272,000 people. Without such a rapid increase in African slavery, the impressive expansion of Cuba's sugar economy would have been impossible.

A second, related development during the 1700s was a deeper, if sporadic, trade relationship between Cuba and North America. While illicit trade and smuggling occurred throughout the 1700s between the two regions, international developments on occasion accelerated the exchange of goods and people. In 1762, in the midst of the Seven Years War, British troops occupied the city of Havana for 10 months. Previous limits on trade with North America imposed by Spain disappeared immediately, and a flood of goods, including an astounding 10,000 enslaved workers (as many in one year as had arrived throughout the previous decade), entered the country. At the same time, new international markets for Cuban sugar, tobacco, and other goods also opened. Though Spain soon reoccupied Havana, a decade later the American Revolution and Spanish support of the 13 colonies opened trade once again between Cuba and North America. Commercial exchange flourished, as the annual number of ships traveling between Havana harbor and the American colonies rose from 4 in 1776 to 368 in 1782. In 1784, however, Spain returned to restrictive trade policies for Cuba and drastically limited trade with other countries. The nearly 400 annual ships leaving Havana a year earlier for North America fell to only 10 by 1785.

Despite such commercial setbacks, trade between Cuba and the new United States was a significant component of the island's economy by 1800. One hundred and fifty American ships arrived in Cuban ports in 1796 and more than 600 in 1800. According to one historian, the ships "originated from Boston, New York, Philadelphia, Savannah, and New Orleans and provided Cubans with box shooks, staves, caskets, barrels, hoops, nails, tar, textiles, salt, fish, corn, lard, flour, and rice. They returned loaded with sugar, cocoa, tobacco, molasses, and coffee" (Pérez 2003, 13). In the next century, the fates of the two countries and their people would be drawn even closer together.

In the three centuries from roughly 1500 to 1800, Spanish settler colonialism spread into major sections of North America, into much of what is now the western United States, and throughout the Caribbean, including the islands of Española (now Haiti and the Dominican Republic), Puerto Rico, and Cuba. This Spanish presence is at the root of Latina/o history, from the continued prominence of the Spanish language, to the profound mixing of European, African, and Native American cultures, to the acceptance of more fluid and dynamic racial categories.

Over the course of the next century, the Spanish empire would disappear from the Western Hemisphere, from Mexico at the beginning of the 1800s and finally from Puerto Rico and Cuba in the 1890s. Nonetheless, the Spanish colonial legacy would endure in what would become the United States long after the last Spanish soldiers, explorers, and settlers departed the Americas.

PROFILE: MALINTZIN TENEPAL ("LA MALINCHE")

Born in the late 1400s in a Nahua-speaking indigenous community in what is now Mexico, Malintzin, who was also known as Malinalli,

Chicana feminists have recovered the contested figure of Malintzin Tenepal ("La Malinche"), a Native Mexican woman who was a guide and translator for Spanish invaders like Hernán Cortés. *La Malinche Tenía Sus Razones* ("Malinche Had Her Reasons") by Cecilia Alvarez, 2004. (Property of Cecilia Alvarez)

Malinche, and Marina, was an expert in languages and an indispensable guide to the Spanish forces invading Mexico.

Malintzin Tenepal (the name Tenepal was a term, possibly of honor, representing linguistic skill and aptitude) was reportedly forced to join the Spanish invasion when it arrived in Mexico in the early 1500s. Some scholars have described her as a gift from a powerful Native leader, while others view her as a slave given to the Spanish. Likely coerced in some manner to serve the Spanish, Malintzin acted as a personal translator for Spanish leader Hernán Cortés. Given the Spaniards' unfamiliarity with Native communities in Mexico and the complexity of political dynamics under Aztec rule, she was also undoubtedly an important advisor in terms of guiding Cortés's alliance-making efforts as the Spanish made their way to the Aztec capital of Tenochtitlan.

Possibly forced into a sexual relationship with Cortés, Malintzin gave birth to a child, Martín, who would eventually be awarded a Spanish knighthood. She later married another elite Spanish man, Juan de Jaramillo, and had a daughter, María. Historical accounts differ as to Malintzin's exact date of death, ranging from 1531 to the 1550s.

Malintzin, more commonly referred to as La Malinche, has been a controversial and contested figure in Mexican and Latina/o history. Mexican Nobel Prize–winning writer Octavio Paz, in his classic work *Labyrinth of Solitude*, titles one of his chapters "The Sons of La Malinche." Paz, though attempting to acknowledge the enduring indigenous presence in Mexican culture, also reinforced the image of a sexually promiscuous Native woman who "betrayed" the Aztec people. Pointing to the fact that Malintzin was not an Aztec (and thus was hardly a traitor to her people for helping Cortés invade the Aztec empire) and that accusations of cultural betrayal by women are frequently used to reinforce women's inequality and subordination, Chicana feminists have more recently presented a contrasting, more positive view of Malintzin. "Women writers," according to historian Asunción Lavrin, "such as Rosario Castellanos, Sabina Berman, Gloria Anzaldúa, Pat Mora, and others, critical of the patriarchal models created by the traditional masculine view, give her a more independent and assertive role and extol her importance as a founder of the Mexican nation" (Lavrin 2006, 366). It is thus apt that a 1997 painting of Malintzin by artist Cecilia Concepción Alvarez is titled *La Malinche tenía sus razones* ("La Malinche had her reasons").

PROFILE: ÁLVAR NUÑEZ CABEZA DE VACA

Álvar Nuñez Cabeza de Vaca, one of four survivors of the ill-fated Narváez expedition, was born in the last decade of the 1400s to a prominent

Spanish family from the region of Andalusia, Spain. Cabeza de Vaca's grandfather had been a military hero, and the young man followed him into military service. Beginning in his early twenties, he joined several Spanish army campaigns and earned distinctions for his service. After a 15-year military career, and with the help of influential family friends, Cabeza de Vaca was appointed the royal treasurer of the Pánfilo de Narváez expedition. Among Cabeza de Vaca's duties as royal treasurer were to oversee spending on the voyage and to verify that the Spanish government was receiving its proper amount of profit from the expedition. In this respect, as an official appointed by the Spanish crown, Cabeza de Vaca was one of the most powerful members of the Narváez expedition.

After nearly a decade as a castaway, Cabeza de Vaca returned in 1536 to Spanish society and sought to rebuild his life. As one of the highest-ranking members of the Narváez expedition, he attempted to capitalize on his standing as a royal official by petitioning the Spanish crown for the right to lead another colonizing expedition of "la Florida," the region he had explored and lived in for years. Authority to settle the region, however, had already been granted elsewhere, and Cabeza de Vaca had to settle for authorization to lead a settlement of an uncolonized region of South America. While the ensuing colonization effort was not a disaster at the level of the Narváez expedition, the settlement was hardly a success. After four disappointing years, Cabeza de Vaca was forced to return to Spain. He abandoned his plans to lead another colonization effort and remained in Spain for the rest of his life.

Cabeza de Vaca's most lasting contribution, however, was not his attempt to lead settlements in Spanish America but a chronicle he wrote describing his experiences during his years wandering through North America. In 1542, his narrative of the ill-fated Narváez voyage was published. Cabeza de Vaca's *Narrative* became one of the earliest and most influential accounts of European exploration in the Americas and, despite its clear biases, describes life in Native America in the 1500s with a level of detail and sensitivity that has fascinated readers for centuries.

PROFILE: JUANA LA COYOTA

The mixture of Spanish and Native American cultures, whether by force or through less violent means, was profound across the Southwest in the 1600s and 1700s. The extent of these cultural crossings is especially evident from the perspective of Spanish homes and domestic situations. Take, for instance, the life of one New Mexican woman known, depending on the historical record, as either Juana la Coyota ("coyote" was one of several Spanish racial classifications indicating mixed heritage) or Juana Galván.

Juana was born in 1673 to a Pueblo Indian mother from Zia Pueblo. Juana's mother, the sister of a prominent Zia leader, had a sexual relationship—likely coerced in some manner—with a married landowning Spanish man named Andrés Hurtado.

Although Hurtado did not formally acknowledge his daughter, the girl was living with the family in the summer of 1680 when a group of Navajo Indians attacked the Hurtado estate. Juana la Coyota, along with her half-sister, also named Juana, and her half-sister's daughter, were captured by the Navajo. The three remained in captivity among the Navajo for 12 years, from the onset of the Pueblo Revolt, which began soon after their capture, to the return of Spanish soldiers in 1692. By the time she was a teenager, Juana had thus experienced three cultures, the Zia Pueblos of her mother, the Spanish of her father, and the Navajos of her captivity.

Four years after returning to Spanish society, Juana reasserted her Zia Pueblo connections, asking for and being granted a tract of land in Zia territory. From her newly acquired lands, Juana maintained relationships with Zia, Spanish, and even Navajo people, who continued to visit her on a regular basis. Juana also maintained a long-term relationship with a man with the last name Galván from Zia Pueblo. By 1727, the couple had four children and Juana occasionally used the name Juana Hurtado Galván. When she died in 1753, Juana was exceedingly prosperous and commanded respect from across the region. According to her will, she owned "two ranches with three houses, 330 head of goats, ewes, and rams, 42 cows with calves, 6 oxen, 3 bulls, 38 heifers and steers, 31 mares and stallions, a jenny and a jack mule, and a respectable amount of personal property" (Brooks 2002, 100). Her children prospered as well. One daughter, who died in 1735, 18 years before her mother's death, listed two dozen cows, horses, and sheep in her will, and Juana's son assumed a leadership role in the governing of Zia Pueblo.

Juana la Coyota is one of a long line of remarkable women in the Latina/o past. She was clearly resilient, surviving over a decade of captivity; multilingual; capable of speaking with Zia, Spanish, and Navajo peoples; and an adept businesswoman.

REFERENCES

Barr, Juliana. *Peace Came in the Form of a Woman: Indians and Spaniards in the Texas Borderlands*. Chapel Hill: University of North Carolina Press, 2007.

Brooks, James. *Captives and Cousins: Slavery Kinship and Community in the Southwest Borderlands*. Chapel Hill: University of North Carolina Press, 2002.

Lavrin, Asunción. "La Malinche (Malinalli Tenepal)." *In Latinas in the United States: A Historical Encyclopedia*, edited by Vicki L. Ruiz and Virginia Sánchez-Korrol, 364–66. Bloomington: Indiana University Press, 2006.

Pérez, Louis A., Jr. *Cuba and the United States: Ties of Singular Intimacy.* Athens: University of Georgia Press, 2003.

Pubols, Louise. *The Father of All: The de la Guerra Family Power and Patriarchy in Mexican California.* Berkeley: University of California Press, 2010.

Chapter 2

Independence and Empire, 1800–1835

As the nineteenth century began, movements for independence coursed through the Americas. Like countries throughout the region in the late 1700s and early 1800s, Mexico achieved its independence in 1821, while Spanish rule would endure in Cuba, Puerto Rico, and the Philippines for almost 80 more years. The nearly four decades between 1800 and 1835 extended from the last decades of the Spanish empire in the Southwest to the war between Mexico and Texas. Social divisions within Latina/o communities persisted during this period, such as inequalities between men and women and enduring racial divides targeting Native Americans and Latina/os of African descent. The relationship between Anglos (Americans of northern European descent) and both Mexicans in the Southwest and Puerto Ricans and Cubans in the Caribbean also deepened. Intermarriages, as well as other cross-cultural sexual intimacies, and trade relationships between the United States on the one hand and Mexico and the Spanish Caribbean on the other also blossomed in the early nineteenth century. Finally, the period witnessed the development of new and enduring bonds between separate Latina/o groups, especially between exiled Cuban and Puerto Rican independence leaders who made new homes and formed new activist communities in the United States.

In the first decade of the 1800s, the vast majority of Mexico's population was either of Indian or of African descent (in 1810, 70% of Mexico's population was "Indian" and 10% were "Mulato" or "Negro"), and most Mexicans struggled with poverty and harsh work conditions. Meanwhile, a small number of Mexican elites, including significant numbers of Spanish-born whites, controlled the country's major political and economic institutions. Political instability in Spain and poor crop conditions further heightened tensions in Mexico during the period.

Led by Father Miguel Hidalgo y Costilla, the Mexican Independence movement began in 1810. (Charles & Josette Lenars/Corbis)

In the fall of 1810, these tensions erupted into widespread revolt. Miguel Hidalgo y Costilla, a priest in the Mexican town of Dolores, organized mass protests against the Spanish and the country's ruling elites. His September 16th proclamation, the "Grito de Dolores," rallied followers, and the insurgency gathered momentum as tens of thousands of working-class Mexicans joined the revolt. Though Hidalgo's rebellion was eventually defeated by forces loyal to the Spanish crown and the priest was executed for treason, independence movements persisted throughout the decade in Mexico, as did liberal reforms targeting church property and efforts to grant citizenship to the country's Indian population. In 1821, Augustín de Iturbide, a wealthy military officer, issued a statement—the Plan de Iguala—that declared Mexico independent of Spain. The Plan de Iguala, which protected the property rights of large landowners and the Church, and instituted a constitutional monarchy to rule Mexico, was more conservative than Father Hidalgo's program, yet also granted citizenship to Indians and to Mexicans of African descent.

During this period of revolution and independence, Texas, New Mexico, Arizona, and California, despite certain clear differences, had much in common. All four regions were located on the borders of first Spanish and then Mexican control, leading to significant levels of cross-national, cross-cultural mixing between Mexican, Native American, and eventually U.S. born communities in the Southwest. The regions were also bound by profound cultural similarities, such as the Spanish language, Catholicism, and gender roles and expectations. In fact, while inequalities between women and men were often stark throughout the region, Mexicanas could be capable defenders of their rights and privileges.

As revolutionary violence overwhelmed central Mexico, some northern provinces like New Mexico experienced economic growth and population expansion. A central feature of this expansion was the increased integration and interdependence of Spanish villagers and Indian communities in northern New Mexico. Mixed Spanish and Indian communities could at times even join forces in opposition to Spanish government officials. One such alliance emerged in the village of San Miguel del Vado, located east of the Sangre de Cristo mountains and along the Pecos River in New Mexico. The village was founded in 1794, when 52 Santa Fe residents petitioned the governor for land in the fertile Pecos valley, 20 miles from the Pecos Indian Pueblo. Intercultural mixing was evident throughout the village's early years, from its founding by both Spanish and genízaro (former Indian slaves or descendants of slaves) families, to the use of Indian weapons like bows and arrows to defend the town, to the town's first recorded marriage, where a Spanish woman married a Pecos Indian man. While villagers engaged in some agricultural production, trade dominated the economy, and San Miguel del Vado was a critical link between the rest of New Mexico and Indian groups like the Comanche to the east. As part of this trade, villagers exchanged manufactured goods like saddlebags, iron products, and textiles for horses, mules, buffalo hides and meat, and male and female slaves. For Spanish officials, such east–west trade networks jeopardized the important north–south trade routes between New Mexico and central Mexico. As a result, the Spanish government after 1800 increasingly attempted to limit trade between villages like San Miguel del Vado and Indian communities to the east.

Another form of cross-cultural contact was also built around trade and commerce: the growing relationship between New Mexico's Mexican communities and newcomers from the United States. Under Spanish policy, trade between Spanish colonies and foreigners had been strictly controlled and limited. After independence, Mexican officials changed that policy almost immediately, allowing greatly expanded foreign trade. New Mexico merchants and traders had previously focused on Chihuahua and Mexico City to the south, but in 1821, just two months after formal Mexican independence, William Becknell, who was seeking new trade opportunities in order to hold off the impending bankruptcy of his business in Missouri, made the overland journey to Santa Fe. The United States in the early 1820s was in the throes of a financial crisis, so while there were many goods available to buy and sell, there was a shortage of cash with which to buy those goods.

Becknell brought to Santa Fe a wide range of goods and merchandise and found an eager market. New Mexicans discovered that U.S. goods were less expensive than the prices that traders from Chihuahua to the south were offering, and a broad trade network soon developed between Santa Fe and St. Louis. Santa Fe became an important stop in an east–west trade artery that came to be known as the Santa Fe Trail. The growth of trade along the Santa Fe Trail shifted the orientation of many Mexicans in the region from focusing southward, along a north–south axis to central Mexico, to looking eastward to the United States.

Unlike the family-dominated settler colonists from the United States who would come to rule the Southwest by the end of the nineteenth century, the Anglos who first arrived in New Mexico, and then California, were largely single men. These men were quickly incorporated into Mexican culture— they were taught Spanish and instructed in the customs and practices of Mexican communities. Critical to this process of acculturation were significant numbers of Mexican women, many of whom married and formed families with these Anglo newcomers. Among these mixed families were the families of prominent Anglos like Kit Carson and Charles Bent.

As intermediaries of trade from St. Louis to Chihuahua along the Santa Fe Trail, Mexican merchants in New Mexico prospered in the 1820s. Another trade route, known as the Old Spanish Trail, was established later in the decade, linking New Mexico to California. Both trade routes expanded significantly New Mexico's traditional economic reliance on livestock, especially sheep ranching, and small-scale agriculture. The economic expansion and the region's growing prosperity had uneven effects, however. Certain elite families, like that of eventual governor Manuel Armijo, grew much wealthier and more politically powerful. At the same time, many ordinary Mexican and Native American villagers struggled in small farms or ranches. New Mexico's Pueblo Indian communities had managed to endure several centuries of Spanish colonialism and by 1821 numbered about 10,000, or roughly a quarter of New Mexico's total population. While some Pueblos, as well as other non-Pueblo Indians, continued to live in Spanish and Mexican communities, most lived in separate, relatively autonomous villages and towns.

Accompanying these economic transformations in New Mexico was the emergence of important new cultural institutions. Father Antonio José Martínez of Taos, one of the region's most influential church leaders, spearheaded the drive to bring the first printing press into New Mexico. As a result, the first newspaper in New Mexico, *El Crepúsculo de la Libertad*, was published in 1834. Martínez also helped open a school in Taos and was a strong advocate for literacy and the spread of education to broader sectors of New Mexico society.

Like New Mexico, California's politics and economy had been oriented toward the south and Mexico City in the late 1700s. Political turmoil and revolutionary violence in Mexico in the early 1800s, however, led to a series of important shifts, especially when communication and trade networks between the two regions were cut off by civil war. Although annual supply ships from the south no longer arrived in California ports when war broke out in 1810, Spanish trade restrictions, which had severely limited trade between California and other regions of the Americas, were finally eased during the war, and California merchants eagerly entered this broadened market for their goods and agricultural produce. Among California's most important new trading partners was the United States, and commerce between Mexico and the United States would become a defining feature of the region's history.

In Spanish and Mexican California, the family was a cornerstone of politics, business, and social life. Elite Californio politicians and business leaders extended their positions as male heads of families (or patriarchs) to father-like authority over Spanish-Mexican society in general. This authority included members of their own families, as well as less wealthy Mexicans, and Indians residing in their households and in the broader community. California patriarchs like José de la Guerra turned to family relationships to augment business prospects—using, for instance, relatives to establish connections with other trading establishments—and found commercial success that, in turn, enriched their families and bolstered their social status.

Intermarriages between Mexican women and Anglo men were an extension of the significant role of family ties in California's economic development. While intermarriage rates were never exceptionally high in California (accounting for, on average, between 10 and 20% of all marriages), many of the intermarriages united elite Mexican families with prosperous Anglo merchants. One such union occurred in the mid-1830s with the marriage of Anita de la Guerra, the daughter of patriarch José de la Guerra, and Alfred Robinson, an accomplished American trader, a marriage that brought together both family interests and business matters.

For Mexican women, this emphasis on strong families and family connections was accompanied by persistent gender and sexual inequality. Most Mexican women worked long hours and were expected to submit to male authority and control over their lives. As in the United States during this period, a rigid sexual double standard punished women far more severely than men for violating sexual norms. Mexican women also had less sexual freedom than men, and considerable pressure was placed on women to behave in ways that brought honor, and not shame, to the family. Anastacia Zuniga, for instance, was a widow from Los Angeles who became pregnant in 1818 after an extramarital affair with a man from a nearby community.

Zuniga was forced to appear in church with her head shaved and was confined in a secluded place for six months. Her male lover, by contrast, was compelled to provide a month of forced labor.

At the same time, Mexican women in the early 1800s possessed rights (such as the right to own land) that most women in the United States would not receive until decades later. Female property holders in California acquired their land most often through inheritance, though a handful of women were awarded land grants by the Mexican government. One of the largest estates was owned by Manuela Nieto, who inherited a portion of her father's property when he died in 1804. After Mexican independence, Nieto and her siblings, who had also received land from their father, sought to have the new government confirm their title to the land. A lengthy legal dispute followed, ending nearly a decade later when Nieto's title was ruled legitimate. Besides the land, Nieto's major possessions also included 2,000 head of cattle, corrals, and a house, property that she eventually left to her husband and children upon her death in 1843. Another widow, Juana Pacheco, received 20,000 acres of land in Northern California in 1834.

For both male and female California Indians, on the other hand, the early 1800s witnessed continued suffering, with repeated bouts of deadly disease, forced labor, and violent attacks. Nonetheless, Indian communities resisted Spanish control in multiple ways. In 1810, for instance, Indians at the San Gabriel mission in Southern California planned a revolt in cooperation with nearby Mojave Indians, who had conducted previous raids on Spanish settlements in the region. According to an informant, who revealed the plans to Spanish authorities, the uprising would have targeted both the San Gabriel mission and the town of Los Angeles and would have mustered a combined force of 400 Indian men and women. The revolt was repelled by Spanish troops and local villagers, and the captured Indian rebels were punished with sentences of hard labor for the men and forced service in Spanish households for the women.

Tragically, for California's Native population, many of the traumas associated with Spanish colonialism did not end with Mexican independence. In the early 1800s, for instance, a new mission was founded nearby indigenous communities in the Napa and Sonoma regions of Northern California. These communities already had decades of experience with European colonialism. Indians fleeing north from Spanish missions that had been established in the late 1700s at times found refuge among Napa and Sonoma villages. So too did epidemics related to European arrival make their way into the Napa/Sonoma region. Indian women also continued to suffer sexual attacks by Spanish and Mexican men in the early 1800s. Accompanying this sexual violence was often the spread of sexually transmitted diseases like syphilis into Native communities. "The effects of the disease," according to one historian, "resulted in massive population losses" among Indians throughout the region (Chávez-García 2004, 12). By the 1830s, syphilis is estimated to have caused up to one-third of Indian deaths in the missions and may have inflicted a similar number of deaths throughout California.

Unlike California, the region that would eventually become Arizona experienced only limited Spanish or Mexican population growth in the early 1800s. Native American communities effectively resisted such settlements, including the establishment of religious missions, for much of the period. Groups like the Apache had successfully forced the Spanish to supply goods to their people in exchange for relative peace. After Mexican independence, however, funds for such negotiations dwindled and violence soon overcame the region. By the mid-1830s, one historian notes that "five thousand Mexicans were reported as killed on the northern frontier and four thousand others were known to have left the area" (Gómez-Quiñones 1994, 150). In 1835, the governor of the Mexican state of Sonora went so far as to authorize a reward of 100 pesos for every scalp of an Apache male 14 years of age or older.

For Tejana/os, the new century brought a set of challenges similar to that faced by other regions of northern New Spain like California, Arizona, and New Mexico. Despite significant regional differences—the Tejana/o economy, for instance, relied far more heavily on cattle ranching—Texas Mexicans shared with their New Mexico and California counterparts a sense of distance from Spanish imperial control. Likewise, the revolutionary movements that spread throughout Mexico in the 1810s had a significant effect on Mexican communities in Texas.

In fact, Texas was one of the flash points of the Mexican independence movement. Soon after the "Grito de Dolores," a series of violent uprisings in Texas challenged Spanish rule and drew the support of both elite and nonelite Texas Mexicans. In both 1811 and 1813, anti-Spanish insurgents led uprisings against Spanish authority. In January 1811, only months after Father Miguel Hidalgo's famous call for independence, Juan Bautista de las Casas, a former Spanish military officer, led a coup occupying the town of Bexar. Though the Spanish government was reestablished in Bexar two months later, another revolt involving many of the members of the failed 1811 rebellion soon followed. The leader of this second uprising was Bernardo Gutiérrez de Lara, who had been born in Spain but lived much of his life in northern Mexico. Gutiérrez raised an army from his base in Louisiana that was largely Anglo-American, and in late fall 1812 the troops marched into Spanish Texas. Gutiérrez and his soldiers occupied Bexar in April 1813 and held the town until the fall, when Spanish forces defeated the insurgency.

When Mexico finally achieved independence in 1821, one of the major issues facing the young country was the security of its northern border, especially the region of Texas. Rather than immediately closing their border and turning inward for protection, the Mexican government actively sought immigrants from the United States. Their hope was that U.S. immigrants would quickly assimilate into Mexican culture, become Catholic, and then, if bloodshed should occur, take up arms to protect Mexico from U.S. expansionist intentions. Mexico's government encouraged immigration by offering large grants of land to groups of U.S. colonists, but Mexican officials hoped eventually to recruit other foreigners to dilute the U.S. presence. As a result, though trade (much of it in the form of smuggling) and military campaigns, like the 1813 revolt, had drawn some U.S. newcomers into Texas before the 1820s, Mexican independence, in fact, marked the beginning of large-scale U.S. immigration to the region. Illegal immigration also grew, as scores of unauthorized U.S. settlers crossed into Mexico. By the mid-1820s, there were several thousand "illegal aliens" in Mexico from the United States.

One of the initial legal settlement contracts arranged by the Mexican government was an agreement with Moses Austin to bring 300 Catholic families to settle in Texas in exchange for a large land grant. In general, foreign groups, including those hailing from the United States, were eligible for 4,500 acres of grazing land and 170 acres of farmland for a very small fee. By 1830, 7,000 U.S. immigrants resided in Texas, twice as many as the Mexican residents there. These newcomers included Stephen F. Austin, the son of Moses Austin, who inherited title to his father's land grant as well as three more grants for settling additional families in Texas. Tejana/o elites initially supported these measures, and through much of the 1820s, U.S. immigration worked to the benefit of both Mexican elites and newcomers from the United States.

Besides increased involvement with U.S. immigrants, Mexican communities in Texas, like the rest of the region, sustained deep links with local Indian groups. These links could take many forms. The town of Bexar, for instance, was the site of extensive trade between Indian communities like the Comanche and Spanish and Mexican merchants and government officials. Indians also helped shelter Mexican rebels fleeing Spanish troops after failed revolts. Francisco Ruiz, a prominent Bexar resident, found refuge among the Comanche after the 1813 insurgency was defeated by the Spanish. Ruiz lived with the Comanche for the next eight years until Mexican independence in 1821. Under Mexican rule, Ruiz continued his connection with Indians in Texas by serving as Indian commissioner.

In a pattern common throughout the Southwest, Mexican women in early 1800s Texas experienced hardships and gender inequities, while at the same time exercising what could be impressive control over their lives and communities. María Josefa Becerra, for instance, the wife of prominent politician Erasmo Seguín, was deeply involved in Tejano politics, serving as an intermediary during her husband's frequent trips to Mexico City and elsewhere in the region, and relying on her familial links to men like her uncle Gaspar Flores, a Bexar mayor and councilman. As occurred in California as well, Mexican women also played an important role in cross-cultural interaction with U.S. and other non-Mexican newcomers.

On occasion, this interaction led to Mexican-Anglo courtship and intermarriage, though intermarriage rates would not rise significantly until later in the century. On other occasions, Mexican women engaged in other, less formal forms of cultural brokering and relationship building. Maria Josefa Becerra, though married to another Tejano and not intermarried, again is notable. Becerra's family formed a strong alliance in the 1820s with another prominent family, the immigrant Austin family, which was instrumental in bringing hundreds of Anglo settlers to Texas and owned considerable landholdings in the region. Becerra played a critical role in cementing this relationship, hosting the Austin family during their visits to Bexar and maintaining written communication between the two families. In 1824, for instance, Becerra wrote a letter to Moses Austin expressing her family's condolence at the death of Austin's mother. Becerra's son, Juan Seguín, would maintain these strong intercultural relationships (see the profile of Seguín at the end of chapter 3).

By the 1830s, the spirit of cooperation and cross-cultural partnership between Mexicans and U.S. immigrants, exemplified by Maria Josefa Becerra and the Austin family, had begun to deteriorate. While some Anglos, like Stephen F. Austin, attempted to assimilate to Mexican culture by learning Spanish and respecting Mexican laws and customs, others behaved differently in their new homes. Anglo commitments to cultural mixing and cooperation were increasingly replaced, in the words of one historian, by "an underlying resistance to fully embracing Mexican civil society" (Ramos 2008, 155). Escalating tensions in the early 1830s widened this divide between Anglos, especially Anglo newcomers, and Tejana/os.

This fraying of relations occurred for several reasons. In 1830, the Mexican government passed a new law abolishing slavery in Texas and eliminating new U.S. immigration to the region. Concern by Texans, Anglo and Mexican alike, about the consolidation of political, economic, and military power in Mexico City further stoked discontent. In the fall of 1835, war broke out between Texans, mostly Anglo but with a significant Tejana/o contingent, and the central government of Mexico. The ensuing war for Texas independence (see chapter 3) would transform the region and would be one of the major events in Latina/o history.

While waves of independence rolled through Mexico and the rest of the Americas in the 1800s, Spain retained its empire in Puerto Rico and Cuba. In Puerto Rico, whose population was more than 150,000 in 1800, the economy was shifting toward a far greater reliance on exports. The Puerto Rican economy benefited from upheavals elsewhere in Latin America, especially in Haiti, where revolutionary wars disrupted that country's vast sugar plantations. Sugar, coffee, and tobacco production increased during the period, as did trade with European countries and the United States. According to one historian, "foreign trade increased 2000 percent" between 1814 and 1854 (Flores 2010, 55). As in Mexico, women in the Spanish-speaking Caribbean often took active roles in business and politics. San Juan, Puerto Rico, for instance, experienced considerable population growth in the early nineteenth century, due in part to significant numbers of women who moved to the city. San Juan's population grew from 7,800 in 1803 to nearly 9,000 in 1816 to 11,500 in 1827. As sugar production accelerated after 1800 in Puerto Rico, San Juan's proximity to sugar-growing regions and its accessible port helped draw new business, including a heightened trade in African slaves, and new residents, such as wealthy merchants and planters from elsewhere in the Caribbean, Spain, Ireland, and the United States.

The shift toward an export-oriented economy limited the production of subsistence goods on the island, leaving Puerto Ricans increasingly dependent on imports from other countries such as the United States. Another important aspect of this deepening trade relationship with the United States was the creation of commercial networks linking Puerto Rico with major U.S. cities on the East Coast like New York, Philadelphia, and Boston. Puerto Rican merchants shipped products like sugar and molasses to North America, while U.S. ships brought more basic food supplies, such as rice, to Puerto Rican ports. This network of merchants and trading centers was developed enough by the 1830s to support the establishment of the Socieded Benéfica Cubana y Puertorriqueña (Cuban and Puerto Rican Benevolent Society) in New York City, where merchants from both Puerto Rico and Cuba gathered. In coming decades, these commercial relationships linking Puerto Rico and the United States would grow even stronger.

Like the United States, Puerto Rico would continue to rely on slave labor well into the 1800s. Puerto Rico's economic growth in the early 1800s, in fact, increasingly relied on African slavery. Although Spain agreed to end the formal slave trade in 1820, the importation of slaves actually accelerated in the first half of the nineteenth century, when approximately 50,000 slaves entered the country. In fact, more slaves arrived in Puerto Rico between 1800 and 1873 (when slavery was finally abolished) than had arrived in the previous 300 years. Compared to other Caribbean countries, slaves represented overall a relatively small percentage (5%) of the island's total population; however, their presence was much higher in sugar-growing regions, which depended heavily on slave labor.

Despite generally brutal work and living conditions, Afro-Puerto Rican slaves actively resisted their bondage, at times even engaging in coordinated revolts. By one count, there were more than 40 planned slave uprisings in Puerto Rico between 1795 and 1873. One revolt, covering several planta-tions near the city of Bayamón, was planned in 1821. Though ultimately unsuccessful—slave owners discovered the plot and captured more than 50 of the revolt's organizers—the uprising was aimed at the overthrow of slav-ery on the island and the establishment of a republic led by former slaves similar to the Haitian government.

Like Puerto Rico, Cuba remained under Spanish imperial control for most of the 1800s. This control, however, was inconsistent, as political instability in Spain contributed to dramatic shifts in colonial policy. Successive regimes would alternate between offering greater freedom to Cubans and imposing tight restrictions on their political and economic activity. As Spanish control over the island wavered, new links developed between Cuba and newly inde-pendent countries in the Americas such as the United States. One of the most important trends, in fact, in nineteenth-century Cuba was a blossoming trade with its northern neighbor. By mid-century, the United States had replaced Spain as Cuba's most important trading partner. Increasing num-bers of North American ships docked at Cuban ports (600 in 1800, nearly 780 in 1826, and approaching 2,000 annually by the 1840s), and expanding U.S. companies established major new regional offices in Cuba. U.S. busi-ness interests also invested in sugar plantations and steam-powered sugar mills, mining operations, and railroad construction. In the 1830s, a 50-mile railroad track was completed to Havana, the first railroad line of such length in Latin America and built decades before such a track was constructed in Spain itself.

At the center of this transformation was sugar. By 1840, sugar accounted for 60 percent of Cuba's earnings from exports (the percentage would rise to almost 75% by 1860). With the rapid growth of the sugar economy came the expansion of the African slave trade. Between 1790 and 1820, 385,000 slaves were imported to the island. In the next three decades, another 272,000 enslaved people arrived. As a result, by the end of the 1830s, Cuba's slave population was approaching 50 percent of the entire island.

Deepening trade between Cuba and the United States in the early 1800s was accompanied by more sustained interaction between Cubans and North Americans. This interaction took many forms. On the one hand, U.S. new-comers associated with commercial interests moved to Cuba and established their homes on the island. Two U.S. men, a sugar planter and a sugar mer-chant, even founded a city in Cuba, named Cárdenas, which soon attracted

In the nineteenth century, Cuba and the United States developed increasing economic ties, and the sugar industry was a primary link between the two countries. Seen is a Cuban sugar train, circa 1920. (Library of Congress)

other U.S. immigrants. Other, more transient North Americans resided in boardinghouses in Cuban cities. "In their modest way," one historian notes, "the boardinghouses served as centers of cultural diffusion, a point at which North Americans and Cubans converged socially, talked politics, trade, and commerce, and gradually come to know each other" (Pérez 2003, 21).

From a broader perspective, U.S. political leaders frequently expressed interest in the early 1800s in annexing Cuba to the United States. Cuba was strategically located at the opening of the Gulf of Mexico and alongside important shipping lanes between the Atlantic Ocean and the Caribbean. U.S. business interests and politicians as notable as John Quincy Adams, Daniel Webster, and Thomas Jefferson saw the importance of Cuba to U.S. economic prosperity and political strength. Some prominent North Americans, in fact, openly advocated the annexation of the island. "The annexation of Cuba to our federal republic," John Quincy Adams observed, "will be indispensable to the continuance and integrity of the Union itself" (Pérez 2003, 39). Similar calls for annexation emerged from within Cuba as well during the period.

At the same time, many island elites profited handsomely from the boom in sugar production and the acceleration in the slave trade and, as a result, were often hesitant to support Cuba's independence from Spain and potentially jeopardize their financial prosperity. Elites expressed fears that rebellion against Spain could lead to broader social revolts, such as the slave uprisings that upended French rule in Haiti. Another force stifling change in Cuba was diplomatic, as rival European powers like France and England and newly independent countries like the United States supported continued Spanish rule over either the fractures and unpredictability of an independent Cuba or the island falling under the control of a rival nation. According to historian Gerald Poyo, the United States discouraged an attempt by the new republics of Colombia and Mexico in the 1820s to support a military expedition to liberate Cuba from Spanish control. Although U.S. officials like Secretary of State Henry Clay believed that Cuba would eventually be incorporated into the United States, the nation was reluctant to intervene or provide assistance to insurgents, whether located on or off the island. England took a similar stance to the planned invasion, fearing, in Poyo's words, "that it would disturb international relations sufficiently to pose a threat to their own possessions in the Caribbean" (Poyo 1989, 3). Thus, the prosperity of Cuban elites and the reluctance to intervene by foreign countries hindered the development of a broad-based and well-supported independence movement in Cuba.

Another notable trend in the relationship between Cuba and the United States in the early 1800s was the United States' new role as a base for exiled Cuban independence leaders. While the overall migration of Puerto Ricans and Cubans to North America remained small in the early nineteenth century, political exiles exerted special influence during the era. Spain's common response to political agitation (force the dissidents into exile in a foreign country) led to the resettlement of significant numbers of Puerto Rican and Cuban opposition leaders in the United States. Throughout the 1800s, Spanish exiles thus maintained political bases in the United States, especially in New York City. José Martí, for instance, who would lead the final, successful war for Cuban independence in the 1890s, spent considerable portions of his life in exile in New York City, planning and advocating for revolution. This trend of Cuban exiles organizing for revolution from American shores had roots in the early 1800s.

One such exile was José Alvarez de Toledo y Dubois. Educated in Spain, Alvarez rose through the ranks of the Spanish military and was eventually elected as a representative of Santo Domingo to the Spanish parliament. In 1811, however, Alvarez fled Spain after reports written by him criticizing the Spanish government surfaced. After a period in London, he settled in Philadelphia, joining a wider group of exiled activists and writers from throughout Spanish America, including Argentina, Venezuela, and Mexico. From Philadelphia, he published attacks on the Spanish crown and called for the independence of Spanish America. In 1811, he wrote an 83-page denunciation of Spain, "The Manifesto," which, according to literary historian Nicolás Kanellos, is a "call to all Spanish Americans to rise up in rebellion for their independence, basing their mission on the rights of man and using language similar to that in the United States declaration of independence" (Kanellos 2008, 89). Alvarez's revolutionary gaze soon sharpened to focus on Mexico, and he became deeply involved in Mexico's decade-long battle for independence from Spain. While meeting with powerful U.S. officials like James Madison, the secretary of state, and President James Monroe in Washington, D.C., Alvarez met Bernardo Gutiérrez de Lara, who was seeking U.S. support for the rebellion against Spain that was building in Texas.

Alvarez eventually joined Gutiérrez de Lara in Mexico, but not before publishing at least one pamphlet, and possibly two, in Philadelphia advocating for Mexican independence. While in Texas, Alvarez helped found the first newspaper in the region, *La Gaceta de Texas*, which was later renamed *El Mexicano*. After a series of successful political and military maneuvers, including being named a general in the Mexican Army and serving as an ambassador from Mexico to the United States, Alvarez betrayed his fellow revolutionaries and sided with Spain against the rebel forces.

Despite this betrayal, Alvarez was a critical figure in Latina/o literary and intellectual history. In the following decades, Spanish-language periodicals would appear in greater and greater numbers. According to Nicholas Kanellos, "scores of newspapers followed during the century," with publishing centers in New Orleans, Philadelphia, and New York (Kanellos 2008, 94). In the long, nineteenth-century tradition of Latina/o political exiles in the United States, these newspapers, and editors and journalists like José Alvarez de Toledo y Dubois, would be vital tools in efforts to topple the Spanish empire in the Americas.

Although Puerto Rico and Cuba followed a different path than Mexico in the early 1800s, with Mexico achieving its independence and the two islands remaining under Spanish rule, certain shared dynamics played out in all three countries. Economic ties deepened with the United States, as expanding U.S. business interests intersected with Mexican, Puerto Rican, and Cuban economies that possessed a renewed orientation to international trade and the production of export goods. African slavery, though outlawed in the Mexican Southwest, continued to be central to both economic development, especially in Puerto Rico and Cuba, and political controversy—most notably in Texas, where Anglo slave owners strongly resisted the Mexican government's attempts to outlaw the practice.

From a cultural perspective, the lives of Mexicans, Puerto Ricans, and Cubans were also intertwined with North Americans. Trade networks were at the center of many such cross-cultural interactions. Recall, for instance, the presence of Puerto Rican and Cuban merchants in North American cities like New York. In the Southwest, where Mexican/U.S. trade networks were also common, this cultural convergence could take on the added feature of intermarriages and informal sexual unions between Mexican women and Anglo men.

After 1835, the historical trajectory of each region would diverge in important ways. As the next chapter will discuss, Mexico would lose Texas in 1836, and then much of what would become the U.S. Southwest in 1848, while Puerto Rico and Cuba—despite active independence movements— would continue to be colonies of Spain for several decades to come. Nonetheless, significant patterns apparent in the early 1800s would persist, especially the heightened role of Puerto Ricans, Cubans, and Mexico in the economic, political, and cultural life of the United States.

PROFILE: VICTORIA BARTOLOMEA REID

While the social worlds of New Spain and Mexico offered some chances for advancement and higher status for individuals, few women or men improved their lives as much in the early nineteenth century as Victoria Bartolomea Reid. Born near the San Gabriel mission in Spanish Alta California around 1810, Victoria Bartolomea was a Comcrabit Indian and was raised by her parents until about the age of six, when she was forced to relocate to the nearby mission. There, she learned Spanish and was forced to convert to Christianity and to adopt Spanish customs and practices. She became an assistant to one of the Spanish women helping to run the mission, and in her early teens was compelled to marry a fellow convert, Pablo Maria, from a nearby Native community. The couple had four children, the first when Bartolomea was 15 years old. In a rare accomplishment for Native peoples in California, the couple also managed to be given land by the overseers of the mission. In 1836 Bartolomea's husband, Pablo, died, leaving her in full control of the two parcels of land, a valuable possession in early nineteenth-century California.

That year, 1836, Victoria Bartolomea married once again, to Hugo Reid, a Scottish immigrant and entrepreneur, who also assumed guardianship of his new wife's four children. For several years, the couple jointly ran their two ranches, and Victoria Reid was widely praised for her financial and management skills, as she often oversaw the family's business enterprises. Although the couple eventually separated and Victoria Reid would end her life in poverty, her life and achievements point to the intimate connections that bound together Indian, Mexican, and U.S. cultures in the borderlands region in the nineteenth century, as well as offering one of many examples of talented and business-savvy women in Latina/o history.

PROFILE: CONCEPCIÓN ARGUELLO

In 1806, 15-year-old Concepción Arguello was a member of a small Spanish settlement in Northern California. Though her father was the commander of the Spanish fort, or presidio, at San Francisco and her family was hardly destitute, Arguello seemed eager to leave the region and her family. With many employment and travel opportunities declared off-limits to women in Spanish society, Arguello turned to one of the few other options available to women in the early 1800s: marriage. She and 50-year-old Nikolai Rezanov, a high-ranking Russian government official and merchant stationed along the Pacific coast, began courting each other and, despite her parents' misgivings, married. The marriage, however, was short-lived. Within the year, Rezanov died during a return voyage to Russia, and Arguello, who due to limited communication networks only learned of his death five years later, was left a widow.

Barely 20, Arguello retained the same independence and strong will that led her to pursue her marriage to Rezanov over her parents' clear objections. In 1816 James Wilcox, a California newcomer from Boston, offered to convert to Catholicism in order to marry Arguello. Not content to trade her independence for an unappealing marriage, Arguello remained unmarried throughout the rest of her life. Despite new chances to leave California, she apparently developed a great fondness for the land of her birth and led a life increasingly committed to religion. According to one historian, in 1852, in her early sixties, Arguello "became the first nun initiated into the newly established Dominican convent in Monterrey" (Casas 2005, 83). Concepción Arguello, though exceptional in many ways, represents a recurring theme in both the history of California in the early 1800s and Latina/o history in general: Latinas' determination to exercise, even in the face of imposing challenges, individual rights and freedoms.

PROFILE: JOSÉ IGNACIO DE LA GARZA

José Ignacio de la Garza was born in 1772 to an indigenous community in the region of the Rio Grande River, at the time known as the Río Grande del Norte. Taken from his family at a young age by Spanish authorities, de la Garza and his sister were raised as domestic servants in a Spanish household near what is now South Texas. Running away at a young age from his forced service, he found a series of jobs as a manual laborer in the region. He was also arrested several times by local authorities. One arrest resulted in imprisonment when he attempted to rescue his sister from domestic servitude in the household of a wealthy Spanish family. Another arrest occurred after he took an employer's property in what he described as a misunderstanding over wages owed to him.

In 1804, de la Garza was arrested for a different offense, though he once again displayed an unwillingness to accept his subordination to Spanish villagers. After an incident one night with a Spanish soldier and landowner, where de la Garza had been restrained and publically humiliated by the man, de la Garza confronted him the next day at the home of a local Spanish merchant. De la Garza reportedly issued a challenge to the soldier. "If he was a man," he taunted him, he would be willing to fight de la Garza (Valerio-Jiménez 2012, 17). No duel ensued, but de la Garza was arrested on charges of using insulting language. Though outnumbered in court and, like most Mexicans of indigenous background, lacking either wealth or social status, de la Garza refused to give ground, stating that he had merely been responding to disrespectful treatment on the part of the Spanish soldier. The court eventually dismissed the charges against de la Garza. Three years later, however, he was again involved in a dispute with Spanish villagers. On this occasion, de la Garza was badly beaten by several Spanish men. At the age of 35, José Ignacio de la Garza died of injuries sustained in the beating.

While the historical record is limited in terms of more information on the life of José Ignacio de la Garza, his determination to liberate himself and his sister from forced domestic labor and his refusal to defer to the views of supposedly superior Spanish villagers point to the enduring presence of Native resistance to Spanish colonialism in Latina/o history.

REFERENCES

Casas, María Raquel. "Victoria Reid and the Politics of Identity." In *Latina Legacies: Identity, Biography, and Community*, edited by Vicki L. Ruiz and Virginia Sánchez-Korrol, 19–38. New York: Oxford University Press, 2005.

Chávez-García, Miroslava. *Negotiating Conquest: Gender and Power in California 1770s to 1880s.* Tucson: University of Arizona Press, 2004.

Flores, Lisa Pierce. *The History of Puerto Rico.* Santa Barbara, CA: Greenwood Press, 2010.

Gómez-Quiñones, Juan. *Roots of Chicano Politics, 1600–1940.* Albuquerque: University of New Mexico Press, 1994.

Kanellos, Nicolás. "José Alvarez de Toledo y Dubois and the Origins of Hispanic Publishing in the Early American Republic." *Early American Literature* 43, no. 1 (2008): 83–100.

Pérez, Louis A., Jr. *Cuba and the United States: Ties of Singular Intimacy.* Athens: University of Georgia Press, 2003.

Poyo, Gerald E. *"With All, and for the Good of All": The Emergence of Popular Nationalism in the Cuban Communities of the United States, 1848–1898.* Durham, NC: Duke University Press, 1989.

Ramos, Raúl A. *Beyond the Alamo: Forging Mexican Ethnicity in San Antonio, 1821–1861.* Chapel Hill: University of North Carolina Press, 2008.

Valerio-Jiménez, Omar S. *River of Hope: Forging Identity and Nation in the Rio Grande Borderlands.* Durham, NC: Duke University Press, 2012.

Chapter 3

Los Americanos, 1835–1848

The decade and a half between 1835 and 1848 was one of the most tumultuous and transformative periods in the history of Latina/os in the United States. The simmering conflict in Texas over issues like slavery and local political control burst into full-scale war in the winter of 1835 and 1836. Organized violence continued in the Southwest for the next 10 years, cresting in the war between Mexico and the United States in 1846 and the signing of the Treaty of Guadalupe Hidalgo in 1848, one of the foundational documents in Latina/o history. Similar disputes over slavery and independence, some also escalating into violence, coursed through Puerto Rico and Cuba as well during the period.

Though the era was characterized by turmoil and change, certain prominent themes in Latina/o history endured and were even amplified. Latinas continued to challenge unequal treatment and assume leadership positions in civic society. Likewise, business, political, and personal interactions between Anglos from the United States and Mexicans, Puerto Ricans, and Cubans broadened, just as internal tensions (of race, class, and gender and sexuality) continued to divide Spanish-speaking communities in the Mexican north and the Spanish Caribbean. As always, many Latina/os who were excluded from full participation and membership in society—women of all social classes, individuals and communities of African and Native American heritage, and poor people in a variety of settings—struggled mightily to challenge their marginalization and subordinate status.

By the middle of the nineteenth century, the Mexican population of California, New Mexico, and Texas grew to, according to one detailed account, "a grand total of 80,302 Mexican Americans in the Southwest in 1850" (Nostrand 1975, 383). During this period, the vast region encompassing what are now the states of California, Nevada, New Mexico, and Texas and parts of Colorado, Arizona, and Utah was transformed through war and annexation from the Mexican North to the U.S. Southwest. This monumental change, which was responsible for the establishment of a major portion of the United States' continental empire, was the result of a convergence of a great many factors, including tensions in Mexico between regional and national governments, U.S. support of African American slavery, Mexican political instability, and U.S. expansionist and imperial desires.

Among the many leading to political instability in Mexico in the first half of the nineteenth century was the tension between the Mexican government and the Catholic Church. A central goal of reformers and Mexican independence leaders was to abolish certain kinds of economic privilege, while at the same time protecting the rights of private property. The secularization process, which focused on curtailing the special treatment of religious institutions and making it possible for others to acquire church land, was a pillar of this liberal program. In actual practice, however, the transfer of church property to the Mexican government and its people led to the rapid accumulation of large parcels of land by wealthy Mexicans, including elite families in the northern Mexican territories of California and New Mexico. Secularization also dramatically diminished the presence of priests in the region. There were only eight priests in New Mexico in 1829, two in Texas in 1830, and a total of five in California in 1846. More pointedly, by 1840, there were no Franciscans, the order that had dominated religious life in New Mexico for several centuries under Spanish rule, left within the province of New Mexico.

In California, Native American residents of church land, many of whom had suffered mightily under the control of religious missions, found themselves in similarly dire and impoverished situations as they became manual laborers on the estates of a handful of wealthy California/o families. In New Mexico, certain well-connected individuals received huge land grants from the Mexican government. By one count, 22 million acres of church land in New Mexico were distributed, mostly to private individuals. These large estates were especially prominent in the Río Abajo region, the area below La Bajada hill outside Santa Fe. In Río Abajo, which included the towns of Albuquerque and Bernalillo, large estates depended on good grazing land for sheep. A system developed, similar to sharecropping in the U.S. South later in the century, that enriched a small percentage of landowners and accelerated the poverty of the majority of families in the region. Above La Bajada Hill, in Río Arriba, the region that included the towns of Santa Fe and Taos, and contained more mountainous terrain, the relative absence of arable soil capable of supporting large farms or ranches led to more of a reliance on subsistence agriculture and smaller-scale livestock production.

The effects of secularization were far less pronounced in Texas than in California and New Mexico; however, political instability also plagued the region. The early 1830s had witnessed escalating conflict between regional political and economic leaders, composed of both Anglo immigrants and Tejana/o elites, and Mexico's central government. While disputes arose over broader issues like the region's political autonomy and ability to govern itself, a core component of the standoff was slavery. During the early decades of the 1800s, few people of African descent lived in Spanish and Mexican Texas. Most of the several hundred Afro-Spanish and Afro-Mexicans, in fact, were free and not enslaved. After Mexican independence in 1821, however, some U.S. immigrants, including the members of the colony sponsored by Stephen F. Austin, brought enslaved workers with them to Texas, especially into East Texas. As a result, slaves represented about a quarter of Texas's population by 1825.

While Anglo newcomers were initially allowed to bring enslaved people into Texas, the new republic of Mexico was increasingly hostile to slavery and there were growing attempts either to abolish slavery or to limit significantly the slave trade. Worried that their ability to own slaves, and their substantial financial investment in slaves, would be limited or declared illegal in Mexico, fewer Anglos immigrated to Texas with slaves in the late 1820s and early 1830s. In fact, during that period, the percentage of slaves actually decreased in Texas. By 1836, the year of independence, about 5,000 slaves lived Texas, or about 12 percent of the population. Despite this decreasing percentage of slaves in Texas, and the fact that some Texans, including both Tejana/os and Anglos, disapproved of slavery, Mexico's attempts to limit and even abolish slavery were clearly a factor in the movement for independence in Texas.

The Texas revolt, which had begun in 1835, continued through the winter and into the spring of 1836. In early March, Mexican forces numbering in the thousands laid siege to a former mission near San Antonio that was defended by Texan soldiers. After brutal fighting, including the deaths of 1,500 Mexican soldiers and the nearly 200 people killed inside the fort, Mexican soldiers assumed control of the fortress, which would become popularly known as the Alamo. Although Anglo-Americans predominated among the Texan forces, a significant number of the rebels were of Mexican descent. In fact, a wealthy rancher named Juan Seguín had been the head of a group of Tejano volunteers inside the Alamo. As Mexican troops approached, Seguín and his men were sent to gather reinforcements. The men were able to talk their way past the troops surrounding the mission by claiming to be countrymen of the Mexican soldiers. Seguín and his men, however, returned too late with their reinforcements and found among the dead seven Tejano volunteers. For all that the Alamo was a major victory

The overwhelming victory of the Mexican army at the Alamo in San Antonio, Texas, helped invigorate the Texas independence movement (Siege of the Alamo, 1836). (Library of Congress)

for the Mexican government, two months later, after several severe Mexican defeats, Texas won its independence in late spring 1836.

Emblematic of the complicated nature of Tejano politics during the war is the fact that at least two sets of brothers fought on opposite sides of the war. In one case, Francisco Esparza fought for the Mexican Army in the battle to retake Bexar and the Alamo, while his brother Gregorio was a Tejano soldier for the Texan revolt. After the Mexican victory, Francisco was granted permission to find his brother's body at the battlefield and bury it properly.

As violence, and finally war, overtook the region in the 1830s, the vibrant mixing of Mexican and Anglo culture, including business and political alliances and cross-cultural intimacy and marriage, which had once characterized social life in Texas, began to deteriorate. In its place emerged a rigid, deeply racialized cultural divide that enforced distance and hostility between the two groups. Texas independence in 1836 also ushered in new, more focused attempts to limit the rights and opportunities of both enslaved and free African Americans. The 1836 Texas constitution, like laws passed in following years, upheld slavery and the rights of slave owners, in addition to denying citizenship to free African Americans. Without the rights of citizens, free African Americans had great difficulty defending their titles to land they had bought. As a result, a great many African Americans lost their land in the 1830s. New laws also targeted African Americans that either directly or indirectly challenged slavery or white supremacy. One law passed in 1837 subjected enslaved and free African Americans alike to whippings if they used abusive language toward or threatened any Anglo. The same law forced any free African Americans who helped enslaved individuals to escape to themselves become a slave. Other laws made manumission, or giving freedom to slaves, more difficult and forced those slaves who had been freed previously to leave Texas. Another law made it illegal for free African Americans to enter Texas.

In 1837, the Texas congress also prohibited all marriages between individuals of European descent and African Americans, regardless of whether enslaved or free. This 1837 law significantly broke from the judicial precedent of Spanish and Mexican law. Before Texas independence, cross-racial marriages involving those of European, African, and Native background had been legal. The law also overturned the Spanish and Mexican law that allowed a slaveholder to marry his or her enslaved worker and effectively free that individual, and the children of the marriage, from slavery and give them full citizenship. Under the new Texas law, even if a slaveholder had wanted to marry a slave and free the slave and children, it would be illegal.

As a result of such laws, Anglo slave owners, who had previously hesitated to immigrate to Texas and risk losing their slave property under Mexican rule, flocked to the new republic of Texas. The number of African American slaves grew rapidly after 1836, especially in eastern Texas, reaching 40,000 or 20 percent of Texas's total population, by 1840. This increasing reliance on African American slavery would continue after the annexation of Texas to the United States in 1845. By 1850, 56,000 enslaved African Americans lived in Texas and by 1860, on the eve of the U.S. Civil War, there were 180,000 African Americans working as slaves in Texas, accounting for about a third of the state's total population.

Tensions between Mexico's central government and its northern provinces reverberated outside Texas as well during the 1830s. In New Mexico, the appointment and subsequent tumultuous administration of Governor Albino Pérez, an appointee of Mexican president Antonio López de Santa Ana, sparked dissatisfaction and eventual armed rebellion. *Nuevomexicana/os* rebelled against increased taxes and the consolidation of power and authority in Mexico City. Unlike Texas, according to one historian, "the revolt represented a protest against the territory's existing relationship to the national government, not a desire for independence or absorption into the United States" (Mora 2011, 40). New Mexico's Pueblo Indians were similarly threatened by changes in the national government's approach to its provinces. Pueblos found the forced conscription by the Pérez administration of scores of Pueblo men to battle Diné (also known as Navajo) raids and the government's seeming unwillingness to protect Pueblo lands against illegal settlements and squatters especially objectionable.

The Pérez administration thus managed to draw the ire of both Mexicans and Pueblo Indians in New Mexico; and when revolt finally broke out, rebels executed the governor, parading his head on a pole through the streets of Santa Fe, and killed some 20 more of his officials during the uprising. The revolt soon fizzled, however, especially as Mexican elites faced the unpleasant, for them at least, possibility that Pueblo Indians would successfully resist political control from any Mexican authority, whether from Mexico City or from within New Mexico itself. In the fall of 1837, a group of Mexican elites from the Albuquerque region organized a militia under Manuel Armijo and managed to force a peace treaty with the rebels in northern New Mexico. Rebel leaders were pardoned and Manuel Armijo effectively became New Mexico's new governor. Although New Mexico did not follow Texas's route to independence, tensions between the centralizing tendencies of Mexico's national government and Mexicans' desire for regional political and control were persistent themes during the period.

Despite such political turmoil, Mexican society continued to expand in New Mexico in the 1830s and 1840s. By 1850, there were 55,000 Mexicans living in New Mexico, accounting for 90 percent of the total population of nearly 60,000 in the territory (there were an estimated 3,300 Pueblo Indians and 1,500 Anglos also residing New Mexico in 1850). Despite continued inequalities, Mexican women persisted during this period in using the legal system to challenge their subordinate civic status. Barbara Roybal, for example, filed several complaints against her husband in 1830s Santa Fe. Her husband, she told the court, had "swatted her with a shoe and bruised her in the mouth" and had also been sexually involved with another women (González 1999, 31). Several years later, Roybal again appeared in court, complaining that her husband had pursued another sexual affair and that he refused to support her and their children. A significant number of other *Nuevomexicanas* similarly turned to both civil courts and religious authorities for protection and support.

Mexican men in New Mexico also relied on the courts during the late 1830s and 1840s. As in previous eras, legal proceedings in Mexican communities could arise from an array of conflicts, ranging from the filing of criminal charges to disputes over contracts, land sales, personal conduct, inheritances, and wills and any number of other business and personal interactions. Amid the growing influence of U.S. newcomers in business and political matters in New Mexico, Mexicans proved willing to use the courts, which were, after all, still under the full control of the Mexican government until 1846, to address perceived injustices. In April 1846, for instance, Marcelo Pacheco sued an American named William Messervy for slander. Both men were businessmen and Pacheco, according to one historian, "call[ed]

the Euro-American merchant 'a trespasser who thinks he owns everything' "
(González 1999, 49). Pacheco eventually won his slander case, pointing
once again to the determination of Mexicans, even on the eve of U.S. occupation, to assert publicly their rights to fair treatment in the face of U.S.
"trespassers."

While California experienced some political turmoil in the 1830s and
early 1840s, the region did not, in contrast to New Mexico and Texas, erupt
into widespread violence and revolt against Mexican rule. The intertwining
of family networks and obligations with political and business matters,
which had proven so successful in California in previous decades, once again
served elite Mexican men and women well.

The endurance of this patriarchal system in California, though plagued
with inequalities, offered certain opportunities to Mexican women, especially elite Californias. Nonelite women in California were at times also able
to carve space for themselves within male-dominated California society. In
1836, for example, California's governor sought to replace a local priest in
Santa Barbara. The priest, popular in the town, had angered the governor
by accusing him of sexual improprieties and troops were sent to forcibly
remove him from the church. Hearing rumors of the priest's expulsion, local
women, many of them devoted parishioners of the church, gathered to pre-
vent troops from leading the priest onto a waiting ship. The protesters were
soon joined by men from the town, and together the townspeople managed
to convince the military to release the priest and avoid a violent confrontation. "Although Santa Bárbara's women did not have a formal voice in
government," according to one historian, "non-elite women did have
recourse to riot and public demonstration to express their opinions" (Pubols
2010, 202).

The lives of Californias like the above women in Santa Barbara, and Mexicans throughout the region, were irrevocably changed by the war between
Mexico and the United States. The Mexican-American War began in 1846
and ended two years later, in 1848. As Anglo-American rule solidified in
Texas, the entire region encompassing the Mexican North became the target
of strengthening expansionist interest in the United States. In 1844, James
Polk was elected president of the United States. Polk had run on a platform
calling for the annexation of Texas, as well as other expansionist goals,
and his election fueled U.S. imperial desires. In 1845, the United States
annexed Texas. Less than a year later, a controversy erupted between the
United States and Mexico over the southern boundary of the new state of
Texas. The United States had accepted Texas's claim to the land north of
the Rio Grande River, while Mexico claimed land between the Rio Grande
and the more northern Nueces River. President Polk sent General Zachary
Taylor to the Texas side of the disputed area between the Nueces and the

Rio Grande with 3,500 U.S. troops. Polk also secretly ordered the navy to seize ports in Mexican California if war were to begin.

In the fall of 1845, Polk sent a negotiator to Mexico City with an offer of $30 million in exchange for New Mexico, California, and the area between the Rio Grande and the Nueces. Mexican officials, however, refused even to meet with the U.S. envoy, and the enraged U.S. president ordered troops to cross the Nueces River into the disputed territory. The following spring, a small skirmish broke out between Mexican and U.S. troops in that border region, and Polk proceeded to call for, and receive, a declaration of war from Congress.

The war with Mexico was deeply divisive in the United States. Many abolitionists were especially suspicious that it was an attempt to extend slavery. Over the next two years, Mexican and American troops battled, at times viciously, in northern and central Mexico. In California, the war began in the early summer of 1846, when "a motley collection of American trappers, horse thieves, and runaway sailors dressed in torn buckskin, many of them barefoot," forced a prominent Californio military leader, his brother, and an American in-law to accompany them under armed guard to their camp (Pubols 2010, 241). Meanwhile, another set of Anglo newcomers declared California an independent republic, free of Mexico. Unaware that war between Mexico and the United States had, in fact, been declared a month earlier, in May 1846, these would-be rebels soon dissolved into the larger U.S. military presence that established itself in California in early July 1846. Warfare continued in California until January of the following year, when California/o leaders agreed to abandon the war and sign a peace treaty with the United States. Characteristically, elite Mexican women played an important role in subsequent negotiations and helped convince U.S. leaders to assure, in the words of one historian, "Californios of the rights of American citizens: life, property, and movement" (Pubols 2010, 262). Three months later, the new U.S. government installed military rule over formerly Mexican California.

One of the most violent episodes in the war occurred in New Mexico in 1847 in what would come to be known as the Taos Revolt. Early in the war, U.S. troops had invaded northern New Mexico and established a military government in 1846. Charles Bent was appointed governor of New Mexico. Bent, an Anglo, had deep ties to the region, including his marriage to Maria Ignacia Jaramillo, a member of a prominent *Nuevomexicana/o* family. Although U.S. officials perceived little resistance to the imposition of military rule, opposition to U.S. authority simmered in Mexican and Native American communities.

In January of 1847, an armed rebellion of 2,000 Mexicans and Pueblo Indians based in the northern New Mexican town of Taos and led by

Mexicans Pablo Montoya and Manuel Cortés and Tomas Romero, a Taos Indian, swept across the region. The rebels targeted U.S. officials, including both Anglos and Mexicans. More than two dozen Anglos and Mexicans were killed, including Governor Bent himself, before the U.S. military arrived and, over a two-week period, forced the rebels to retreat to Taos. The final battle left 150 Mexicans and Pueblo Indians dead and was followed by mass trials for treason. U.S. officials ultimately executed more than a dozen northern New Mexicans for their participation in the uprising. Although the Taos Revolt signaled the end of large-scale opposition to U.S. rule, resistance by Mexicans and Native Americans to U.S. colonialism and federal control would persist, at times violently, in New Mexico and elsewhere in both the nineteenth and twentieth centuries.

The broader Mexican government, meanwhile, after suffering brutal defeats like the sacking of Mexico City by enemy soldiers, finally called for peace. In February 1848, a peace treaty between Mexico and the United States, the Treaty of Guadalupe Hidalgo, was signed, ending the Mexican-American War. According to the provisions of the treaty, the Rio Grande, not the Nueces River, became the new border between the two countries. In addition, large portions of the Mexican North (territory covering the current states of California, Nevada, New Mexico, and parts of what are now Colorado, Arizona, and Utah) were placed under U.S. rule and Mexico received $15 million from the United States. The treaty also included a provision stating that Mexicans who decided to stay in formerly Mexican, now U.S., territories and not immigrate to the south would be guaranteed protection of their property rights. In March 1848, the U.S. Congress approved the treaty, with one exception: the provision protecting the property rights of Mexicans choosing to remain in the United States. The Mexican Congress objected to the deletion of this provision, and the U.S. Congress agreed to add a statement affirming the rights of Mexicans in the United States to the protection of their legal rights to the land.

A critical provision of the Treaty of Guadalupe Hidalgo is thus the promise that Mexicans remaining in the United States and "elect[ing] to become citizens of the United States" would be "incorporated into the Union of the United States, and be admitted at the proper time (to be judged of by the Congress of the United States) to the enjoyment of all the rights of citizens of the United States." While these laws were often ignored under newly installed U.S. colonial rule, Mexicans continued in subsequent decades to point to the Treaty of Guadalupe Hidalgo as the basis of their rights as full U.S. citizens.

Like Mexicans, Puerto Ricans and Cubans faced both persistent economic inequality during the period and continued tensions between advocates of local authority and independence and those in favor of centralized, in this case Spanish, government. In Puerto Rico, such conflicts emerged within the context of a growing population and an expanding economy. In 1830, Puerto Rico's population was nearly 325,000, which represented a growth of more than 100,000 people, close to a 50 percent increase, in just 15 years. Fifteen years later, the island population had grown by another 125,000 people, reaching a population of almost 450,000. The enslaved population grew as well during the same period, from 42,000 in 1834 to 51,000 in 1846, as did the much larger group of free Afro-Puerto Ricans, which rose from 126,000 in 1834 to 176,000 in 1846. Contributing to this population growth was a significant level of immigration from elsewhere in Latin America and the Caribbean, including several thousand from Venezuela and from the Spanish portion of the island of Hispaniola (now the Dominican Republic).

Between 1830 and 1845, Puerto Rico's economy was increasingly tied to sugar production. The amount of land devoted to sugar, and to a lesser extent tobacco, cultivation rose dramatically during the period, limiting subsistence farming in favor of a focus on commercial and export crops. Puerto Rico, in fact, came to compete with Cuba as the Caribbean's major exporter of sugar. Despite the fact that Cuba was a much larger island and devoted much more land to sugar cultivation, Puerto Rico proved to be a strong commercial rival to Cuba. Puerto Rico exported nearly 40,000 tons of raw sugar in the period 1838 to 1842 and more than 50,000 tons between 1848 and 1852. Coffee exports were also significant during the period, averaging 5,000 tons per year by mid-century.

Trade with the United States was an especially important aspect of the success of Puerto Rico's sugar production. While Cuban exports to North America were largely refined or semirefined sugar, Puerto Rican exports to the United States were proportionally larger and contained more raw sugar and molasses. In 1845, the United States purchased over 40 percent of all Puerto Rican sugar exports, while over 10 percent went to Great Britain and France, respectively, and less than 5 percent was sent to Spain. Puerto Rico had benefited from loosening trade policies such as an 1845 British decision to allow the importation of foreign sugar. That decision in Great Britain led to a dramatic rise in sugar purchases from Puerto Rico, which jumped from 3,600 tons of sugar in the early 1840s to more than 9,000 annual tons by the end of the decade.

As in Puerto Rico, Cuba's relationship with the United States deepened and expanded during the 1830s and 1840s. Small numbers of Cubans, recall, had settled in U.S. cities, especially in New York, Philadelphia, and New Orleans, in the 1820s and early 1830s. Cubans established trading houses and merchant organizations in the United States and, according to one historian, "increasingly sent their children to the United States to be educated" (Poyo 1989, 1). Although relatively few in numbers (fewer than a thousand by one estimate), Cuban newcomers tended to be politically influential and financially stable members of Cuba's middle and upper classes.

Conflicts over slavery and continued Spanish rule also occurred in Cuba as mid-century approached. Afro-Cubans, of course, led many of these protest movements. One of the largest uprisings occurred in the mid-1840s, when a series of slave revolts swept through Cuba. In 1843, slaves organized three major uprisings, including a rebellion in Matanzas where hundreds of slaves on sugar and coffee plantations in western Cuba coordinated a sustained attack on multiple estates before government troops on horseback managed to defeat the rebels.

The Spanish responded to such uprisings with a violent attack on a range of Cubans. The year 1844, in fact, became known as the "Year of the Lash," and Spanish officials named the slave conspiracy "La Escalera," or the ladder, after the form of torture inflicted on rebellious slaves, who were tied to ladders as they were whipped. Spanish authorities targeted those involved in the planned uprising as well as free Afro-Cubans in general. Accused leaders of the revolt were executed, including acclaimed Afro-Cuban poet Gabriel de la Concepción, also known as Plácido. Although free Afro-Cubans represented a small percentage of the island's population (15%), according to historian Michele Reid-Vasquez, they "comprised over 67 percent of those sentenced" during the initial Spanish repression (Reid-Vasquez 2011, 3).

The Spanish also lashed out at the broader community of free Afro-Cubans. Free Afro-Cuban women and men were prohibited from certain types of employment, while scores of others were forced into exile and banished from their native land. Among the destinations for exiled Afro-Cubans was the United States. Afro-Cubans based in the United States, in fact, played an important role in mid-century exile politics. In one instance, a collaboration between a Spanish diplomat and New York City police led to reports of a strong Afro-Cuban abolitionist and independence network operating in U.S. cities in the mid-1840s. The report was based on information provided by a police informant, a formerly enslaved woman, who was romantically involved with one of the men. The man, known as "El Secretario" due to his business skill, was one of the "negros españoles" who organized against Spanish rule in the Caribbean. According to the informant, El Secretario and his fellow exile leaders, who were also of Afro-Cuban and Afro-Spanish descent, traveled between New York City, Philadelphia, Washington, D.C., and New Orleans. They held regular meetings in those cities and tried to raise money to support their fight for independence. The meetings at times drew dozens of other activists. At one gathering in New York City, according to historian Michele Reid-Vasquez, officials "observed forty-three *negros españoles*—twenty from New York, twenty from Philadelphia, and three from Baltimore—gather to meet for five consecutive nights on the outskirts of the city" (Reid-Vasquez 2011, 92). Another set of meetings occurred in New Orleans, confirming similar reports from Spanish officials that Afro-Cuban political leaders were active in Louisiana as well.

New Orleans, in fact, was a frequent destination for Cuban and Puerto Rican political exiles. The busy port city was linguistically and racially diverse and linked northeastern and western regions of North America through the nearby Mississippi River to the Gulf of Mexico and the Caribbean. New Orleans was also the site of a dynamic Spanish-language print culture in the nineteenth century. *El Misisipí*, the first U.S. Spanish-language newspaper, was published in New Orleans in 1806 and, by 1860, New Orleans outpaced New York as the home of Spanish-language periodicals with, by one count, 23 titles, compared to New York's 13. Although many of these newspapers lasted only a handful of years, and many issues have sadly been lost, their influence was widespread.

U.S. census records point to the prominent place of New Orleans as a site of immigration from the Spanish-speaking Caribbean. In 1850, Jean Fernandez, a sailor born in Cuba, appeared in the U.S. census in New Orleans's Jefferson Parish. Thirty-year-old Fernandez lived with his wife, Consuela, and infant son. The household also included 12-year-old "M. Lopes," who may have been either a relative or a domestic servant. Next to the Fernandez family lived two men born in "Spain," birthplaces that could have, of course, referred to Spain itself, or to Cuba, Puerto Rico, or any of a number of other Spanish colonial outposts in the early nineteenth-century Caribbean and Latin America.

José Hernandez, a Cuban-born sugar manufacturer, also lived in New Orleans with his wife and three children, all four born in Louisiana. Hernandez appears to have been relatively prosperous. Unlike many of his neighbors, he listed himself as owning real estate worth $400. In one remarkable neighborhood in Orleans Parish lived several Spanish-born merchants and their Spanish-surnamed Cuban, Mexican, and Louisiana-born clerks. In another, more working-class neighborhood, Mexican laborers resided alongside Spanish-surnamed Texans, such as Concepción Estrada and Juan Pares. This New Orleans neighborhood even included intermarriages, with the households of Encarnación (born in Mexico) and James (born in Pennsylvania) Higgins and Manuel (born in Mexico) and Martha (born in Kentucky) Acosta. While exile politics provided one arena for pan-Latina/o organizing and community building, commerce and trade was clearly another critical space for cross-Latina/o affiliation.

Juan Pablo Duarte (1813–1876) is one of the heroes of the Dominican Republic, which became independent in 1844. (Library of Congress)

Like Puerto Ricans and Cubans, migrants from the Dominican Republic also traveled to the United States in the mid-nineteenth century. One of the most prominent visitors to the United States was Dominican independence leader Juan Pablo Duarte. Duarte, according to literary scholar Silvio Torres-Saillant, studied English in New York City for a period before the nation's independence in 1844 and may have "added to the bulk of his writings during his North American sojourn" (Torres-Saillant 1993, 255). Another Dominican independence leader, Matias Ramón Mella, also used the United States as a base for organizing against Spanish rule in the Caribbean. Writer Alejandro Angulo Guridi not only spent several years in the United States, but celebrated a second marriage in the state of Virginia and even became a U.S. citizen.

At times, these mid-nineteenth-century journeys could lead far beyond coastal cities and into the interior of the continent. Williams Wilks, for instance, was born in Santo Domingo in 1813 and at nearly the age of 40 had moved to eastern Michigan. Wilks worked as an "omnibus driver" (a driver of a horse-drawn wagon or carriage) and appeared relatively prosperous compared to many of his neighbors; he owned $400 in property in 1850. Living with his U.S.-born wife and son, and a male lodger, Wilks and his household were also identified as "Mulatto" in the 1850 U.S. census.

The Wilks household were the only "Mulattos" in an otherwise all-"White" neighborhood (at least according to the racial categories of the U.S. government). While certainly differentiated by race, Wilks seemed otherwise fairly well integrated into his community.

As the first half of the nineteenth century drew to a close, a gap seemed to develop between the major Latina/o groups in North America. While Mexicans living in California, New Mexico, and Texas found themselves, by mid-century, citizens of the United States, Puerto Ricans and Cubans remained, despite sustained efforts by independence leaders on both islands, under Spanish rule.

Despite these diverging paths, similarities endured that continued to bind the groups together. Latinas, for instance, sustained their active role in their communities, refusing to accept marginal status either among other Latina/os or in broader U.S. or Spanish society. Affiliations across Latina/o groups also deepened during the period, especially between Puerto Ricans and Cubans, who formed merchant associations and made common cause as political exiles and independence leaders.

At the same time, broader American society tended to consider different Latina/o groups in a similar, unflattering light. This negative vision of Latina/os was especially evident in discussions of American expansion and the settlement of new land by Anglos. In these accounts, Mexicans, Puerto Ricans, Cubans, and other Latin Americans were routinely viewed as racially inferior and incapable of productive land use and proper governance. Notwithstanding such demeaning depictions of Latina/os by Anglos, Latina/os throughout North America struggled mightily to create positive representations of themselves and their communities and fought to resist attempts to limit their political participation and inclusion in American culture and society.

PROFILE: GERTRUDIS BARCELÓ

Latina businesswomen have a long and distinguished history in the United States. This history stretches back hundreds of years in North America, and among the most successful Latina entrepreneurs was *Nuevomexicana* Gertrudis Barceló.

In 1830s and 1840s New Mexico, few women, or men, were as visible or as controversial as Barceló. Also known as "La Tules," or "the reed," a sarcastic reference to her supposedly excess weight, Barceló owned and operated liquor and gambling establishments that served both Mexicans and Anglos. She had begun her career in the 1830s as a card dealer, specializing in the card game known as monte, and steadily expanded her business to include saloons and other real estate holdings. Though operating less reputable businesses like gambling and bars, Barceló was also engaged in more respectable activities. She was married and gave generously to a local church.

Anglo newcomers to Santa Fe, though clearly aware of her entrepreneurial skills and talent for business, routinely disparaged Barceló. She was described as sexually promiscuous, for instance, a depiction that Anglo writers often extended to include *Nuevomexicanas* and Mexican women in general. Yet, despite these demeaning accounts by Anglos, Barceló managed to endure and even profit from U.S. expansion and emerging Anglo domination in the region. During the tumultuous times leading up to, during, and after the Mexican-American War, her savvy business sense allowed her to accumulate a considerable fortune. By the time she died in 1852, her wealth was an estimated $10,000.

PROFILE: FÉLIX VARELA

Félix Varela was born in Cuba in 1788 to a Spanish father and a Cuban mother. Left an orphan by the age of six, Varela moved with his grandfather, a military officer, to St. Augustine, Florida. Deciding against a career in the military, the young man chose to study religion and become a priest. A talented and committed student, Varela soon graduated from San Carlos Seminary and College in Havana in 1808 and was ordained a priest in 1811. In addition to his scholarly accomplishments, the young man also helped found the Philharmonic Society of Havana a year later. At the age of 23, Varela was hired as a professor of philosophy at San Carlos.

Félix Varela soon became one of Cuba's leading intellectuals. He argued for the increasing autonomy of Spanish possessions in the Americas like Cuba and Puerto Rico. He also called for the eventual abolition of slavery, adding that slave owners should be compensated for their lost property and labor. Active in Cuban independence politics, Varela was forced to flee the Spanish government to New York City in 1823. He lived in New York for nearly the next 30 years, editing and contributing essays to Spanish-language exile newspapers like *El Habanero*. He also established himself as one of the leaders of New York's Catholic community. Varela helped found and financially support the Church of the Transfiguration in New York City. He served as its pastor and helped lead it from 1836 to 1850.

Chronically ill, with a persistent cough, Varela moved to St. Augustine, Florida, in 1850. He continued to serve as a Catholic priest in St. Augustine, performing Mass when his health permitted, and received visitors and well-wishers. He died in St. Augustine in 1853. Throughout his life, Varela maintained his strong support for Cuban independence and the abolition of slavery.

PROFILE: JUAN SEGUÍN

Juan Seguín was one of the heroes of Texas independence. Seguín was born in 1806 to an elite family in Spanish Texas. The Seguín family traced its roots in Texas back several generations and was both wealthy and politically prominent. Though still in his teens, Seguín helped his mother manage the post office in San Antonio and became more deeply involved in local and regional politics. Seguín's political career included many interactions with Anglo newcomers to Texas such as the family of Stephen F. Austin. Seguín, in fact, had established a strong relationship with the Austin family as a young man, exchanging letters as a teenager with Stephen Austin and helping to host Austin's brother when he visited San Antonio.

In 1826, Seguín married Gertrudis Flores de Abrego, whose family was similarly wealthy and well respected in Texas, and embarked on a career in politics. He was elected the alcalde (or mayor) of San Antonio and was appointed to a position overseeing portions of southern Texas in 1834. As tensions accelerated between residents of Texas, including both Tejana/os and Anglo Texans, and the central government in Mexico City, Seguín was a powerful advocate of local and regional autonomy, and like many other Tejana/os, he actively supported the Texas independence movement. During the ensuing war with Mexico, Seguín was a captain in the army of Texas, and in his capacity as commander of the forces at San Antonio led the burial services after the defeat at the Alamo.

After the war, Seguín served several terms as a senator and fought for the rights of Tejana/os in the newly established Texas legal system. In 1842, accused of divided loyalties between Texas and Mexico, Seguín was forced to abandon his position as mayor of San Antonio and flee to Mexico. He returned to the city after the Mexican-American War in 1848 and served in a series of important political positions, including justice of the peace in Bexar County and judge in Wilson County, and remained active in the Democratic Party in Texas for many years. Seguín also led troops in Mexico in the 1850s and 1860s. Juan Seguín died in Nuevo Laredo in 1890.

REFERENCES

González, Deena J. *Refusing the Favor: The Spanish-Mexican Women of Santa Fe 1820–1880.* New York: Oxford University Press, 1999.

Mora, Anthony. *Border Dilemmas: Racial and National Uncertainties in New Mexico, 1848–1912.* Durham, NC: Duke University Press, 2011.

Nostrand, Richard L. "Mexican Americans Circa 1950." *Annals of the Association of American Geographers* (September 1975): 378–90.

Poyo, Gerald E. *"With All, and for the Good of All": The Emergence of Popular Nationalism in the Cuban Communities of the United States, 1848–1898.* Durham, NC: Duke University Press, 1989.

Pubols, Louise. *The Father of All: The de la Guerra Family Power and Patriarchy in Mexican California*. Berkeley: University of California Press, 2010.

Reid-Vazquez, Michele. *The Year of the Lash: Free People of Color in Cuba and the Nineteenth-Century Atlantic World*. Athens: University of Georgia Press, 2011.

Torres-Saillant, Silvio. "Before the Diaspora: Early Dominican Literature in the United States." In *Recovering the U.S. Hispanic Literary Heritage*, Vol. 3, edited by Ramón A. Gutiérrez, Genaro M. Padilla, María Herrera-Sobek, 250–67. Houston, TX: Arte Público Press, 1993.

_____ *Chapter 4* _____

Separate Paths, 1848–1868

In 1848, Mexico and the United States signed the Treaty of Guadalupe Hidalgo, one of the key events in Latina/o history. The treaty transferred huge swaths of land from Mexico to the United States, and tens of thousands of former residents of Mexico became U.S. citizens. For Mexicans on newly U.S. territory, the next two decades forced major adjustments, with new forms of government, new systems of property ownership, and a new authority for U.S. culture and customs. Great losses accompanied many of these changes for Mexicans: losses in land, political and economic status, and prestige. At the same time, some Mexicans, including Mexican women, found new opportunities in their transformed world.

Unlike Mexicans, who shifted from Spanish to Mexican to U.S. governments in the first half of the nineteenth century, Puerto Ricans and Cubans remained subjects of the Spanish crown throughout the period. Nevertheless, independence efforts persisted on both the islands and in exile communities in New York, Philadelphia, and New Orleans. Two decades after the end of the Mexican-American War, another major confrontation erupted in the Caribbean. In 1868, Cuban independence leaders led an armed rebellion against Spanish authorities. The ensuing war (the Ten Years War) would last until 1878. At the same time, Puerto Rican rebels, based in the mountain town of Lares, took up arms against both slavery and continued Spanish rule on their island in the Lares Revolt of 1868.

Latina/os in the mid-nineteenth century, whether newcomers to North America or remaking their homes in the aftermath of the Mexican-American War, displayed characteristic grit and determination in managing to carve space for themselves and their communities amid a violent and war-torn era.

The decisive victory of the United States in the Mexican American War
(1846–1848), included the invasion of Mexico City and the storming of
Chapultepec Castle, which housed Mexico's military academy. (Library of
Congress)

As the U.S. Civil War, the bloody battle between defenders of the U.S.
slave system and opponents of slavery, raged in North America in the first
half of the 1860s, another war over slavery accelerated in the Spanish Caribbean during the same decade. In the 1850s and 1860s, for instance, antislavery politics spread throughout Puerto Rico. By the end of the 1860s, Puerto
Rico's population had risen to 600,000. The free Afro-Puerto Rican population grew rapidly, from 175,000 to 237,000, while the population of predominantly European descent increased from 216,000 to 323,000. The
number of enslaved people in Puerto Rico actually decreased during the
same period, from more than 50,000 to 39,000. According to the census of
the island in 1869, 40 percent of Puerto Ricans were free Afro-Puerto
Ricans, 54 percent were "white," and 6 percent were slaves.

While supporters of slavery contended that agricultural production on the
island was completely dependent on slave labor and would collapse in its
absence, abolitionists challenged this claim. Pointing to the 1860 census,
where they claimed that the number of free workers was "seven times
greater (70,000) than that of slave workers (10,000)," abolitionists argued
that the Puerto Rican economy could easily survive the end of slavery
(Wagenheim 1997, 160). Antislavery activists also published strong critiques of Spanish rule on the island, such as the poem "Agüeybaná el Bravo"
("Agüeybaná the Brave"), which appeared in the newspaper *El Ponceño* in

1852. The poem, named after the famous Native leader who battled Spanish occupation of Puerto Rico in the 1500s, called on Spain to abandon the island and relinquish its control of Puerto Rico.

The Spanish response to such activism was their usual practice of forced exile, and the United States often served as a base for many abolitionist and independence leaders of the mid-nineteenth century. One prominent target of the Spanish government was Ramón Emeterio Betances, a physician of mixed African and European descent from Mayagüez, Puerto Rico. Betances and a fellow physician had been accused of organizing an abolitionist society and were forced to flee, as so many exile leaders did, to New York City. In New York, they continued to call for the end of slavery on the island. In 1867, with allies in the Sociedad Republicana de Cuba and Puerto Rico, they issued from New York a series of demands on Spain, including Betances's "Ten Commandments of Free Men" ("Los Diez Mandamientos de Hombres Libros"). The proclamation would become one of the key documents of the Puerto Rican independence movement. The first of the 10 demands called for the abolition of slavery, and the list included claims of freedom of speech, of worship, of the press, of the right to bear arms, and of the right to elect one's own government officials. A year later, in 1868, Betances would help organize an armed uprising against Spanish rule in Puerto Rico, the Lares Revolt. Though the rebellion was quickly turned back by the Spanish military, Betances and the Lares rebels would inspire abolitionists and independence leaders to continue their attacks on Spanish rule in the Caribbean.

Another independence and abolitionist leader, Julio Vizcarrondo, was also forced to live in exile in the United States in the mid-nineteenth century. When he returned to Puerto Rico in 1854, he released the slaves that he had inherited from his family and founded an abolitionist newspaper, *El Mercurio*. Vizcarrondo was soon forced once again to flee the island, and, from Madrid in the 1860s, he founded more antislavery publications. According to historian Olga Jiménez de Wagenheim, Vizcarrondo helped form "the *Sociedad Abolicionista Española* (Spanish Abolition Society), to pressure the government into ending slavery" (Wagenheim 1997, 158). As the activist journeys of Betances, Vizcarrondo, and others make clear, both antislavery and anti-Spanish politics were deeply intertwined among Puerto Rican and Cuban exiles communities in North America.

The deep antislavery tradition in independence movements in nineteenth-century Latin America (recall the explosive tension in Texas between the newly independent Mexican government that banned slavery and slave-owning Anglo newcomers) appeared with special intensity in the abolitionist exile newspaper *El Mulato*, published by Cubans in New York City in the mid-1850s. *El Mulato* also developed a strong critique of the United States

and its reluctance to end slavery. While many exile leaders sought the support of the United States, including slave-owning sections of the country, in
the 1850s *El Mulato* strongly opposed slavery. In one issue from 1854, editors stated bluntly that their goal was "to attack slavery in whatever form
it takes, out of a belief that it is baneful and incompatible with legitimate
and true liberty" (Lazo 2005, 141). Where other exile newspapers echoed
the fears of many antislavery leaders in the United States that Cuba's multiracial society, especially its large Afro-Cuban population, was a threat, *El
Mulato*, according to literary historian Rodrigo Lazo, "called on Cubans
to recognize the African racial and cultural influence" (Lazo 2005, 141).
As the United States careened toward a brutal war over slavery in the
1850s—the American Civil War would begin in 1861 and last for four
bloody years—one of the strongest voices in opposition to slavery and in
support of equal treatment for those of African descent in the Americas
emerged from the Cuban immigrant community in the United States.

Despite a shared commitment on the part of many activists to both end
slavery and gain independence, however, ending Spanish rule for some exiles
took precedence over ending slavery. Alliance with proslavery forces in the
United States often proved expedient, as when a New York exile group
sought the aid of a proslavery leader from the state of Mississippi in organizing a plot to invade the island in the early 1850s. In the 1840s and
1850s, that is, Latina/o exiles at times supported the U.S. annexation of
Cuba and were occasionally willing to abandon or postpone their antislavery sentiments in order to escape the Spanish government.

Political exiles from Spanish-controlled islands in the Caribbean were not
the only Latina/os or Latin Americans advocating independence, or
abolition, during this period. In 1865, Benjamin Vicuña Mackenna, a Chilean government official stationed in New York City, founded a Spanish-
language newspaper aimed at discrediting and undermining Spanish rule in
the Americas. *La Voz de América* included prominent members of the
Cuban and Puerto Rican exile communities in the United States and contained writings critical of Spanish control of Puerto Rico and Cuba. Vicuña's
efforts, which extended beyond propaganda to what one historian describes
as "provid[ing] funds to equip a privateer to harass Spanish shipping," eventually led to his arrest by U.S. officials and his return to Chile (Poyo 1989,
12). Despite Vicuña's departure, *La Voz de América* continued publishing
as its leadership transferred to Cuban and Puerto Rican editors.

Poets provided another influential voice that was critical of Spanish rule in
the Caribbean. In 1858, a group of exiled Cuban poets in New Orleans published *El laúd del destierro* (*The Exile's Lute*). According to literary historian Kirsten Silva Gruesz, the collection was "the first exclusively Spanish-
language poetry anthology to be published in the United States" and

attempted to fuse artistic production with calls for revolution and Cuban independence (Gruesz 2002, 146). In California, other exile leaders helped found important Spanish-language newspapers such as *El Nuevo Mundo*, which began publishing in San Francisco in 1864. The paper supported independence from Spain for Caribbean islands and the abolition of slavery throughout the Americas, including celebrating the reelection of U.S. president Abraham Lincoln through full-page advertisements. Like other nineteenth-century periodicals, the paper combined news articles and political essays with prose and poetry.

One poet who published in *El Nuevo Mundo* was Isabel Prieto. Mexican-born Prieto, who was fluent in four languages, began writing poetry at a young age (her first poem was published when she was 16) and also wrote plays. During the French occupation of Mexico in the 1860s, her family relocated to California, and Prieto wrote in the poem "¡Oh patria mía!" of her longing to return to Mexico and her distaste for San Francisco:

"Yo no puedo vivir entre estas nieblas,
Que me sofocan en su espeso velo;
De nuestra patria el transparente cielo
Siempre limpio y azul voy a buscar."

("I can't live among these fogs,
That suffocate me in their dense veil;
I'm off to seek the transparent sky—
Always clean and blue—of our homeland.") (Gruesz 2002, 183)

Prieto's writings were published in periodicals in the United States in both California and New York into the 1870s. Tragically, however, she died of breast cancer in 1876, at the age of 43. Had she lived, Prieto would have likely continued to write movingly of themes common to Latina/o history: exile, longing for home, adjustments and triumphs in new lands.

Political exiles and journalists tended to be some of the most visible and vocal members of the Latina/o community in the mid-century United States; however, they were not the only Latinas and Latinos in cities like Boston, New York, and Philadelphia. In 1860, the family of Julia and Louis Gasper lived in Philadelphia in a predominantly Irish and native-born U.S. neighborhood. Louis Gasper was Puerto Rican and listed his occupation as "Barber," while his wife, Julia, was born in Pennsylvania, as were two young men in the home, a 15-year-old son and a 21-year-old lodger. Besides their nationality, the Gasper family was also set apart by race. Louis Gasper and his son were both described as "Black" by the U.S. census, and Julia was listed as "Mulatto," a broad racial category covering those of mixed Anglo and African American, or in this case Afro-Latina/o, heritage. The Gasper family is thus notable not only for being among the pioneers that helped establish the Puerto Rican community in the nineteenth-century United States but also for highlighting the presence of Afro-Puerto Ricans in North America in the decades before 1900.

Puerto Ricans also lived farther north along the U.S. Atlantic coast in Connecticut and Massachusetts. In 1860, according to historian Ruth Glasser, 10 Puerto Ricans lived in New Haven, Connecticut, including a soldier, Augustus Rodriguez, who fought for the Union army during the Civil War. After the war, Rodriguez continued to live in New Haven and worked as a firefighter, as the owner of a cigar store, and as a saloon keeper. Records of passenger ships suggest a lively trade between Puerto Rico and Connecticut in the 1860s as, in Glasser's words, "ships ferried wealthy tourists, merchants, planters, and skilled workers of both nationalities between Bridgeport or New Haven, Connecticut, and Mayagüez, Ponce, or Guayanilla, Puerto Rico" (Glasser 2005, 176). In one case, from the mid-1860s, a 29-year-old dentist from Ponce sailed to New Haven with plans to make a new home in the United States. Similar links tied Puerto Ricans to Boston, where a handful of Puerto Ricans born on the island appeared in the 1860 census for the city.

Like the above newcomers to North America, many of the Puerto Ricans and Cubans living in U.S. cities in the mid-nineteenth century made homes in mixed ethnic and racial neighborhoods where they were not the majority population. In some cases, however, small enclaves developed where Latina/os were not the minority. In New York City in 1860, one stretch of households contained 22 Cubans (of 40 total) as well as 1 Spaniard and several children of Cuban-born parents. The Cubans living in this neighborhood included merchants, a teacher, a druggist, and a doctor, and several families also seemed to be able to afford to employ domestic servants.

Another prosperous household of Spanish Caribbean descent in New York City belonged to the Gimbernat family. In addition to Florentine Gimbernat and his wife, who was listed in the census only as "Mrs. F. Gimbernat," the household contained seven of the couple's children and a domestic servant born in Ireland. The varied birthplaces of the Gimbernat family point to the diverse origins of the Latina/o community in the United States. Florentine Gimbernat, a merchant, was born in Havana, Cuba, while his wife and three of his children were born in Puerto Rico. A daughter was born on the island of St. Thomas, a son in Venezuela, and the youngest child, a daughter, in New York City.

The Gimbernat family not only was wealthy enough to afford to employ a domestic servant, but was listed with substantial wealth, with nearly $20,000 in real estate and personal property, a significant sum in the mid-century United States. The Gimbernat family also possessed enough social status that the sudden death of 30-year-old Florentino Gimbernat Jr., the family's oldest child, in 1865 was announced in the *New York Times*. Though of multiple origins, occupations, and political orientations, and overall small in number, such immigrants helped create the foundation for the much larger Latina/o community that would emerge in eastern cities in the twentieth century.

Another important Latina/o immigrant group who arrived in small but significant numbers in the 1800s were Dominicans. Unlike Puerto Rico and Cuba, the Dominican Republic was an independent nation by the mid-nineteenth century, achieving its independence from Haiti in 1844. In the immediate postindependence period, leaders of the Dominican Republic and the United States established diplomatic relations and increasingly discussed the annexation of the newly independent nation to its larger neighbor to the north. The administration of President James Polk, for instance, which was best known for its expansionist policies and appropriation of Mexican land after the Mexican-American War (1846–48), also expressed interest in drawing the Dominican Republic under U.S. rule. Desire by U.S. leaders to establish a military base in Samaná Bay led post–Civil War presidents Andrew Johnson and Ulysses Grant to discuss annexation with even greater interest. Johnson even voiced his support of Dominican annexation in one of his inaugural addresses, and Grant managed to convince Congress to support an inquiry into annexation that featured a visit to the Dominican Republic by a congressional committee including several senators and the esteemed African American leader Frederick Douglass. Though annexation efforts in both the United States and the Dominican Republic were ultimately unsuccessful, the bonds established between the two countries in the nineteenth century proved durable and would stretch into the coming century.

In addition to annexation attempts and developing diplomatic relations, individual Dominicans traveled between the two countries and, at times, made their homes in the United States. One native of the Spanish-speaking Caribbean lived in Baltimore in the early 1850s. The man, whose name is hardly legible in the census (it is perhaps "N. Mercuelt"), had been born in the first years of the nineteenth century in Santo Domingo. More is known about the military leader José Gabriel Luperón, who reportedly joined the U.S. Civil War on the side of the North. Luperón, in fact, is said to have been appointed a captain in the U.S. Army by President Abraham Lincoln.

Like immigrants from the Caribbean, Central and South Americans also established small communities in the United States in the nineteenth century. In 1850, according to the U.S. census, there were 1,500 South Americans and 150 Central Americans in the country, and 3,200 South Americans and 230 Central Americans a decade later. One of the primary destinations of Central and South American immigrants to the United States was California. Many Chileans were drawn to the gold-mining districts of Northern California, where they joined Mexican immigrants from mining regions in northern Mexico as well as newly arrived settlers from throughout the world hoping to make their fortune in the California Gold Rush. The immigrants from Chile were often young men, as in the household recorded in an 1860 census of Sacramento where nearly a dozen Chilean men, all working-class laborers, lived together. In neighboring households also lived men from Mexico, Nicaragua, Ecuador, and Panama. A Mexican woman, Cruz Ramirez, headed a nearby household with her two daughters, and her neighbor was a Chilean woman who lived with another woman, likely her mother, and two men, one born in Chile and the other born in Spain. While alliances between Puerto Rican and Cuban political exiles were common in the nineteenth century, these examples of households composed of different Latina/o groups (Mexican, Chilean, Nicaraguan, Ecuadorian, and Panamanian) point to a long history of intimate associations between ordinary, working-class Latina/os in the nation's past.

Unlike many Latin American and Caribbean immigrants to the United States in the mid-nineteenth century who were new arrivals to the country, Mexicans in the United States after 1848 faced the devastating effects of U.S. war and conquest on their homes and communities. For Mexicans in southern Arizona and New Mexico, the Treaty of Guadalupe Hidalgo was not the only important international treaty in the middle of the nineteenth century. Soon after the Mexican-American War ended in 1848, a dispute arose between the United States and Mexico over the exact location of the borderline dividing the two countries. After the conclusion of the war, most Mexicans had chosen to remain in newly U.S. territory. A significant number of others, though, had chosen to relocate to Mexico in order to avoid being subject to U.S. rule, including some who moved to the southern New Mexico town of Mesilla. In 1853, the Gadsden Treaty was passed to resolve the borderline dispute and, perhaps most importantly, to ensure a southern route for a proposed transcontinental railroad. According to the treaty, the United States paid $10 million to Mexico for nearly 30 million acres of land that encompassed much of what is now southern Arizona, including the city of Tucson, and portions of southwestern New Mexico and the above-mentioned town of Mesilla. Whether incorporated into the United States through the Treaty of Guadalupe Hidalgo of 1848 or, like the newly U.S. residents of Mesilla, through the Gadsden Treaty of 1853, Mexicans living in U.S. territory in New Mexico and Arizona faced many of the same challenges as did their counterparts in California and Texas.

In California, the Mexican-American War itself led to substantial losses in property and personal belongings. More than 40 individuals in Los Angeles,

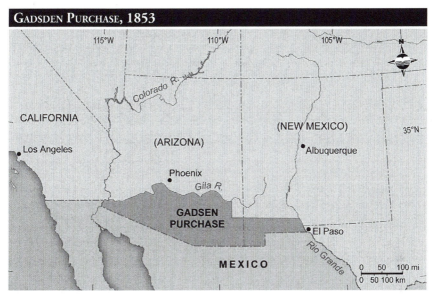

The Gadsden Purchase (1853) added nearly 30,000 square miles of formerly Mexican land to the territorial empire of the United States. (ABC CLIO)

14 of whom were women, filed claims after the war for unnecessary damages caused by American troops. One woman, Juana Rendon, asked for compensation after troops made off with furnishings from her kitchen and bedroom as well as large quantities of corn, beans, potatoes, and firewood. Another woman, María Villalobos, asked to be reimbursed for stolen beds, tools, and food, including more than a dozen bushels of wheat and several bushels of corn and beans.

After the war, Mexicans faced more long-term challenges to their ability to own property and maintain financial stability. In 1851, the U.S. Congress passed a bill to determine the ownership of land granted to individuals in California as the region shifted from Mexican to U.S. property systems and law. The 1851 Land Claims Act required that owners of parcels of land granted during Spanish and Mexican rule prove their ownership of the land in court. While large numbers of Mexican landowners had their grants confirmed by the court and received title to the land (in the Los Angeles region, for instance, 600 of the 800 total land claims were confirmed), the process of defending the land proved very expensive and time consuming for a significant number of Mexicans. In fact, according to historian Miroslava Chávez-García, "nearly half (46 percent) or the original owners in the Los Angeles area went bankrupt in the process of defending those claims" (Chávez-García 2004, 125). Legal fees, such as hiring an English-speaking lawyer, which was especially important in the increasingly English-dominated legal culture of mid-century California, and burdensome new property taxes, as well as a fluctuating economy and the effects of droughts, floods, and a deadly smallpox epidemic in the 1860s led to financial ruin for many Mexicans. By the 1870s, Chávez-García notes, "a Californio-Mexican man and woman held less in personal wealth—cash, bank notes, or other movable goods—than he or she did in the 1850s" (Chávez-García 2004, 146). Anglo men, on the other hand, had their personal wealth, on average, quadruple during the same period. Similar losses for Mexicans occurred in terms of real estate holdings, as in the case of Maria Antonia Tapia, who was forced to sell her home in 1860 in order to repay a $200 debt that she owed to an Anglo attorney. Nicolasa Carreaga also lost property, two lots of 10 acres each in Los Angeles, when she could not afford property taxes and her lots were sold at an auction in 1853.

For all the dislocation and dispossession that Mexicans faced after the Mexican-American War, the period was especially horrific for Native Americans in California. Repeated raids by the U.S. Army targeted Native Americans, forcing as many as possible to live on reservations. Those Native Californians that refused relocation to reservations were often killed if they resisted military orders. In 1850, moreover, the Indenture Act was passed, which allowed Indian "vagrants" and minor children to be placed in indentured servitude to largely Anglo families. Impoverished Native Americans who committed any crime or minor offense could thus be placed in servitude. In 1860, the law was amended to stipulate that if an Anglo-American lodged a complaint against the moral or public behavior of a Native person (such as a complaint of loitering or begging) that within a day that Native American could be placed in bondage and sold at an auction. The Native population in California soon plummeted, from an estimate of about 150,000 in 1850 (some scholars placed the number even higher, at around 300,000), to 50,000 in 1855, and fewer than 30,000 in 1870. Although thousands of Indians were forced to abandon their homes, many refused to relocate to reservations and chose instead to live in towns like Los Angeles, where Native Americans soon formed a significant community.

Over the first half of the nineteenth century, the city of Los Angeles emerged as the political, economic, and cultural center of Mexican life in Southern California. On the eve of the war with the United States, the population of Los Angeles had grown from 650 in 1820 to more than 1,600 in 1844. While ethnic Mexicans remained the majority in Los Angeles, as did Catholics, large numbers of Anglo newcomers lived alongside significant communities of Chinese and French immigrants and African Americans. The heart of the Mexican community in Los Angeles was the plaza. The Los Angeles plaza was a gathering place for Mexican celebrations and festivals and was located nearby the Catholic church and important government buildings.

After the Mexican-American War and during the first decades of U.S. rule, Los Angeles retained its place at the center of business, politics, and social life in Southern California. Nonetheless, the once dominant Mexican elite in Los Angeles faced a rapidly growing Anglo population in the city. In 1850, census takers counted 1,600 residents, with fewer than 400 Anglos (25% of the population) and an overwhelming majority of Mexicans. In the next 10 years, the racial composition of the city changed radically. By 1860, the city was the home of nearly 4,400 people; the new majority, however, was not Mexican but of Anglo descent. There were 2,300 Anglos (53% of the population) and 2,000 Mexicans (47%). A decade later, the gap between Anglos and Mexicans had widened, bolstered by migrants from the post–Civil War U.S. South, and Mexicans comprised less than 40 percent of the population of Los Angeles (2,100 of 5,700 total inhabitants) in 1870. In coming decades, Mexicans would be forced further onto the economic and political margins of Los Angeles, a pattern that would be repeated throughout California and the broader Southwest.

In Texas, which had been annexed to the United States in 1845, attacks on Mexicans and Mexican communities accelerated after the Mexican-American War. One of the major trends in Texas was the large-scale loss of land by Mexicans. In 1850, property in Texas was relatively evenly distributed between Mexican and Anglo landowners. Mexicans were one-third of the workers and owned one-third of the wealth of the state. Twenty years later, however, Mexicans had become 50 percent of the workforce but owned only 10 percent of the wealth of the state. Between 1848 and 1855, to take another example, fewer than 15 Anglos in Texas managed to take possession of 1.3 million acres from 358 Mexican owners.

The dispossession of Mexican land that occurred in Texas appeared throughout the borderlands region. Anglo men, some of whom married into wealthy Mexican families, exploited their knowledge of U.S. legal codes and business practices, their personal connections with newly appointed Anglo judges, land office officials, and other bureaucrats, and their ability to speak and write English, and managed to purchase or to be given or, in some cases, to steal huge amounts of land from Mexican landowners. Anglos also took advantage of the widespread fear among Mexicans that the United States would refuse to honor the land claims of Mexican citizens as the Treaty of Guadalupe Hidalgo had promised and offered to buy their land to avoid such a predicament. Many Anglos also served as lawyers for Mexicans who sought to have their land claims verified and to receive title to their land, and, in payment, the Anglo lawyers often received land.

The criminal justice system in Texas contributed mightily to the challenges facing Mexicans in the mid-nineteenth century. At the Huntsville penitentiary in 1860, 70 of the 200 prisoners (35%) were Mexicans, despite the fact that less than 5 percent of the state's adult male population was of Mexican origin. The percentage of Mexicans at Huntsville had decreased by the end of the decade but by 1870 still far exceeded their share in the overall population (African Americans were similarly overrepresented at the prison, comprising more than half of the inmates, a proportion well higher than their overall population in the state). Mexicans faced similar disadvantages at the county level of the judicial system. In Cameron and Webb counties, Mexicans received significantly higher conviction rates than their share of the population and were also more likely to be sentenced to the penitentiary or given other severe penalties, while Anglos tended to receive lighter sentences like fines or short prison terms.

Defendants in criminal proceedings similarly faced a judicial structure that could be dramatically skewed against Mexicans. While juries in some regions were relatively balanced by race (in Webb County, for instance, Mexican participation in juries even outpaced their percentage of the population), in certain counties the disparity between Anglos and Mexicans on juries was stark. In Cameron County, where 75 percent of the adult men were of Mexican origin, less than 20 percent of jury members were Mexican and an even smaller percentage (11%) served as jury foremen. Judges and attorneys were also overwhelmingly Anglo in Texas. "During the first eighteen years of American rule," according to historian Omar Valerio-Jiménez, "seven district judges and six chief justices presided over courtrooms in Cameron County; all were Anglos" (Valerio-Jiménez 2012, 168).

Demeaning descriptions of Mexicans were common in mid-century Anglo newspapers in Texas. Poor Mexicans were targeted with special scorn and were described as thieves, murderers, and prone to violence. One article, from the 1860s, described two Mexican teenagers involved in a fight with each other as "murderous devils" (Valerio-Jiménez 2012, 160). At times, these local newspaper accounts reached beyond the state, spreading negative images of Texas Mexicans to a national audience, as in an editorial from a New Orleans newspaper that suggested in 1866 that authorities in Brownsville should execute more than a dozen Mexican prisoners as a warning against future criminal activity by "the community of 'greasers' at large" (Valerio-Jiménez 2012, 161). A writer from nationally circulated *Harper's Magazine* described Mexicans in Texas as "the laziest living beings in the world." "Eating, sleeping, smoking, riding, and herding cattle," he wrote, "is about all they are good for." "But let them get excited, and they become crazy," the piece added, "they go in masses like sheep" (Harrington 1867, 624).

Juan Nepomuceno Cortina led one of many resistance movements, both violent and non-violent, challenging Anglo rule in the U.S. Southwest in the nineteenth century. (Library of Congress)

In the face of such scornful descriptions, Mexican resistance to the imposition of Anglo rule took on many forms. Some forms of resistance were more direct and more violent. One of the most famous events occurred in 1859, when Juan Nepomuceno Cortina led a group of Mexicans across the Rio Grande from Matamoros to overtake Brownsville, Texas (see the profile of Cortina at the end of this chapter). Religion was another space of Mexican resistance. Tensions over religion, especially between Protestants and Catholics, emerged throughout the mid-century U.S. Southwest. Predominantly Catholics, Mexicans in the Southwest did not escape the sharp criticism directed at the Catholic Church by the majority Protestant population in the United States. Anti-Catholic hostility was widespread in the nation, leading to riots and political mobilization against Catholic immigrants from Ireland and Germany. One solution proposed by Catholic leaders was to use the church to Americanize and assimilate Catholic immigrants to the United States as rapidly as possible.

In Mexican communities in the Southwest, the transfer of authority from the Mexican government to the United States after the Mexican-American War was accompanied by the rapid replacement of Mexican clergy by European, especially French, priests. "By 1870," writes historian Anthony Mora, "thirty-seven European priests had arrived to assume control of churches throughout the territory, including southern New Mexico" (Mora 2011, 108). The best known of these European newcomers was Jean-Baptiste Lamy, who was archbishop of Santa Fe for more than 30 years beginning in 1850 and was made famous by novelist Willa Cather in her novel *Death Comes for the Archbishop*. Lamy was notoriously critical of Mexicans, including Mexican priests, stating at one point that Mexicans "cannot be compared to Americans in the way of intellectual liveliness, ordinary skills, and industry" (Mora 2011, 109). Unfortunately, Lamy was not alone among his immigrant colleagues in harboring such views of Mexicans.

Such animosity, however, did not deter Mexicans from challenging the displacement of Mexican religious, as well as political and cultural, authority in the region. One leader of opposition to the Europeanization and Americanization of Catholic leadership was the bishop of Durango, Mexico, José de Zubiría y Escalante. For several years, Zubiría and José Jesús Baca, who Zubiría appointed to "supervis[e] all of the major parishes in southern New Mexico, including San Albino's in Mesilla and Santa Genoveva (St. Genevieve's) in Las Cruces," thwarted attempts to replace Mexican religious authorities with non-Mexican leaders (Mora 2011, 110).

Other forms of resistance arose from within the U.S. legal system. Criminal appeals cases, for example, were one arena where Mexicans resisted Anglo attempts to marginalize them and to deny them the full rights of U.S. citizenship. The Treaty of Guadalupe Hidalgo in 1848 had promised that Mexicans remaining in the United States and "elect[ing] to become citizens of the United States" would eventually receive "all the rights of citizens of the United States." These rights of citizens could appear in many forms, of course, including the right to call upon the support and protection of the criminal justice system. While there were many inequities in U.S. courts and law enforcement, Mexicans throughout the second half of the nineteenth century also often appeared to approach the use of the legal system as an important right. Mexicans used the courts for a variety of reasons, such as bringing lawsuits, determining the distribution of inheritances, and requesting divorces and custody of children. Mexicans also turned to the courts to appeal criminal convictions. Between 1850 and 1859, for instance, Spanish-surnamed individuals appealed more than 100 civil and criminal cases to higher courts in Texas, California, and New Mexico.

In traditional narratives of U.S. history, the Civil War dominates accounts of the middle decades of the nineteenth century. In fact battles, many of them violent, over slavery played a critical role in Latina/o history during the period as well. For Mexicans, however, the major developments in the mid-nineteenth century emerged not from the U.S. Civil War but from the U.S. war with Mexico. The Mexican-American War and the resulting Treaty of Guadalupe Hidalgo in 1848 irrevocably altered the lives of tens of thousands of Mexicans. Faced with an inundation of Anglo newcomers, especially in regions like California after the discovery of gold, and the assertion of U.S. legal, political, and economic dominance, Mexicans suffered many losses in terms of land and property, social and cultural status, and economic and political power.

At the same time, Mexicans displayed remarkable powers of endurance and creativity in resisting Anglo domination. As they had in earlier periods, Latinas, whether Mexicanas or women in Puerto Rico, Cuba, or elsewhere in the Spanish Caribbean, adapted with great skill to transformed and challenging situations. Mexican women, for instance, continued to assert their rights to use U.S. courts to demand justice as they had for scores of years under Spanish and then Mexican rule.

For Puerto Ricans and Cubans, the first half of the nineteenth century had delivered neither independence from Spain nor the demise of slavery. Nonetheless, the intertwining of independence and abolitionism animated widespread political movements both on the islands and in exile communities in the United States throughout the 1850s and 1860s. In 1868, these movements led to violent, armed uprisings, as insurgents in Puerto Rico organized the Lares Revolt and rebels began a decade-long civil war, the Ten Years War, in Cuba. While Spain was determined to maintain its last colonial outposts in the Americas, Puerto Ricans and Cubans of working class and elite status continued, albeit in limited numbers compared to Mexicans in the United States, to make new homes in North America. Among these newcomers to the United States, the most visible were political exiles in cities like New York, Philadelphia, and New Orleans. These activists include editors and founders of newspapers, essayists, and even poets determined to wrest independence from Spain and to end slavery in their homelands.

PROFILE: APOLINARIA LORENZANA

Apolinaria Lorenzana was born in 1779 in Mexico City. An orphan, Lorenzana was among a group of orphaned children sent to California by the Spanish government in 1800. Seeking to encourage Spanish settlement in the region, officials placed the children with families in the towns of Monterey, Santa Barbara, and San Diego. Lorenzana was first assigned to the family of the commander of the military post in Santa Bárbara and moved with the family when the commander accepted a new position at the San Diego Presidio.

After working in the home of another military family in San Diego and suffering from a temporary paralysis of her left hand, Lorenzana began training to be a nurse in the San Diego mission. In addition to teaching

Native children and helping to care for the sick, she eventually rose to a supervisory position at the mission. She became the head housekeeper at the San Diego mission and oversaw the purchase and distribution of food and other goods, as well as being responsible for religious education. Though not known as particularly violent or exploitative toward Native children or adults, Lorenzana actively participated in and helped sustain a Spanish, and eventually Mexican, mission system that took a terrible toll on indigenous communities in California. As Bárbara Reyes notes, Lorenzana contributed to "one of the mission's projects—to exploit the labor of neophytes (mission Indians)" (Reyes 2006, 407).

Like so many Mexicans in California, Lorenzana's life was thrown into turmoil by the U.S. invasion of Mexico during the Mexican-American War. In the 1840s, she had received two government land grants near San Diego and later bought another parcel of land in California. Unable to defend her title to the land under U.S. rule, Lorenzana fell into poverty as an older woman. In 1878, at the age of 84, she provided an oral history interview, leaving behind an important, and rare, first-person account by a Mexicana of life in early nineteenth-century California.

PROFILE: JUAN CORTINA

Juan Cortina was born in 1824 to a prominent family in South Texas. His family, who had faced the onslaught of Anglo settlers and U.S. colonial land policy in the Brownsville area in the mid-nineteenth century, was beset by Anglo squatters, land speculators, and real estate attorneys.

With tensions in the region high in the summer of 1859, an Anglo Brownsville marshal savagely beat an inebriated Mexican man and insulted Cortina when he intervened to protect the man. Cortina then shot the marshal and fled the area. Unable to have the charges dismissed and unwilling to surrender, Cortina drew the support of the besieged Mexican community in South Texas. By the fall of 1859, a widespread revolt was developing in the region.

In September 1859, Juan Cortina led a group of nearly 100 Mexicans to overtake the town of Brownsville. The raid overwhelmed Brownsville officials and only the arrival of the Mexican military managed to force the invaders to withdraw from the town. Gathering at a ranch owned by Cortina's mother, the "Cortinistas" issued a proclamation in both English and Spanish defending their actions and asserting their rights as U.S. citizens to protect themselves against, according to historian Omar Valerio-Jiménez, "those persecuting and robbing them for 'no other crime on our part than that of being of Mexican origin' " (Valerio-Jiménez 2012, 222). The rebellion eventually numbered several hundred and controlled a substantial portion of South Texas before federal troops and Texas Rangers finally managed to defeat Cortina and his men.

After the defeat, Cortina moved to Mexico and embarked on a career in politics. He was a commander in the Mexican Army and became governor of the Mexican state of Tamaulipas as well as, in 1875, the head of the *ayuntamiento* (or city council) of the border city of Matamoros. Accused of engineering cattle raids across the border into Texas, Cortina was arrested under the order of Mexican president Porfirio Díaz. He spent the next 16 years in prison and died in 1894 while under house arrest. Cortina's life points to the transnational links binding Mexicans to both the United States and Mexico in the nineteenth century and to the forms of resistance, at times violent, that Mexicans adopted in the face of Anglo land seizures and U.S. settler colonialism.

PROFILE: JOSÉ AGUSTÍN QUINTERO

Born in 1829 in Havana, Cuba, José Agustín Quintero was of mixed heritage—his mother was English and his father was Cuban—and the family owned a tobacco plantation in Cuba. As a young man, he attended Harvard, even taking a job teaching Spanish while in school in order to cover expenses after his father died and his family faced financial difficulties. In Boston, Quintero was reportedly friends with leading North American intellectuals like Ralph Waldo Emerson and Henry Wadsworth Longfellow.

Quintero returned to Cuba in 1848, where he became active in the independence movement. He was arrested in 1850 and sentenced to be executed; however, he managed to escape the prison and eventually arrived in New Orleans. For Quintero, poetry played a critical role in the independence movement. While in Cuba and New Orleans in the 1850s, he wrote poems expressing romantic and patriotic sentiments and corresponded for many years with Longfellow, even translating several of Longfellow's poems into Spanish.

In 1855, Quintero moved to Texas to help the former president of Texas, Mirabeau Lamar, translate his Spanish documents and organize his personal library. Quintero, in addition to continuing to write poetry, helped support the Tejana/o community in San Antonio by founding a Spanish-language newspaper, *El Ranchero*, in the mid-1850s. During the same period, Quintero married Eliza Bournos, a French creole woman from New Orleans. By 1860, Quintero had relocated to New York City, where he served as an editor for publisher Frank Leslie's illustrated Spanish-language weekly, *La Ilustración Americana*.

The outbreak of the U.S. Civil War drew Quintero to the side of the Confederacy, where he served on diplomatic missions to Mexico. After the

Confederate defeat, he sought a presidential pardon for his actions. He was eventually named a U.S. consul for Costa Rica and then for Belgium and continued to be a practicing journalist. During the 1860s and 1870s, he also lived in New Orleans and wrote editorials for one of its major newspapers, the *Daily Picayune*. Quintero died in 1885 of cirrhosis at the age of 56.

REFERENCES

Chávez-García, Miroslava. *Negotiating Conquest: Gender and Power in California 1770s to 1880s*. Tucson: University of Arizona Press, 2004.

Glasser, Ruth. "From 'Richport' to Bridgeport: Puerto Ricans in Connecticut." In *The Puerto Rican Diaspora: Historical Perspectives*, edited by Carmen Teresa Whalen and Víctor Vázquez Hernández, 174–99. Philadelphia: Temple University Press, 2005.

Gruesz, Kirsten Silva. *Ambassadors of Culture: The Transamerican Origins of Latino Writing*. Princeton, NJ: Princeton University Press, 2002.

Harrington, George F. "The Virginians in Texas." *Harper's New Monthly Magazine* 34, no. 203 (April 1867): 621–33.

Lazo, Rodrigo. *Writing to Cuba: Filibustering and Cuban Exiles in the United States*. Chapel Hill: University of North Carolina Press, 2005.

Mora, Anthony. *Border Dilemmas: Racial and National Uncertainties in New Mexico, 1848–1912*. Durham, NC: Duke University Press, 2011.

Poyo, Gerald E. *"With All, and for the Good of All": The Emergence of Popular Nationalism in the Cuban Communities of the United States, 1848–1898*. Durham, NC: Duke University Press, 1989.

Reyes, Bárbara O. "Apolinaria Lorenzana." In *Latinas in the United States: A Historical Encyclopedia*, edited by Vicki L. Ruiz and Virginia Sánchez-Korrol, 407–8. Bloomington: Indiana University Press, 2006.

Valerio-Jiménez, Omar S. *River of Hope: Forging Identity and Nation in the Rio Grande Borderlands*. Durham, NC: Duke University Press, 2012.

Wagenheim, Olga Jiménez de. *Puerto Rico: An Interpretive History from Pre-Columbian Times to 1900*. Princeton, NJ: Markus Wiener Publisher, 1997.

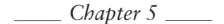

_____ *Chapter 5* _____

Wars of Independence, 1868–1898

For many historians of the United States, the last three decades of the nineteenth century are filled with the dramas of Reconstruction, westward expansion, and industrial and urban growth. In some respects, these traditional U.S. history themes are also at the heart of Latina/o history during the period, especially U.S. expansion and the consolidation of colonial rule in the formerly Mexican territories of the Southwest.

In other respects, however, traditional U.S. history does not reflect the paths of many Latina/os during the period. For Puerto Ricans and Cubans, wars of independence continued throughout the end of the century, including the Lares Revolt in Puerto Rico and the Ten Years War in Cuba, both of which began in 1868. As in earlier decades of the nineteenth century, significant numbers of Latina/o newcomers to the United States were political exiles like José Martí, the famous Cuban essayist and revolutionary. Martí and his compatriots helped organize and lead the final wars against Spanish rule in the Caribbean; and, in 1898, the Spanish-American War and the resounding military victory of the United States over Spain led to the long-awaited end of Spanish control over Cuba and Puerto Rico. The year 1898 thus joined 1848, which marked the end of the Mexican-American War and the signing of the Treaty of Guadalupe Hidalgo, as one of the critical dates in Latina/o history.

Although large-scale Puerto Rican and Cuban immigration to the U.S. mainland would not occur until the twentieth century, significant immigrant communities in East Coast cities, many of which had existed since mid-century, continued to expand. In addition, a range of exile communities emerged, many advocating the abolition of slavery and independence from Spain for Caribbean islands. In the U.S. Southwest, the late nineteenth century witnessed continued Mexican land loss and political and economic marginalization. As in earlier periods, however, Mexicans, including large numbers of Mexican women, challenged such attacks on their communities and adopted multiple forms of resistance, including the strategic use of U.S. courts and the legal system.

In Puerto Rico, sugar and coffee production formed the cornerstone of the island's economy in the nineteenth century. As the century came to a close, however, coffee had begun to outpace sugar in Puerto Rican agriculture. By the 1880s, in fact, coffee exports took the lead over sugar exports from the island. In another critical development during the period, slavery was abolished in Puerto Rico in 1873. Rather than gaining their immediate freedom, however, former slaves were forced to remain in apprenticeship positions for a period of three years. Although freedmen and freedwomen were allowed to choose new employers during their term as apprentices, and to move freely to new locations, they received little assistance in relocating or finding new employment. As a result, according to one historian, most were compelled "to remain in close proximity to the hacendados who knew them and who might offer them paid employment and subsistence plots once the apprenticeship ended" (Wagenheim 1997, 180). For their part, slave owners had hoped to be compensated by the government for the full price of their slaves once slavery was ended but discovered that the annual payment they received did not cover the new wages they would have to pay to hire the newly emancipated workers.

The abolition of slavery and other transformations in Puerto Rico did not, however, lead to widespread migration to North America. In the late nineteenth century, Puerto Ricans relocated in relatively small numbers to North America. The primary destinations of the Puerto Rican newcomers were large East Coast cities. Puerto Ricans were drawn to Philadelphia, for instance, by the city's cigar-manufacturing industry and, alongside Cuban immigrants, they helped establish strong mutual aid societies and Spanish-speaking chapters of local cigar worker unions. One of Philadelphia's new Puerto Rican arrivals in the late nineteenth century was Francisco Aguilar. In 1880, Aguilar lived on South Street in Philadelphia with his wife, Rebecca, and their four sons. Rebecca Aguilar had been born in Pennsylvania, as had her parents, suggesting that the Aguilars were an intermarried couple and that their children were of mixed Anglo and Puerto Rican heritage. Francisco Aguilar's occupation appears in the census as "Cigar maker," while Rebecca Aguilar is listed as "Keeping house." The Aguilar's neighbors, including butchers, peddlers, and servants, were native-born Americans like Rebecca Aguilar, as well as immigrants from Prussia, Ireland, Bavaria, and England. While large-scale Puerto Rican communities did not develop in Philadelphia for several decades, Puerto Ricans like Francisco Aguilar helped form small but visible Latina/o communities in northeastern cities well before the twentieth century.

Enslaved people in the Spanish Caribbean helped drive both the independence movement and the anti-slavery movement in the nineteenth century (formerly enslaved people in Puerto Rico, circa 1880). (Library of Congress)

A significant number of Puerto Ricans in the United States took active roles in the Puerto Rican and Cuban independence movement. In 1875, for instance, at least one Puerto Rican nationalist was aboard a Cuba-bound ship that sailed from Boston intending to join anti-Spain forces on the island (the voyage was short-lived, however, as the ship almost sank shortly after setting sail). Two decades later, as proindependence forces gathered strength, Puerto Ricans in New York City joined the Cuban Revolutionary Party, founded by José Martí in Tampa and based in New York. Branches of the same group, likely also with strong Puerto Rican representation, were formed in Philadelphia and Boston.

During the last three decades of the nineteenth century, the Cuban immigrant population also grew significantly. At mid-century, only about 1,000, mostly middle-class, Cubans lived in the United States. By the middle of 1870s, however, there were an estimated 2,000 Cuban immigrants in the country of various class and racial backgrounds. One of the most prominent and influential Cuban communities was located in Key West, Florida. Spurred by favorable trade policies and the availability of Cuban cigar workers, a thriving cigar-manufacturing center developed in Key West. In less than a decade, cigar production jumped from fewer than 10 million cigars per year to 25 million annually and would reach an annual rate of 100 million by 1890. The number of factories also expanded rapidly. "By 1880," according to historian Gerald Poyo, "Key West had about forty-four factories employing an average of almost 1,400 cigar workers" (Poyo 1989, 43). Five years later, 5,000 Cubans lived in Key West, representing one-third of the city's population. While most Cuban cigar workers were male, about 10 percent were Cuban women.

U.S. census records point to the vibrancy of the Cuban community in Key West in the late nineteenth century. In 1880, Cubans predominated in certain neighborhoods in the city, with household after household composed of Cuban families. Like so many Cuban (and Puerto Rican) immigrants during the period, newcomers to Key West were drawn to work in the cigar industry. Residents of one 40-person section of a Cuban neighborhood, for instance, included five cigar makers, a reader in a cigar factory (that is, an individual who read the latest news aloud to entertain and inform the workers as they assembled the cigars), several clerks, the prosperous, Spanish-born owner of a cigar factory, and a physician. More than a third of the individuals were also under 15 years old, suggesting that Cuban immigrants planned to make new homes and build communities in the United States and were not simply temporary workers hoping to labor in the United States for a handful of years and return to Cuba.

Immigrants from other regions in Latin America and the Spanish-speaking Caribbean also made new homes in the United States in the late nineteenth century. Between 1870 and 1900, the number of Central Americans grew from 300 to 4,000, and the South American population rose from 3,500 to 4,700. New York City was a popular destination for both Central and South Americans. Farther north, near Poughkeepsie, New York, in the town of Hyde Park lived the Serrano family in 1870. José Serrano, born in Colombia, worked as a dentist in Hyde Park, which is best known as the hometown of U.S. president Franklin Delano Roosevelt, and resided with his wife, Mary, born in Ireland, and their children Mary, Vicente, and Mercedes. The large household also included servants and laborers hailing from Costa Rica and Colombia, including the famous South American poet and diplomat Rafael Pombo. Though surrounded by Anglo, native-born New Yorkers, José Serrano was easily among the wealthiest and best educated of his Hyde Park neighbors.

West Coast cities like San Francisco were also destinations for Central and South Americans in the late nineteenth century. Census documents from one San Francisco neighborhood list individuals from both Guatemala and Panama residing among an eclectic mix of Mexican, Irish, Jamaican, French, and Portuguese immigrants. Uliseo Flores, for instance, a 28-year-old boot-black from Guatemala, lived as a lodger in the home of Juana Patron, a

45-year-old Mexicana. Also lodging in the same household were two other Mexican men, one a cook, the other a musician.

While immigration from Spanish-speaking countries to the United States occurred in increasing numbers in the late nineteenth century, North Americans also migrated from the United States to locations like the Dominican Republic in the second half of the nineteenth century. Silvio Torres-Saillant notes that Tomás Cocco y Alum migrated from New Orleans to Puerto Plata, where he "achieved distinction as a Dominican patriot" (Torres-Saillant 1993, 258). Arturo Lithgow, of Maine, and Ana María Pellegrín, of New Orleans, similarly relocated from the U.S. mainland to Puerto Plata, where their son Federico Lithgow, who would become a prominent Dominican military leader, was born.

For a great many immigrants to the United States, especially Cubans and Puerto Ricans, the cause of independence was a central concern in the late nineteenth century. Cuban exiles worked diligently to draw the support of the U.S. public for their cause, and one particularly effective strategy was to portray the Spanish government as scheming, evil men and the Cuban people as innocent women. In fact, the association of Cuba with women and femininity was a major theme in U.S. popular culture.

As an example, take the case of Evangelina Cosio y Cisneros. Cisneros came from a prominent Cuban family and was imprisoned by Spanish authorities for supposedly aiding Cuban revolutionaries in 1897. The *New*

Support for the Cuban independence movement in the United States in the late nineteenth century often highlighted deeply gendered and racialized differences. (Library of Congress)

York Journal covered the story with numerous accounts, claiming that Cisneros had been arrested and jailed because she resisted the sexual advances of a lustful Spanish officer. The paper also reported that when thrown in jail, Cisneros had been put in a cell with a gang of prostitutes. According to the paper, Cisneros was to be sentenced to a Spanish penal colony in Morocco, a "Spanish hell" where "no woman prisoner has ever been sent," a place full of "murderers, robbers, and ravishers." So bad was this place that the prison sentence, according to the paper, meant "dishonor [or rape] first and death within a year" (Hoganson 1998, 58). Soon, other newspapers picked up the story, and the tale of Cisneros's arrest spread across the country.

These newspaper articles depicted Cisneros as representative of all Cuban women and encouraged its readers to sympathize with her predicament. Besides writing about Cisneros, the *New York Journal*, led by its editor William Randolph Hearst, organized petition drives and letter-writing campaigns on her behalf. Hearst focused special attention on American women, and according to the newspaper's figures, 15,000 women soon signed the petition, including the mother of President William McKinley. Other prominent women wrote letters, such as Varina Davis, widow of Jefferson Davis, the head of the Confederate army during the Civil War, who wrote to the queen of Spain, and Julia Ward Howe, author of "Battle Hymn of the Republic," who wrote to the pope. Due in part to such accounts in U.S. newspapers, sympathy for Cuba and Cuban revolutionaries in their struggle for independence from Spain was widespread in the United States in the 1890s. In one rally in 1895 in New York City, 2,000 supporters of Cuban independence gathered in a mass parade, and during the presidential election of 1896, both the Republican and the Democratic parties contained planks in their party platforms supporting Cuban independence.

Driving the independence movement, of course, were Cubans and Puerto Ricans who had struggled for decades, and at times sacrificed their lives, for the end of Spanish rule in their homelands. This struggle would finally end in 1898 when Spain and the United States went to war in what has come to be known as the Spanish-American War. In 1895, under the leadership of poet and political organizer Jose Martí, a broad-based movement of Cuban revolutionaries including peasants, elites, and middle-class Cubans organized to create a "Cuba Libre," a free Cuba. Spain responded to this independence movement by tightening their control of the Cuban people. The Spanish government appointed General Valeriano Weyler to enforce Spanish authority in Cuba. Weyler became known as "Butcher" Weyler in large measure because he established a "reconcentration" policy that forced rural Cubans into Spanish-controlled towns where they could be monitored and policed. Then, to hamper the guerrilla soldiers who still remained in the countryside, Weyler ordered the destruction of crops and other goods that the guerrillas might have used. Meanwhile, the rural people forced into towns faced overcrowding, disease, and mass starvation. Tens of thousands of Cubans died in these camps. This Spanish policy not only did not end the rebellion, but also convinced many Cuban moderates to side with the rebels. Weyler's actions also drew the sympathy of the U.S. public and heightened popular U.S. support for Cuban independence.

In 1897, Spain developed an autonomy plan that would grant Cubans greater control over domestic affairs on the island but would continue Spanish rule. This plan was endorsed by the United States. In January 1898, a group of Havana residents who supported continued Spanish control over the island and opposed Cuban autonomy rioted in Havana. This riot was seen by the U.S. president William McKinley as being anti-American because the United States had supported the autonomy plan for Cuba. McKinley, claiming to fear for U.S. lives in Cuba, sent in the battleship USS *Maine* to the Havana harbor. After waiting in the harbor for more than a month, the *Maine* mysteriously exploded and sank on February 15, 1898, killing more than 250 U.S. sailors. The United States accused Spain of bombing the battleship (an investigation later discovered that a boiler had actually exploded, causing the destruction of the ship) and declared war. The U.S. military strategy focused on Cuba and the Spanish fleet stationed in the Philippines. On May 1, 1898, the U.S. Navy destroyed the Spanish fleet in Manila Bay in the Philippines. In late June, U.S. troops launched a major offensive into Cuba. By July 1898, Spain surrendered and the war ended. After the war, the United States proceeded to occupy Cuba and Puerto Rico with a military government.

Despite their decades of activism for self-determination and independence from Spain, Puerto Rican calls for autonomy were largely ignored in the aftermath of the U.S. defeat of Spain in 1898. Rather than declaring Puerto Rico to be an independent country, the Treaty of Paris, which officially ended the Spanish-American War, placed the island under U.S. rule. As a result, according to historian Carmen Whalen, "a highly centralized military rule dismantled and replaced the institutions of self-government and the greater autonomy that Puerto Rico had wrested from Spain in the final days of its rule" (Whalen 2005, 6). Denied either self-determination or full status as an American state, Puerto Rico in 1898 found itself ensnared in the newly expanding American empire. Cubans, on the other hand, managed to gain their independence but continued, as the new century began, to struggle for autonomy from the political and economic control of the United States.

For Mexicans in the last third of the nineteenth century, the period was characterized by both continued Anglo expansion and widespread Mexican resistance to political and economic marginalization. Mexicans in the biggest states in the region, California and Texas, suffered great losses between

1850 and 1900: in land, in wealth, in status, in political power, even in percentage of the population. In California, the ethnic Mexican population had dropped to 48,579 in 1900, or 3.2 percent of the state's population, while the nearly 200,000 ethnic Mexicans in Texas still constituted only about 6 percent of the total population.

Of the many transformations in the United States in the nineteenth century, few had as broad and as lasting an effect as the development of the railroad. For Mexicans, and the wider U.S. Southwest, this effect was especially jarring, as railroads enabled the arrival of vast numbers of Anglo newcomers and helped usher in a massive growth in agriculture, mining, and ranching. These changes would transform the region's economy, vault Anglos into economic and political dominance, and threaten to overwhelm most Mexican communities in the region.

Los Angeles was one of the many cities irrevocably altered by the arrival of the railroad. In 1876, the Southern Pacific Railroad linked LA with San Francisco, and the city's population soon began to rise, especially its Anglo population. The 1870 population of LA of 5,700 almost doubled in 1880 to 11,000. The city ballooned in 1890 to 50,000 and doubled once more, to more than 100,000, in 1900. LA's population thus grew 20-fold in the three decades between 1870 and 1900. The new Anglo majority in Los Angeles forced Mexicans to the political, economic, and cultural margins of the city.

Mexican loss of land, political power, and social status was dramatic throughout California in the late nineteenth century. Shifting employment patterns for Mexicans reflected the increasing marginalization of ethnic Mexicans as the century drew to a close. In Ventura County, located just north of Los Angeles, for instance, the overall population jumped from 5,000 in 1880 to more than 10,000 in 1890 to 14,000 in 1900, with a significant (75–80%) Anglo majority. "Mexicans," according to sociologist Tomás Almaguer, were "the largest minority group in the county, representing approximately 15–20 percent of the total population during this period" (Almaguer 1994, 99). While Anglo men came to dominate the professional and managerial classes of occupation (such as doctors, lawyers, bank cashiers, and real estate agents) and skilled laborers, Mexicans were largely confined to working-class jobs. In 1880, more than two-thirds of Mexican male workers toiled in unskilled jobs or worked as farm laborers. Twenty years later, that percentage had risen to almost 80 percent. By comparison, only one-third of all Anglo men were unskilled workers or farm laborers in 1900.

Like employment, changes in property ownership among Mexicans point to the depth of losses in Mexican communities during the period. In Ventura County, ranching dominated the economy entering the second half of the nineteenth century. In one area around the township of San Buenaventura in 1860, livestock was valued at $450,000 while agricultural products accounted for less than $20,000. Although the largest landowner was an Anglo, according to Almaguer's analysis of the 1860 population census, "twenty-two of the twenty-nine ranchers or pastoralists had Spanish surnames, as did six of the ten farmers reported" (Almaguer 1994, 77). Nine of the 10 largest landowners in the township also had Spanish surnames.

The next two decades proved devastating to this group of property-owning Mexicans in Ventura County. Through a combination of poor business decisions, the need in a cash-poor economy to pay lawyers' fees with land, rising property taxes, disastrous droughts during the period, and outright swindles, Mexican land loss accelerated. By 1870, the three largest landholdings in San Buenaventura belonged to Anglos or Anglo-led companies. Moreover, only 6 of the nearly 50 parcels of land with more than 500 acres had Spanish-surnamed owners. Ten years later, in 1880, none of the eight largest landowners were Mexicans. This loss of land, and accompanying political and social status, only worsened in the coming decades in Ventura County, broader California, and the wider Southwest.

Exacerbating the marginalization of Mexican communities in California in the late nineteenth century was the development of an increasingly sophisticated and modern prison system in the state. The inmate populations of penitentiaries like Folsom and San Quentin expanded, as did the number of young men and women incarcerated by the state's juvenile justice system. Although the Anglo population by the end of the century held a considerable majority in the state, Mexicans, alongside Native Americans, were disproportionately confined behind bars. By the 1870s, according to historian Miroslava Chávez-García, Spanish speakers, including ethnic Mexicans and those of Central and South American origin, comprised only 4 percent of the state yet were over 10 percent of the prisoners at San Quentin. The imbalance was even more stark in the case of youth incarceration. The percentage of youth of Mexican and of other Latin American origin in San Quentin was 18 percent in the 1870s and 13 percent in the 1880s, leading Chávez-García to conclude that "Californio and Mexicano immigrant youth—all of them male—were more likely than youngsters of all other ethnic and racial backgrounds to be tried, convicted, and imprisoned in the state penitentiary in the nineteenth century" (Chávez-García 2012, 33). As jails and juvenile detention facilities, key institutions of the modern United States, expanded in size and scope in California, Mexicans bore the weight of this expansion, and their experiences with the criminal justice system point to the racial inequalities that persisted at the core of the nation's modernization.

As in California and throughout the Southwest, Mexican land loss and dispossession in Texas was significant. In Cameron County, for instance, the overwhelmingly Mexican-owned land base that had existed in the mid-nineteenth century had dwindled in the ensuing decades. Running parallel to Mexican land loss was the transformation of Mexicans into a largely working-class population. According to one account, the percentage of Mexican manual laborers had jumped from 34 percent in 1850 to 67 percent in 1900, while skilled laborers had dropped from 29 percent of the population to 12 percent over the same 50-year period. At the same time, the percentage of Anglos owning farms or ranches boomed, rising from 2 percent in 1850 to 31 percent in 1900. Further evidence of Mexican dispossession and marginalization emerges from changes in political leadership. In San Antonio, for instance, historian David Montejano has highlighted the shift from Mexican to Anglo political power in the second half of the nineteenth century. While nearly two-thirds of the city's aldermen were Spanish surnamed between 1837 and 1847, that proportion shifted rapidly after 1848. During the period 1867 to 1874, only 7 percent of aldermen were Mexican, and by 1900, there were no Mexican aldermen in San Antonio. In terms of law enforcement, Montejano adds that after the 1840s, "there were no Mexican county sheriffs or city marshals in San Antonio" (Montejano 1987, 41).

Despite their increasing economic and political marginalization in the Southwest, Mexicans continued to exercise their rights in the U.S. legal system. In 1880, for instance, there were 19 Spanish-surnamed appeals of criminal convictions in Texas (of 587 total). In the same year, there were 14 appeals (of 543) in California and 1 appeal (of 6) in New Mexico. During the years 1865 to 1880, moreover, 2 of the 38 total cases appealed to the Arizona Supreme Court involved Spanish-surnamed individuals. Though judges in appeals cases often wrote disparagingly of Mexicans, Mexicans could at times find success in the legal process. In Bee County, Texas, for instance, Felipe Greta appealed a murder charge to a Texas higher court. The judge's decision in the appeal described the crime as "instigated by conjugal jealousy—an emotion which is generally assumed to be potent among the Mexican race, to which all the parties belonged" (Mitchell 2012, 130). Despite this sentiment (judges presiding on higher courts in Texas and elsewhere in the Southwest appear no less immune to denigrating and insulting views of Mexicans than the rest of the Anglo population), Greta won his appeal and a new trial was ordered for him. At times, Mexican appeals cases could even provide the space for relatively positive characterizations of Mexicans. In a theft case from Travis County, Texas, in 1880, the court ruled that Antonio Jorasco merited a new trial and stated, "To deprive a citizen of his liberty, the law demands that his conviction shall be based upon legal evidence of such force and character as to satisfy the minds of his peers beyond a reasonable doubt; and without this amount of legal evidence, his condemnation shall not stand" (Mitchell 2012, 130). The strong assertion in the second case of the rights of Spanish-surnamed Antonio Jorasco was accompanied, as in the first case, by a victory for the appellant and a new trial.

Though often targeted viciously by Anglos as un-American and dangerous to the community, Mexicans could at times join forces with Anglos in race-based attacks on other communities. In Los Angeles in the early 1870s, for instance, two men were killed when they were caught in the crossfire of a gun battle involving two opposing Chinese immigrant groups. The death of the men, a Mexican police officer and an Anglo, sparked an anti-Chinese riot that focused on LA's Chinese neighborhood and Chinese men throughout the city. In one night, at least 19 Chinese men and boys were murdered by members of a multiracial mob and numerous Chinese businesses and homes were destroyed. Spanish-surnamed men were witnessed attempting to lynch Chinese victims, and several men with Spanish surnames were convicted of manslaughter for their actions during the riot and sentenced to prison, though their convictions were overturned on appeal. One of the mob's victims was a Chinese physician who pleaded for his life in both English and Spanish before being murdered. This tragic sign of Los Angeles's bicultural nature was echoed in the two judges who presided over the manslaughter trials, one an Anglo and the other Ignacio Sepulveda, a Los Angeles County judge.

As occurred when Mexicans and Anglos joined forces to attack the Chinese community in Los Angeles, Mexicans in Arizona could at times form alliances with Anglos in order to terrorize and dispossess Native Americans in the region. By 1900, there were 40,000 ethnic Mexicans living in Arizona. With increasing numbers of Anglos moving into the territory in the late nineteenth century, ethnic Mexicans in Arizona negotiated a complex multiracial society that included more recent newcomers from Mexico and immigrants from elsewhere in Latin America, as well as Native American groups like the Apache and the Tohono O'odham. In the post–Civil War era, the U.S. military escalated its attacks on Native communities in the West, and one group drawing special attention was the Apache. Military attacks on Apaches received strong support from Arizona's Anglo population, as well as from Mexicans and Tohono O'odham (who had fought bitter wars against the Apache for many decades). When a group of Apaches sought the protection of the U.S. military and settled nearby a U.S. fort north of Tucson, a multiracial force of Tucsonenses, including several prominent Mexicans, gathered to attack the settlement in 1871. The ensuing assault was one of the worst massacres in North American history, with nearly 150 Apache murdered and more than two dozen Apache children sold into slavery.

While the second half of the nineteenth century was a period of significant setbacks for Mexicans through the Southwest, the view from New Mexico was somewhat different. In New Mexico, Mexicans represented nearly half the population in 1900. The Mexican population, in fact, had expanded markedly in the nineteenth century, rising from 54,000 in 1850 to nearly 100,000 in 1900. The Anglo population had also grown dramatically in the previous 50 years from about 1,500 in 1850 to 100,000 in 1900. New Mexico was also the home of approximately 13,000 Native Americans (representing 7% of the population) and 1,600 African Americans. In this diverse setting, Mexicans, who also called themselves Hispanos or *Nuevo-mexicanos*, were able to assert some relative political and economic power, especially compared to the widespread disenfranchisement and dispossession occurring throughout the region. Hispana/os were prominent landowners, businesspeople, and civic leaders. Significant numbers of Hispanos were also elected to New Mexico's legislature well into the next century.

In the post–Civil War era, images of Latinas/os in mainstream American culture varied considerably, ranging from the racist and demeaning to the exoticized and sexually charged to the sympathetic and approving. Among the many negative descriptions of Latina/os in U.S. popular culture, one of the most vivid involved a religious group from New Mexico known as the Penitentes. In the absence of Catholic clergy in many regions in the Southwest, Penitentes had developed independent rituals and observances that drew considerable Anglo attention. In the late nineteenth century, Penitente rituals were described by Anglo newspaper reporters and other observers as an affront to proper religious practices. Reporters criticized Penitentes for, supposedly, engaging in "flagellations, carrying crosses, and other horrid rites," and newspapers published sensationalized accounts of Penitente rituals (Weigle 1976, 79). Inaccuracies and ignorance aside, for many Anglo readers, these accounts were unfortunately their only knowledge of Mexicans and their communities.

In addition to starkly negative accounts of Latina/os in broader U.S. culture, Latina/os were often categorized as distinct and culturally quite distant from Anglos. Rather than a focus on their shared characteristics and their compatibility, Latina/os were often viewed in much the same way as African Americans, where race was highlighted with non-Anglos (specifying, for instance, a "Mexican" man or a "Negro" woman) but not when describing Anglos. In medicine, for instance, Anglo doctors consistently identified Latina/os (whether Mexicans, Puerto Ricans, or Cubans) as racially different. An 1897 article from the *American Journal of the Medical Sciences* describes two cases of fractures of the clavicle from a Philadelphia hospital. The first involved "P.K., a Cuban, aged twenty-five," who fell from a bicycle in 1896, and the second case began with the following description: "Case II:

P.D., aged twenty-five was received in the accident-room of the hospital July 5, 1896" (Spencer 1897, 447–49). "P.D." (who was presumably Anglo, given the fact that his race and/or nationality is never mentioned) apparently fell off a moving freight car. Though such descriptions of Latina/os were far removed from the overt hostility and racism often directed at Mexican individuals and communities during the period, the seemingly neutral and scientific language of medicine nonetheless reinforced the deep racial divide separating Mexicans, Puerto Ricans, and Cubans (as well as other non-Anglos) from Anglos.

Another arena in U.S. culture where Latina/os were marked as racially different from Anglos was professional sports. Historian Adrian Burgos Jr. has identified two professional baseball players from the late nineteenth century: Esteban Bellán of Cuba and Vincent Nava of Mexican descent. Bellán, of elite background in Cuba, attended college in the United States in the 1860s, where he played on the collegiate baseball team. Between 1869 and 1871, he played professionally for the Troy Haymakers before returning to Cuba and helping to lead the development of the sport of baseball on the island. A decade later, Vincent Nava debuted at catcher for the Providence Grays in baseball's National League. Nava's mother, and likely also his father, was born in Mexico and Nava was raised in California. He began his professional career in 1876, was signed by Providence in 1882, and played until 1886. Hardly a star, Nava was nonetheless a frequent topic of interest for sportswriters, who consistently (mis)identified him in newspaper articles as a "Spaniard" and alluded to his "foreign" background. Spared the ridicule and scorn often inflicted on non-Anglos such as African Americans, Native Americans, and Asian immigrants during the period, Nava was nonetheless clearly distanced both from his Anglo teammates and from full acceptance in broader U.S. culture.

While most accounts of Latina/o lives in the nineteenth century were written by non-Latina/os, some Latina/o authors managed to find success in the nineteenth-century literary world. In 1876, for instance, Cuban-born Loreta Janeta Velásquez published her narrative of her Civil War service to the Confederate army. Velásquez, of mixed Spanish, French, and North American descent, was born into an elite, landowning Cuban family and, like other young women her age, was sent to the United States to attend school. While living with an aunt in New Orleans, Velásquez recounted eloping with an American military officer (she sought to escape an arranged marriage to a Spaniard), the births and tragic deaths of three children, and her Anglo husband's departure to join the Confederate army when the Civil War began in 1861. Eager to join the Confederate forces and undeterred that her husband refused to support her desire to become a soldier, Velásquez cut her hair, put on a false mustache, and from her personal wealth paid to provision nearly 250 men that she had recruited to join the Southern forces. When her husband died, Velásquez completed her transformation, taking on the name Lieutenant Harry Buford and, according to her memoir, fighting in several critical Civil War battles as a male soldier. In the years after the war, Velásquez would go on to write her memoir, *The Woman in Battle: A Narrative of the Exploits, Adventures, and Travels of Madame Loreta Janeta Velásquez, otherwise Known as Lieutenant Harry T. Buford, Confederate States Army*, a chronicle of more than 600 pages. In coming years, Velásquez continued to travel throughout the Americas and was last reported to have been living in Brazil, when she disappeared from the historical record. Though her life was clearly exceptional, Velásquez offers an important example of the transnational links between Cuba and the United States and the presence of Latinas in U.S. literary culture in the nineteenth century.

The year 1898 was a pivotal one in Latina/o history. For decades, Spanish-speaking, largely Mexican communities in the U.S. Southwest fought mightily to survive repeated waves of U.S. colonial expansion that swept into the region after the conclusion of the Mexican-American War. After 1898 and the end of the Spanish-American War, Puerto Ricans and Cubans found themselves in a similar predicament. The United States, its government and its general population, was reluctant to consider Puerto Rican and Cuban newcomers as full citizens. In the coming century, Puerto Ricans and Cubans—with few exceptions, such as light-skinned elite immigrants—would face, and to an extent overcome, a similar level of hostility as they too attempted to make new homes in North America. These early pre-1898 migrations to places like New York, Philadelphia, Boston, and even San Francisco established footholds and small communities in the United States that would be the foundation for later, much larger twentieth-century migrations.

PROFILE: MARÍA AMPARO RUIZ DE BURTON

María Amparo Ruiz de Burton was one of the most successful and best-known Latina writers in the United States in the nineteenth century. She was the author of a five-act play as well as two novels: *Who Would Have Thought It?*, published in 1872, and *The Squatter and the Don*, which appeared a decade later, in 1885.

María Amparo Ruiz was born in 1832 in Baja California to a relatively wealthy family. In fact, her grandfather was the governor of the region in the 1820s. As a teenager, Ruiz could not escape the turmoil caused by the Mexican-American War. Amid the wartime disruption and chaos, however, she met Henry Burton, a captain in the U.S. Army. The couple married in

1849 in Monterey, California. Ruiz, now Ruiz de Burton, and her husband lived in Monterey and then San Diego, California, for nearly 10 years before Burton was reassigned to the East. Entering elite social circles in Washington, D.C., on the eve of the Civil War, Ruiz de Burton was a close friend of First Lady Mary Todd Lincoln. Soon after the end of the Civil War, Ruiz de Burton's husband died, leaving her a widow and a single mother of two children.

Ruiz de Burton had begun her writing career in the 1850s while still living in California, when she wrote a five-act play that was eventually published in 1876. She also published her first novel, *Who Would Have Thought It?*, in the 1870s. Appearing in 1872, the book traces the romance between Lola, a Mexican woman, and Julian, an Anglo man, and is set in Civil War-era Washington, D.C. Written in English, the novel sharply criticizes Northern racism and political and corporate corruption among the country's elite.

Thirteen years later, Ruiz de Burton published another English-language book, her most famous novel, *The Squatter and the Don*. Like her first book, a romance between a Mexican woman, the *California* Mercedes, and an Anglo man is at the center of the narrative. Ruiz de Burton also sustains her critique of U.S. politics and big business, pointedly attacking the displacement and forced land loss of Mexican communities in the U.S. West. *The Squatter and the Don* solidified her place as a pioneer in Latina/o literature.

Despite her literary successes, Ruiz de Burton struggled to overcome formidable financial challenges as a single mother. Like so many Latinas in U.S. history, she fought legal battles to protect her land and refused to relinquish her rights as a full U.S. citizen. María Ruiz de Burton died in 1895 at the age of 63.

PROFILE: JOSÉ MARTÍ

José Martí was born in Cuba in 1853, the child of Spanish parents who had moved to Cuba before he was born. As a child, Martí attended the school of Rafael María de Mendive, a poet and educator who argued both for the abolition of slavery and for Cuba's independence from Spain. From a very early age, therefore, Martí was a devoted nationalist and abolitionist. In 1869, during one of Cuba's many wars for independence in the nineteenth century, 16-year-old Martí was arrested and convicted of writing a letter expressing nationalist, independence-minded sentiments. He was sentenced to jail and spent six months doing hard labor before his sentence was commuted and he was exiled to Spain.

From that point on, at the age of 16, Martí very rarely returned to his native Cuba. He lived for extended periods in Spain, Mexico, Guatemala,

Cuban writer and independence leader José Martí is one of the towering figures in Latina/o History. (Library of Congress)

Venezuela, and the United States. In 1892, Martí founded the Cuban Revolutionary Party, and three years later, the CRP helped orchestrate the invasion of Cuba. Although Martí had been encouraged to stay in the background of the invasion and continue to write articles and give speeches supporting the revolution, he insisted on joining the front ranks of the fighting and was killed in a battle with Spanish troops in May 1895 at the age of 42. It is likely that had Martí lived, he would have been the first head of state of an independent Cuba.

José Martí was also well known as a writer, poet, reporter, and essayist and has become a deeply contested symbol in Cuba. Martí's most influential writing was the essay "Our America," written in 1891. In "Our America," Martí was one of the first writers to describe the link between the descendants of Spanish colonialism, bringing together Mexicans, Puerto Ricans, Cubans, Dominicans, and other Latin Americans under one group. He described this group as fundamentally different from those inhabitants of places influenced by the history of English, French, or other forms of European colonialism. In this way, Martí is one of the earliest writers to speak of a shared Latino history. Martí also identified in the essay the imperialist tendencies of the United States and argued that the annexation of Mexico in 1848 was just the first step in U.S. imperialist ambitions. Martí was thus an important early voice among Latina/os in identifying and challenging U.S. imperialism in Latin America.

PROFILE: TERESA URREA

While Mexican migration to the United States would reach unparalleled levels in the twentieth century, Mexican women and men also crossed the northern border in significant numbers in the nineteenth century. One of the best-known Mexican immigrants of the period was the healer and religious leader Teresa Urrea, also known as "Santa Teresa."

Teresa Urrea was, like many Latina/os, of mixed heritage. Her mother, reportedly a Tehuecan Indian, was a domestic servant in the household of Urrea's father, a rancher in the northern Mexican state of Sonora. As a child, Urrea formed a close relationship with a local healer, or curandera, and learned a great deal from the woman about various treatments and medicinal herbs. In her childhood, Urrea also began to experience extended trance-like states.

Word of her mystical and healing powers soon spread, and Urrea became widely known in northern Mexico in the late 1880s. As opposition to Mexican president Porfirio Díaz's rule built in northern Mexico in the late nineteenth century, Urrea's popularity as a healer drew increasing attention from federal authorities who feared that she might help spark a widespread rebellion. Forced to flee Mexico to avoid arrest, Urrea and her father, Tomás, relocated to Arizona in 1892.

In Arizona, Teresa Urrea's reputation as a healer and spiritual leader soon attracted a new, and broader, audience. In 1900, she began a tour of U.S. cities, which included an audience of more than 1,000 spectators in San Francisco and performances in St. Louis and New York City. After the tour, Urrea moved to East Los Angeles and worked as a healer as well as reportedly helped to support Mexican railroad workers in their labor organizing efforts in the city.

Urrea returned to Arizona in 1903, where she continued to serve as healer and religious guide to the largely poor Mexican community of Clifton, Arizona. Falling seriously ill with what was likely tuberculosis, Urrea died in Clifton in 1906. Her funeral was attended by a large crowd of mourners. Teresa Urrea's life, where she combining tradition healing methods with religious devotion, points to the long history of Latina cultural and social leadership and the enduring links between Mexico and the United States.

REFERENCES

Almaguer, Tomás. *Racial Fault Lines: The Historical Origins of White Supremacy in California*. Berkeley: University of California Press, 1994.

Chávez-García, Miroslava. *States of Delinquency: Race and Science in the Making of California's Juvenile Justice System*. Berkeley: University of California Press, 2012.

Hoganson, Kristin L. *Fighting for American Manhood: How Gender Politics Provoked the Spanish-American and Philippine-American Wars*. New Haven, CT: Yale University Press, 2000.

Mitchell, Pablo R. *West of Sex: Making Mexican America, 1900–1930*. Chicago: University of Chicago Press, 2012.

Montejano, David. *Anglos and Mexicans in the Making of Texas, 1836–1986*. Austin: University of Texas Press, 1987.

Poyo, Gerald E. *"With All, and for the Good of All": The Emergence of Popular Nationalism in the Cuban Communities of the United States, 1848–1898*. Durham, NC: Duke University Press, 1989.

Spencer, George W. "The Treatment of Fracture of the Clavicle by Incision and Suture." *American Journal of the Medical Sciences* 113, no. 4 (April 1897): 445–54.

Torres-Saillant, Silvio. "Before the Diaspora: Early Dominican Literature in the United States." In *Recovering the U.S. Hispanic Literary Heritage*, Vol. 3, edited by Ramón A. Gutiérrez, Genaro M. Padilla, and María Herrera-Sobek, 250–67. Houston, TX: Arte Público Press, 1993.

Wagenheim, Olga Jiménez de. *Puerto Rico: An Interpretive History from Pre-Columbian Times to 1900*. Princeton, NJ: Markus Wiener Publisher, 1997.

Weigle, Marta. *Brothers of Light, Brothers of Blood: The Penitentes of the Southwest*. Albuquerque: University of New Mexico Press, 1976.

Whalen, Carmen Teresa. "Colonialism, Citizenship, and the Making of the Puerto Rican Diaspora." In *The Puerto Rican Diaspora: Historical Perspectives*, edited by Carmen Teresa Whalen and Víctor Vázquez Hernández, 1–42. Philadelphia: Temple University Press, 2005.

_____ *Chapter 6* _____

Birth of a Latina/o Nation, 1898–1930

Like 1848 and the signing of the Treaty of Guadalupe Hidalgo, 1898 was a turning point in Latina/o history. After decades of fighting, and at times dying, for independence, Puerto Rican and Cuban rebels finally achieved their goal: the end of Spanish rule on the islands. In the wake of the decisive U.S. military defeat of Spain in the summer of 1898, however, the long-awaited independence of the two countries was not forthcoming. Despite the ample support of Puerto Rican and Cuban soldiers and a chorus of U.S. denials of imperial intentions in both the Caribbean and broader Latin America, Puerto Rico and Cuba were not granted their freedom at the conclusion of the Spanish-American War. Instead, in the immediate aftermath of the war, both countries were retained by the United States as colonial possessions under military rule.

The impact of U.S. occupation on the lives of Puerto Ricans and Cubans in the early twentieth century was profound. In 1903 the Platt Amendment, which led to the independence of Cuba, was passed, and another piece of legislation, the 1917 Jones Act, granted (or in some views, imposed) U.S. citizenship on Puerto Ricans. The period also witnessed the beginnings of large-scale immigration from Puerto Rico and Cuba to the United States as well as the dramatic rise in Mexican immigration to the United States, which some historians estimate at reaching 1 million people between the years 1900 and 1930. As anti-immigrant sentiment accelerated in the early 1900s, ordinary Mexican, Puerto Rican, and Cuban women and men struggled mightily to defend the rights of themselves, their families, and their communities in their new homes.

In 1898, in the aftermath of the war between Spain and the United States, U.S. troops installed a military government in Puerto Rico. The ensuing U.S. occupation dramatically altered Puerto Rico's economy. The country's

After the Spanish-American War in 1898, U.S. business interests came to dominate sugar production in the Caribbean (Sugar exporting town Yauco, Puerto Rico, circa 1899). (Library of Congress)

primary crop shifted from coffee to sugar, and to some extent tobacco, and the agricultural sector was increasingly based on exports rather than on subsistence farming and addressing the daily living needs of Puerto Ricans. As a result, food and other goods began to be largely imported from the United States. By 1910, Puerto Rico was the 12th-largest consumer of U.S. goods in the world. In this way, Puerto Rico had much in common with Mexico, which underwent a similar transition to export-oriented agriculture in the late 1800s and early 1900s. Both countries also experienced increased migration to urban areas within their own countries and to the U.S. mainland during this period.

Another similarity between Puerto Ricans and Mexicans in the U.S. Southwest was the presence of U.S.-based social service organizations in both regions. As in Mexican communities, there was a concerted effort by North American reformers in Puerto Rico to try to transform Puerto Ricans into proper Americans. A critical feature of U.S. imperialism—one shared with other imperial nations like England—was lifting supposedly inferior peoples up toward what Anglos in the United States tended to think of as higher U.S. standards of civilized behavior. In both the Southwest and

Puerto Rico, this effort focused on women and transforming the supposed inferiority of Mexican and Puerto Rican women and their families

In Puerto Rico, attempts to combat prostitution on the island offer a vivid example of how women figured prominently in the extension of U.S. imperial rule in the early 1900s. In the early twentieth century, Puerto Rico had a policy of reglementación, or registration, for prostitutes. Prostitutes were required by the government to register with local officials and to undergo weekly medical examinations in hospitals. American reform groups like the Women's Christian Temperance Union (WCTU), which opposed the registration of prostitutes and instead supported incarceration for the women and medical treatment during their jail time, took it upon themselves to attempt further suppression of prostitution in Puerto Rico. This attack on prostitutes was part of a broader effort by groups like the WCTU to create middle-class homes in Puerto Rico based on U.S. models of domesticity and proper gender roles. The WCTU, as their name suggests, had been in Puerto Rico originally to promote temperance and abstinence from alcohol, but their larger goal was to improve the supposedly backward Puerto Rican family by transforming women. In jails, Anglo female reformers taught English to women arrested on prostitution charges and held literacy classes. They also taught skills like needlework and hat making and consistently emphasized the creation of nuclear, Anglo-American-like families.

At first, the WCTU's campaign appeared successful. The group managed to persuade the U.S. military to enforce laws that were already in effect on the U.S. mainland that prohibited prostitution within a five-mile radius of military training camps. The military agreed, and women found within this five-mile zone who were suspected of commercial sex work were arrested, jailed, and treated for venereal disease. The suppression of prostitutes soon spread to major urban locations like San Juan, where police arrested large numbers of prostitutes and suspected prostitutes.

Within a year, however, the support for the suppression of prostitutes seemed to fade. The WCTU's antiprostitution campaign, which framed their action as compassionate treatment of sympathetic and downtrodden women, had initially gained the support of the Catholic Church as well as Puerto Rican elites, including local women's groups like the Club de Damas in the large city of Ponce. Local newspapers, however, soon began to represent the women who had been arrested as victims of U.S. colonialism. One paper asked how Puerto Rico could be subject to measures to: "imprison these innocents, with no greater crime than to protect their own lives and those of their children who are dying of hunger, who ask her, beg her for a morsel of bread to eat and a torn garment with which to cover their feeble bodies" (Briggs 2002, 49). At one point, more than 300 imprisoned women in Ponce began a series of riots. They described repeated blood tests and pelvic exams and painful forced treatments for venereal diseases with mercury and arsenic. Pressure quickly built on the U.S. governor of Puerto Rico and the attorney general to release the women. The attorney general refused at first, even cutting the food rations of the female prisoners, but pressure by Puerto Rican political leaders eventually led to the dismissal of the attorney general and the release of the women. The uproar suggests, on the one hand, that the control of sexuality was a central part of U.S. intervention into the lives of Puerto Rican people. The incident also reveals the strength of the anti-imperialist movement in Puerto Rico, even in the early years of U.S. occupation.

The early 1900s is also notable for the beginnings of large-scale migration of Puerto Ricans to the U.S. mainland, especially to the eastern coast of the United States and to cities like New York City. Two main factors influenced Puerto Ricans to leave the island. The first was the continued mechanization and centralization of agricultural production in major areas like sugar, tobacco, and coffee. This modernization (as would occur in Mexico as well) led to increased unemployment, land loss, and migration, both to urban areas in Puerto Rico and off the island in search of better-paying jobs. The second factor in migrating to the U.S. mainland was a rapid growth in the Puerto Rican population in the early part of the 1900s. This population growth was due largely to increased health and a declining mortality rate. Overall, the population of Puerto Rico doubled between 1900 and 1940. It is important, however, to view critically this argument that increased population encouraged Puerto Ricans to migrate to the U.S. mainland. Throughout the twentieth century, population growth in Puerto Rico was often framed by both U.S. and Puerto Rican officials as a result of the supposedly excessive fertility of Puerto Rican women, especially working-class women and women of Afro-Puerto Rican descent. The broader U.S. population has often viewed Puerto Rico (and many other countries around the world) as overpopulated and has fixed the blame for overpopulation on the purported excessive and unchecked sexuality of women. In coming decades, this type of sexual demonization of Puerto Rican women would help justify experimentation on them in trials of birth control drugs as well as sterilization campaigns targeting women on the island. Charges of overpopulation were also a pillar of later attacks on the Puerto Rican family as unstable and dysfunctional. In the 1960s, and to some extent continuing to the present, these attacks dovetailed with critiques of African American families as dysfunctional and with the conservative assault on welfare programs and other social service programs.

While certain aspects of life in Puerto Rico encouraged migration off the island, other factors drew Puerto Ricans to the U.S. mainland. The first major pull factor was the passage of the Jones Act in 1917, which imposed

U.S. citizenship on Puerto Ricans. The Jones Act also required military service for Puerto Rican men. Young men were sent to the mainland with their
army groups and were introduced to U.S. customs and culture. For many
this introduction, although brief, offered a chance to become more familiar
with the United States and nurtured the idea of possibly moving to the mainland after their military service was completed. The second major factor
inducing Puerto Ricans to migrate to the U.S. mainland was the passage of
immigration restriction laws in the United States that were directed, in particular, at migrants from Europe and Asia. Laws limiting foreign migration
to the United States were passed with increasing speed in the 1910s and
1920s, culminating with the 1924 National Origins Act, which severely
restricted immigration to the country. As a result of such laws, a major
source of workers from Europe and Asia was cut off, leaving many more
entry-level, manual labor jobs available for Puerto Ricans, who were newly
designated as U.S. citizens.

Puerto Rican migrants to the U.S. mainland in the early 1900s settled in
various locations around the country. In 1920, Puerto Ricans were listed
by the census as living in 45 states. Nonetheless, the vast majority of Puerto
Ricans during this period settled in New York City. In 1910, 37 percent of
all Puerto Ricans lived in New York City; in 1920, over 60 percent lived in
the city; and by 1930, the percentage had risen to 80 percent. One 1925
report counted 100,000 Puerto Ricans in New York City with 5,000 in
Washington Heights, 25,000 in Brooklyn, and 70,000 in Manhattan. The
same survey in 1925 reported that there were only slightly more men than
women among the Puerto Rican newcomers, that migrants came from urban
rather than rural locales, and that many were either skilled or semiskilled
laborers. Many of the migrants, in fact, had worked in tobacco factories in
Puerto Rico, which was a relatively skilled job on the island.

Puerto Ricans chose New York as a destination for several reasons. Since
the nineteenth century, Puerto Ricans had lived in the city, some as merchants, some as political exiles, others as manual laborers. A group of fellow
Puerto Ricans that could provide support and guidance to migrants moving
to a new area thus already resided in the city. In addition, in the early 1900s,
passenger steam ships running between the island and New York became
increasingly available to a wider range of passengers. Though passenger ship
routes existed between Puerto Rico and southern ports of the United States,
these ships had only first-class seating for private passengers. Ships to New
York, on the other hand, offered different fares by class and were more effi-
cient and faster. In the 1920s and 1930s, fares ranged between $25 and $55
and trips lasted three to five days.

Puerto Rican newcomers to New York City found several types of support
in acclimating to their new homes. A range of organizations focused on

serving the needs of Puerto Ricans and defending the Puerto Rican community. By one count, there were more than 40 such organizations serving Puerto Ricans in the 1920s. One of the most successful of these groups was the Puerto Rican Brotherhood, which was founded in 1923. The Brotherhood's activities included defending a group of Puerto Rican men incorrectly charged with being non-U.S. citizens, providing aid to impoverished Puerto Rican families, and covering the burial expenses of poor Puerto Ricans. The support of social service organizations helped sustain the emerging Puerto Rican community in New York, a community that would experience far more dramatic growth in subsequent decades.

Unlike Puerto Ricans, Cubans eventually wrestled their independence from both Spain and the United States. Cuban independence, however, was not immediate, and the U.S. government forced Cuba to accept a series of concessions in order to achieve their autonomy. The 1903 Platt Amendment, which both countries eventually signed, stipulated the conditions whereby the United States would withdraw troops from Cuba, including the requirement that Cuba provide land for U.S. military installations (land that would eventually become the U.S.-controlled Guantánamo Bay military base). The Platt Amendment was incorporated into the Cuban-American Treaty of 1903, when Cuban leaders realized that they could either endure continued U.S. military occupation of the island or sign the treaty. The Platt Amendment and the Cuban-American Treaty were instrumental in North American businesses' eventual domination of the Cuban sugar industry (after the treaty, U.S. businesses felt secure that their companies, factories, and property would be protected by the U.S. military). The treaty also contributed to decades of anti-U.S. sentiment among Cuban nationalists, who, perhaps not incorrectly, believed that the United States had undermined their goals of Cuban freedom and independence.

Accompanying the presence of U.S. military and colonial government officials in Cuba in the early 1900s was a heightened role for U.S. business on the island. Though Americans had been involved in sugar production for decades, U.S. occupation spurred far more profound involvement in the sugar trade. Widespread destruction during the war and high levels of poverty throughout the island compelled many Cubans to sell land at lowered prices, bargains that were quickly seized by North American companies. U.S. sugar companies purchased vast acreage in sugar plantations, some stretching more than 1,000 acres, and established nearby mills for processing the sugar harvest. By one estimate, nearly one entire sugar-producing region along Cuba's north coast was sold into U.S. control in the span of a single decade.

U.S. businesses expanded into other sectors of the Cuban economy as well. Three-quarters of the cattle ranches in Cuba, worth some $30 million, were owned by North Americans. U.S.-based tobacco companies also dominated cigar and cigarette factories and hundreds of thousands of acres of tobacco farmland. By 1902, according to one historian, a North American group "controlled 90 percent of the export trade of Havana cigars" (Pérez 2003, 119). In all, by 1911 North Americans held more than $200 million in capital in Cuba, a sum that would grow to five times that amount by the 1920s.

As so often happens, U.S. economic control in Cuba moved in lockstep with an expanded U.S. cultural presence on the island. English-language instruction, for instance, spread rapidly in Cuban schools, and Cuban teachers often traveled to the United States on U.S.-sponsored visits designed to familiarize teachers with North American culture and customs. U.S. culture also entered Cuba in the form of religion. As in Puerto Rico and in Mexican communities in the Southwest, Protestant missionaries from the United States flocked to Cuba in the early 1900s. Between 1900 and 1910, for instance, "Baptists in eastern Cuba established forty-four churches, sixty-eight chapel stations, and forty-six Sunday schools in forty-two towns and cities and claimed a membership of more than twenty-two hundred Cubans" (Pérez 2003, 131).

Interactions between Cubans and North Americans thus multiplied rapidly in the early decades of the 1900s. Just as North Americans increasingly traveled to Cuba, Cubans visited, and even relocated to, the United States in greater numbers after 1898. One of the earliest migrations of Cubans to the United States had occurred during the late 1800s as Cubans fled the upheavals of the revolution and U.S. occupation. Many of these early Cuban migrants to the United States were tobacco workers who settled in places like Key West, Tampa, and New Orleans. One example of this early migration was the case of Vicente Ybor and Ignacio Haya, who in 1887 had established a cigar factory near Tampa and called it Ybor City. Ybor City eventually outproduced Havana as a manufacturing center of quality cigars and became known as the "Cigar Capital of the World." A steamship line soon linked Ybor City and Havana in the early 1900s, with tens of thousands of people annually traveling between Cuba and Florida. In 1900, there were more than 100 cigar factories in Ybor City and a population of 15,000. That year the Cuban population of Ybor City was twice that of New York City, and a decade later there were more than 6,000 Cuban residents of the city.

Ybor City continued to grow and prosper through the 1920s and into the 1930s. Several factors soon converged to bring about hard times, however. Cigarette consumption began to grow during that period, and improved machinery for rolling cigars managed to produce a product comparable in workmanship to the hand-rolled variety. At first, these machine-produced cigars could find only a small niche in the market because the hand-rolled "Havana"-type cigar had a strong reputation for quality and taste. The producers of the machine-made cigars, however, launched what came to be known as the "spit" campaign, where they falsely claimed in their advertisements that human saliva played a major role in the production of hand-manufactured cigars, and the sales of hand-rolled cigars began to diminish. Though Ybor City eventually receded as a primary site of Cuban migration, the city served as an important predecessor to Miami as a major Cuban-identified city in Florida.

Puerto Ricans and Cubans were not alone in experiencing military invasion and occupation by the United States at the turn of the twentieth century. In 1916, the U.S. military invaded the Dominican Republic. The military occupation lasted until 1924, and during this period the United States helped train the Dominican military, including the man who would come to dominate the Dominican Republic for the next 30 years, the eventual president Rafael Trujillo. Despite the U.S. presence, immigration from the Dominican Republic to the United States was limited during the period, with a population of only 1,200 Dominicans in the United States in 1930.

New York City was the home of many of these Dominican newcomers. Sebastian Gozan, for instance, was born in the Dominican Republic, as were both his parents, and had lived in the United States for more than three decades in 1900. The 61-year-old Gozan was a naturalized U.S. citizen and worked as a bookkeeper in New York City. Thirty years later, the Dominican community had grown in the city, and in some areas, Dominicans lived alongside Puerto Ricans and Cubans in small Spanish-speaking neighborhoods. Carlos Acosta, a Dominican laundry worker, had immigrated to the United States in 1907 and lived with his Venezuelan wife, Emilia, who arrived in the United States in 1923, on 116th Street in upper Manhattan. The Acosta family lived in a remarkably broad pan-Latina/o neighborhood. The majority of their neighbors were Puerto Ricans; however, living nearby were two couples who, like the Acostas, were intermarried: Joe Cardt, a Cuban, and Carmen Cardt, a Puerto Rican, and Bernadino Perez, a Mexican, and Mary Perez, also a Puerto Rican. In addition to Dominicans, Venezuelans, Puerto Ricans, Cubans, and Mexicans, this stretch of 116th Street included African Americans, Anglo Americans, and Italian, Irish, and Swedish immigrants. A small number of Dominicans also lived outside New York City. One *Dominicana*, Juanita H. Basham, lived in Jumping Branch, West Virginia, in 1930. Basham resided with her Anglo husband, Roy, a manual laborer, and their two-year-old son, John. She had arrived in the United States six years earlier and was the only Spanish and English speaker among her neighbors, nearly all of whom had been born in West Virginia.

Like Dominicans, Central Americans and South Americans arrived in relatively small numbers to the United States in the early twentieth century. Four thousand Central Americans appeared in the U.S. census in 1900. The population rose to 5,000 in 1920 and reached more than 10,000 by 1930. The South American population rose more dramatically during the same period, increasing from fewer than 5,000 in 1900 to almost 20,000 in 1920 and more than 30,000 in 1930.

As the rapid growth of U.S. investments in Cuba and Puerto Rico suggest, the U.S. economy was booming in the early 1900s. This growth was especially dramatic in the U.S. Southwest, where the two most important developments were the expansion of the railroad and the construction of extensive irrigation projects for large-scale agriculture. The rapid construction of railroad tracks linked increasing numbers of communities across the nation to the rest of the country. This expansion of the railroad reached into Mexico as well, bringing trade goods and enabling the movement of peoples and commerce on an unprecedented scale. A second major development was in agriculture, where large federally funded irrigation projects like dams and irrigation canals enabled the cultivation of previously arid and agriculturally unproductive lands. In 1890, the total amount of irrigated land in California, Nevada, Utah, and Arizona was 1.5 million acres. Twenty years later, there were 14 million acres in the Southwest devoted to agriculture. California and Texas came to dominate U.S. agriculture, California with fruits, nuts, citrus, and vegetables, and Texas with fruits, vegetables, and especially cotton. Texas, by the 1920s, grew about 40 percent of U.S. cotton production and between 20 and 30 percent of the world's cotton.

This rapid economic expansion in sectors like agriculture and transportation would have been impossible without affordable and reliable labor. Denied the use of Chinese and Japanese laborers after a series of anti-Asian immigration bills, beginning with the 1882 Chinese Exclusion Act, U.S. businesses in the Southwest turned to Mexican workers. U.S. companies even hired labor recruiters in Mexico to recruit workers to relocate to the United States. The expansion of railroad construction in Mexico further facilitated Mexicans' journey north. During this same period in Mexico, the government of President Porfirio Díaz embarked on an effort to introduce export-oriented agriculture, rather than subsistence farming, to the nation, leading to a rise in food prices, a decline in wages, and thousands of Mexicans being forced off their land. With a worsening economic situation in Mexico and the promise by North American labor recruiters of better wages in the United States, many Mexicans thus began making their way north by the end of the 1800s. In 1890, there were nearly 80,000 Mexican-born people in the United States (not to mention the tens of thousands of

Mexican railroad and agricultural workers formed the backbone of U.S. economic growth in the Southwest in the early twentieth century. (Library of Congress)

Americans of Mexican descent already in the country). The number rose to above 100,000 in 1900, 222,000 in 1910, and 480,000 in 1920.

Mexican workers soon became the backbone of several major businesses in the Southwest, including agriculture, construction, and railroad work. Labor shortages during the World War I era increased the demand for Mexican labor, as did legislation placing limits on European immigration like the previously mentioned 1924 National Origins Act. In Mexico, the social unrest, food shortages, and scarcity of work during the Mexican Revolution spurred many to leave the country. As a result, throughout the 1920s Mexico was the prime source of foreign immigration to the United States.

While Mexican newcomers in the early 1900s settled throughout the Southwest, the highest concentration of Mexicans in the United States lived in Los Angeles. Most Mexican immigrants entered the United States through the border city of El Paso, Texas, and a great many turned westward to California, drawn by plentiful, though low-paying, jobs in agriculture and in Los Angeles's developing industrial sector. Los Angeles as a whole was growing rapidly during the period, jumping from a citywide population of 102,000 in 1900 to 1.2 million in 1930 (in broader Los Angeles County, the population rose from 170,000 in 1900 to 2.2 million in 1930). During the same three decades, the Mexican population of Los Angeles grew from fewer than a thousand in 1900 to 5,000 in 1910, 30,000 in 1920, and nearly 100,000 in 1930.

Although Mexicans in Los Angeles were largely confined to poorly paid, manual labor jobs, their cultural position in the early 1900s at first tended to be more highly regarded than that of Asian immigrants, especially Chinese and Japanese Americans. As a result, though Mexicans experienced severe racism and discrimination in Los Angeles, they also managed to demand, and at times receive, respectful treatment by the city's Anglo leaders and government officials. Unlike Chinese and Japanese American families, for instance, Mexican families were considered potential U.S. citizens. Significant efforts were focused on improving the supposedly inferior parenting techniques of Mexican women in order to create, in the words of historian Natalia Molina, "a population that could conform to American standards and thus become an acceptable workforce" (Molina 2006, 78). This sense of Mexicans as potentially assimilating to U.S. society began to fade, however, by the end of the 1920s. Vicious anti-immigrant attacks spread throughout Los Angeles and the region, and the capacity of Mexican women and men to become full members of U.S. society was increasingly questioned.

Rivaling California as a destination of Mexican immigrants at the turn of century was Texas. In fact, the highest number of Mexicans living in the United States resided in Texas until 1930, when California assumed the mantle of largest population. In 1910, the combined U.S.-born and Mexican-born Mexican population in Texas was 230,000. As occurred throughout the Southwest, Mexicans were drawn to Texas by plentiful jobs in industries like the railroad and agriculture. Mexican men, for instance, helped build the railroad tracks that were vital to the booming economy of the U.S. West. After immigration restriction effectively cut off the supply of low-wage workers from Asia, railroad companies turned to Mexican workers for railroad construction and maintenance. By the end of the first decade of the 1900s, one historian notes, "Mexicans had supplied most of the labor for track maintenance crews in the Southwest" (Foley 1999, 44). Unlike railroad construction, where Mexican men were overwhelmingly employed, agriculture in Texas, especially cotton production, often drew entire families. As a result, the gender balance in Texas tended to be more even, and Mexican women in Texas were significant members of the state's agricultural workforce.

As in California, Mexicans in Texas struggled mightily to hold back the tide of both intense anti-immigrant rhetoric and literal physical attacks on Mexican communities. As calls to limit immigration from Mexico gained momentum in the early 1900s, Mexicans were described by Anglos— including Anglo politicians and civic leaders—as, in the words of one historian, "prone to criminal activity, filth, and disease" (Orozco 2009, 60). Violence against Mexicans was similarly pervasive. In South Texas, a plot to overthrow Anglo authority and reinstitute Mexican rule in the region, known as the Plan de San Diego, was discovered in 1915. Though a member of an elite Mexican family in Texas had helped uncover the uprising and the actual number of Mexican conspirators was relatively small, Anglo officials and law enforcement officers like the Texas Rangers took the opportunity to attack all Mexicans in the state. Violence burned through the South Texas region in particular, with estimates of Mexican deaths ranging from several hundred to several thousand, and the Texas Rangers played an active role in terrorizing and murdering Mexicans. As a result, according to one count half of the Mexican population fled South Texas in the 1910s.

During this challenging period for Mexicans in the United States, Mexicans resisted their subordination in multiple ways. In the legal system where Mexicans often faced many barriers, such as lack of wealth and political status, unfamiliarity with U.S. laws and customs, or poor English-language skills, criminal appeals cases filed by Mexicans point to an insistence by a significant number of Mexican men and women of their legal rights in the United States. In fact, between 1900 and 1930, more than 1,000 Mexicans filed appeals to higher courts in the U.S. Southwest. There were 41 criminal appeals cases by Mexicans in the California Supreme Court and 167 in the Court of Appeal of California. Court records reveal 78 Spanish-surnamed appellants in Arizona and 114 in New Mexico over the same period. In Texas, nearly 750 Mexicans appealed criminal convictions to the Texas Court of Criminal Appeals between 1900 and 1930. While most of the appeals were filed by Mexican men, Mexican women also appealed criminal convictions to higher courts. Moreover, court records reveal that Mexican women who testified during criminal trials were often confident and assertive on the witness stand and were frequently capable defenders of their families and communities in the face of an overwhelmingly Anglo-dominated judicial system.

While a substantial majority of Mexicans in the United States in the early 1900s lived in the Southwest and in states like California and Texas, a small but significant number of Mexican newcomers settled in the U.S. Midwest during those early decades of the century. Most Mexicans who migrated to the Midwest came from Texas, and a great many had worked in the state's expanding cotton economy of the 1910s and 1920s. Cotton picking in Texas had many drawbacks. It was grueling, backbreaking work in unrelenting sun that paid low wages. The annual rainy season also forced extended periods of unemployment, and workers lived in small camps in rural areas where they often suffered racial discrimination and racial abuse from Anglo Texans. Labor agents for midwestern farms and factories could thus make convincing arguments to workers to go north for higher wages and better working and living conditions. Companies adopted various methods to convince Mexicans to go north, including hiring Spanish-speaking labor recruiters to ride the trains and speak glowingly of life in cities like Chicago and Detroit. So convincing could recruiters from the Midwest be that, increasingly, migrants from Mexico did not even stop first in Texas but went directly to the Midwest.

By 1927, the Mexican population in the Midwest totaled 64,000; in the summer months, when migrants from the South moved in to farming regions, the population could grow to 80,000. Half of these newcomers were between the ages of 18 and 30. Most were male and hailed from regions in Mexico like Michoacán, Guanajuato, and Jalisco. Most had also already migrated within Mexico before crossing the border. One man, for example, left his farm outside Guadalajara and found a job in a U.S. owned oil refinery in Tampico, Mexico. He lost his job there, however, and returned to Guadalajara, where he worked in a brick factory. Later, the man went to El Paso and signed a contract to harvest sugar beets in the state of Wyoming. From Wyoming, he moved to Chicago and worked in a meat-packing factory, where he finally settled.

The first major employers of Mexicans in the Midwest were sugar beet producers. During World War I, as occurred in many agribusinesses in the Southwest, Mexicans became the majority of the workers in midwestern sugar beet farms, replacing Russians and Eastern Europeans in the fields. By 1927 in Michigan alone, there were 20,000 Mexican sugar beet work-ers. But farmwork was hardly ideal employment. In Mexican and other communities, farmwork was considered the most difficult, poorest-paying job. Factory work and work on the railroads was considered much more attractive. Factory work, in particular, paid better and was more stable, allowing children to stay in school and not be withdrawn by their families during harvest or picking seasons. Although Mexicans were restricted by racist policies from rising to management positions, factory work was thus desirable for many. By the 1930s, Mexican workers formed significant segments of the labor force in industries in the Mid-west like auto production in Detroit, meatpacking in Chicago, and steel mills in Pittsburgh.

In Lorain, Ohio, for example, which is located west of Cleveland along the shores of Lake Erie, the National Tube factory sent recruiters to Texas and Mexico advertising good wages in the North in the 1920s. One thou-sand Mexican workers, their transportation paid by the company, soon arrived in Lorain and settled in the town. In September 1926, a sociologist studying Mexican American workers in the United States attended a celebra-tion of Mexican Independence Day. The sociologist described a crowd of 300 listening to patriotic speeches and presentations, and the playing of both the Mexican and American national anthems. Such public celebrations affirmed ordinary Mexicans' rights as citizens of the city of Lorain and as members of the U.S. nation.

As the new century dawned, Latina/o populations in the United States had been transformed. Despite heightened anti-immigrant attacks, Mexicans managed to weather the storm and establish a lasting presence both across the Southwest and in the Midwest. Puerto Rican migrants likewise formed strong and enduring communities in the East Coast of the United States, especially in New York City and "Spanish" Harlem. Cuban migrants, though in smaller numbers, joined Puerto Ricans in New York City and expanded existing settlements in southern locations like Ybor City, Florida. In the coming decades, as the United States endured the Great Depression, a second world war, and the onset of the Cold War, these communities would provide the foundation for a much broader expansion of the country's Latina/o population.

PROFILE: LUISA CAPETILLO

Labor activist, feminist, and writer Luisa Capetillo was born in Arecibo, Puerto Rico, in 1879. Her mother, who was French, and her Spanish father raised their daughter to believe in women's rights and the importance of education, and to support labor organizing. Capetillo's father left the family when she was a girl, and by the time she was in her early twenties, she was the mother of two children.

Supported by her mother, Capetillo began a career as a union organizer in 1905. "By caring for her children for extended periods," historian Nancy Hewitt writes, "Luisa's mother enabled her daughter to establish her career as a reader [in tobacco factories] and, later, as an itinerant organizer and lecturer" (Hewitt 2005, 123). Capetillo worked for a tobacco workers union associated with La Federación Libre de Trabajadores de Puerto Rico (also known as FLT) and soon rose to leadership positions, a rare feat for a woman in a union filled with men.

Capetillo was also a prolific writer and journalist. She was the author of several books, including collections of essays addressing women's rights, education, motherhood, and health care. An anarchist feminist, like Emma Goldman, Capetillo, according to Hewitt, "advocated free love and sex education for women and men and condemned conventional marriage as a form of prostitution" (Hewitt 2005, 126). Capetillo further challenged gender norms and expectations by often dressing in men's trousers and a tie.

One of the twentieth century's great transnational organizers, Capetillo traveled from Puerto Rico to Cuba to New York City to Ybor City, Florida, giving lectures, writing articles for local papers, and helping to lead major strikes. In the early 1920s, however, Capetillo contracted tuberculosis and, weakened by the illness, moved to Río Piedras, Puerto Rico. In April 1922, she died at the age of 42. Her feminist writings, U.S.-Caribbean labor organizing, and commitment to anarchism and socialism have served as an inspiration to successive generations of Latina and Latino activists.

PROFILE: JESÚS COLÓN

Puerto Rican author, civil rights pioneer, and community leader Jesús Colón was born in Cayey, Puerto Rico, in 1901. In his teens, Colón joined the Tobacco Workers Union and the Socialist Party in Cayey and continued his commitment to rights for workers and union organizing when he moved to New York City in 1917.

In the 1920s, Colón taught literacy and civics classes at night and started a successful career as a journalist and essay writer. He wrote movingly of the miserable work conditions that Puerto Ricans often faced in the city. He described Puerto Ricans working at jobs such as, according to scholar Linda Delgado, "removing glued-on labels from bottles which required your hands to be constantly in ice water while removing the label with your frozen thumbnail to avoid scratching the bottle," as well as "night shift work on the docks in Hoboken, New Jersey, during the dead of winter, with so little salary that the workers could not afford a winter coat or even a warm pair of gloves" (Delgado 2005, 72). In addition to his blossoming writing career, Colón helped found numerous community organizations that supported the Puerto Rican diaspora in New York City, including Alianza Obrera Puertorriqueña in 1922 and La Liga Puertorriqueña e Hispana in 1928.

As an Afro-Puerto Rican, or in his words, "a Negro and a Puerto Rican," Colón viewed racism within the context of rights for workers and union organizing, seeking to link racial equality with critiques of capitalism and economic disparity (Delgado 2005, 81). Colón was also highly critical of U.S. colonialism and the exploitation of Puerto Ricans under U.S. colonial rule.

A prolific writer, Jesús Colón addressed these themes in his long career as a journalist, community organizer, and public intellectual. He wrote more than 400 essays and in 1961 published a book, *Puerto Ricans in New York City and Other Sketches*. Jesús Colón died in 1974.

PROFILE: ADELINA OTERO WARREN

Unlike the vast majority of Latinas and Latinos in U.S. history, Adelina ("Nina") Otero Warren, born in 1886 in New Mexico, was raised in wealth and privilege. Her mother, Eloisa Luna, was a member of one of New Mexico's most prosperous and politically powerful families, and her father was a well-known politician before his untimely death when his daughter was only two years old.

The family lived in a mansion with several servants in what would become the town of Los Lunas, New Mexico. At the age of 11, Otero attended a Catholic boarding school in St. Louis. She also insisted that she be taught to shoot a gun in order to protect herself and her family members. In 1908, Adelina Otero married Rawson Warren, who was a lieutenant in the U.S. Army. The couple quickly divorced, however, and Otero Warren moved to New York City, where she worked in a settlement house that served a poor community in the city. She returned to New Mexico in 1914 and turned to a career in politics. She was appointed the superintendent of public schools for Santa Fe County and was repeatedly elected to that post for the next 12 years. One of her priorities in public education was to balance English-language instruction with a respect for *Nuevomexicana/o* culture, including a refusal to punish children for speaking Spanish at school.

A strong supporter of women's right to vote, Otero Warren decided to run for Congress in 1922. Though revelations of her divorce, which previously had not been widely publicized, hurt her campaign, she nonetheless lost by only a slim margin in the general election. Undeterred by the loss, Otero Warren continued to serve in important political positions in the decades to come, including a post in the Works Progress Administration in Río Piedras, Puerto Rico, in the early 1940s.

In addition to public service, Otero Warren was an accomplished writer. She was especially interested in folk stories and was also the author of *Old Spain in Our Southwest*, which was published in 1936. After retiring from politics, she and her partner of many years, Mamie Meadors, opened a successful real estate business. Meadors died in 1951 and, though heartbroken, Otero Warren continued running the business until the mid-1960s. In 1965, Nina Otero Warren, a pioneer Latina educator and activist, died at the age of 83.

REFERENCES

Briggs, Laura. *Reproducing Empire: Race, Sex, Science, and U.S. Imperialism in Puerto Rico*. Berkeley: University of California Press, 2002.

Delgado, Linda C. "Jesús Colón and the Making of a New York City Community, 1917 to 1974." In *The Puerto Rican Diaspora: Historical Perspectives*, edited by Carmen Teresa Whalen and Víctor Vázquez Hernández, 68–87. Philadelphia: Temple University Press, 2005.

Foley, Neil. *White Scourge: Mexicans Blacks and Poor Whites in Texas Cotton Culture*. Berkeley: University of California Press, 1999.

Hewitt, Nancy A. "Luisa Capetillo: Feminist of the Working Class." In *Latina Legacies: Identity, Biography, and Community*, edited by Vicki L. Ruiz and Virginia Sánchez-Korrol, 120–34. New York: Oxford University Press, 2005.

Molina, Natalia. *Fit to be Citizens?: Public Health and Race in Los Angeles, 1879–1939*. Berkeley: University of California Press, 2006.

Orozco, Cynthia E. *No Mexicans, Women, or Dogs Allowed: The Rise of the Mexican American Civil Rights Movement*. Austin: University of Texas Press, 2009.

Pérez, Louis A., Jr. *Cuba and the United States: Ties of Singular Intimacy*. Athens: University of Georgia Press, 2003.

Chapter 7

Great Depression and World War II, 1930–1945

The period between 1930 and the end of World War II in 1945 would transform the nation and its Latina/o peoples in many ways. Like their fellow Americans, Latina/os suffered deeply during the Great Depression. In addition to widespread unemployment and poverty in the 1930s, certain Latina/o communities, such as Mexicans, faced organized deportation drives targeting U.S. citizens and noncitizens alike. Attacks on Mexicans continued in the 1940s as well, and all Latina/os struggled to escape poverty and poor work and living conditions. Latina/os adopted a range of strategies to resist these attacks. Moreover, in what has been an enduring theme in Latina/o history, Latinas often took the lead in defending themselves and their communities.

Like other Latina/o communities, the Great Depression had a profound effect on Puerto Ricans, both in Puerto Rico and on the U.S. mainland. The island's agricultural economy was hit especially hard by the Depression. The sugar industry was reduced by nearly a third between 1929 and 1939, and by the end of the 1930s, "the tobacco industry in Puerto Rico was virtually nonexistent" (Sánchez-Korrol 1994, 26). Unemployment and poverty rose quickly in Puerto Rico, but unlike the previous decade, few attractive employment opportunities appeared on the U.S. mainland for Puerto Ricans. In fact, in the early 1930s the island experienced a larger return migration (numbering as many as 10,000 people) from the United States.

For Puerto Ricans remaining in North American cities, employment was limited to blue-collar, menial positions. In New York City, a government office that was formed to find jobs for unemployed workers overwhelmingly placed Puerto Ricans in unskilled or semiskilled positions. More than a quarter of the nearly 2,000 jobs found for Puerto Ricans by this office between 1930 and 1936 were in general labor and construction, with several

Widespread deportation raids targeted Mexican communities during the 1930s (Relatives in Los Angeles wave goodbye to family members being deported.). (NY Daily News Archive/Getty Images)

hundred more in laundries and factories, as well as dozens in service sector employment such as hotel workers, porters, janitors, and waiters. This clustering of Puerto Ricans into poorly paid, entry-level positions is a pattern that would continue well into the second half of the twentieth century.

Although the U.S. economy would improve dramatically by the mid-1940s, aided especially by wartime production during World War II, many Puerto Ricans on the island continued to struggle economically and chose to migrate to the U.S. mainland in hopes of financial stability. One Puerto Rican man described finding work only sporadically in Puerto Rico and even then having great difficulty feeding his family. "These salaries," he recalled, "could barely support one individual let alone a family of six" (Sánchez-Korrol 1994, 43). Eventually, in the spring of 1945, the man borrowed money to purchase ship fare and, like so many of his countrymen and countrywomen, migrated to New York City.

While the majority of Puerto Rican migrants to the U.S. mainland settled in New York City, other cities also received significant numbers of Puerto Rican newcomers. Puerto Ricans migrated to Philadelphia, for instance, in large numbers in the early twentieth century. Latina/os had lived in the city for many decades, especially those associated with the cigar-making industry, and the Puerto Rican population in Philadelphia was initially small compared to the larger presence of Cubans and Spaniards in the city. After World War I, however, Puerto Ricans began to outnumber other Latina/o newcomers. Puerto Rican migrants were increasingly limited to industrial, working-class jobs, and, like African Americans, Puerto Ricans suffered from housing and job discrimination in Philadelphia in the 1930s and 1940s. As new employment and housing opportunities opened for whites in suburbs and outlying areas, Puerto Ricans found themselves trapped in blue-collar jobs and homes in the inner city.

Confined to poor-paying, often grueling jobs and crowded living quarters, Puerto Ricans in Philadelphia turned to a handful of Latina/o organizations for support. La Milagrosa had been founded in 1909 through the Catholic Church to serve the city's Spanish, Cuban, and Puerto Rican populations, and by the 1930s it was a well-established neighborhood institution, offering a space for English classes, baptisms, weddings, and other social activities. The Hispanic American Fraternal Society of Philadelphia, also founded in the early twentieth century, provided a similar set of critical services. Like La Milagrosa, La Fraternal's membership included not only Puerto Ricans but Philadelphians of Spanish and Cuban descent as well.

Though many Puerto Ricans built new lives far from the island in cities like New York and Philadelphia, deep ties with Puerto Rico often endured. The exchange of peoples, ideas, and organizations between Puerto Rico and the mainland took on many forms. In matters of medicine and health, for instance, North American medical professionals joined with their counterparts on the island to address a variety of public health issues. One area of especially intense intervention was in the realm of sex and reproduction. In the early twentieth century, debates over sex, especially prostitution, became an important terrain in Puerto Rico for challenges to U.S. colonial rule. Sex and politics were similarly intertwined in the 1930s and early 1940s in struggles over birth control, reproduction, and motherhood. According to one historian, a birth control movement emerged "in the 1920s under the auspices of the Puerto Rican Socialist Party—before most places on the mainland (outside of New York City) even had an active birth control movement" (Briggs 2002, 90). The island's first birth control group, Liga para el control de natalidad de Puerto Rico (Birth Control League of Puerto Rico), was founded by a socialist activist in 1925.

The birth control movement gained momentum in the 1930s under the leadership of Puerto Rican and North American nurses and social workers. Rosa Gonzalez, for instance, a Puerto Rican feminist leader, started a birth control clinic in the city of Lares, and another clinic was founded in Mayagüez with the support of both North Americans and Puerto Ricans like the physician Dr. Manuel Guzmán Rodríguez. This collaboration strengthened when the U.S. government stepped in to assume leadership of birth control clinics on the island. Under the new U.S. control, Puerto Rican nurses and social workers were placed in charge of the program and continued to be vital figures in providing birth control information and services.

Puerto Rican women were central in another set of exchanges during the period, namely the movement of skills and labor from the island to mainland cities like New York City. In Puerto Rico, sewing and other forms of needlework were taught to girls as young children and were even incorporated into the public school curriculum as early as the second grade. In Puerto Rico, women often found employment both outside and inside the home through their sewing and needlework skills, and migrants brought these skills with them to the mainland. In one study, about half of a group of 600 Puerto Rican women employed in New York City in the early 1930s found work as seamstresses or needleworkers, while the majority of other women turned to domestic service for paid employment.

While Puerto Rican migrants often struggled in their new North American homes with limited employment and housing options, discrimination, and racism, Puerto Rican communities in New York City, Philadelphia, and elsewhere proved resilient in the face of adverse circumstances. Spanish-language periodicals and newspapers, for instance, provided critical sources of news, advice, and support for cultural institutions. The *Revista de Artes y Letras*, one of the most prominent periodicals, was founded by a Puertorriqueña, Josefina Silva de Cintron, in 1933 and lasted until 1945. In *Artes y Letras*, according to historian Virginia Sánchez-Korrol, "community organizational news, advertising, interviews, and advice columns shared space with literary essays and fiction," as well as showcasing the writing of major writers like Julia de Burgos (Sánchez-Korrol 1994, 75). Music played a similarly important role in supporting the Puerto Rican community. Puerto Rican musicians often entertained audiences both in smaller, family-oriented celebrations like weddings and baptisms and in larger dance halls and concerts. Bernardo Vega, the famous Puerto Rican chronicler of life in New York City before World War II, described house parties where "*trios* and *quartets* which consisted of a lead vocalist, a maraca player, guitarist and sometimes a trumpeter provided live music in the living room" (Sánchez-Korrol 1994, 80). Like newspapers, shared cultural production like music helped sustain the Puerto Rican community during times of hardship.

As in Puerto Rico, the Cuban economy, particularly the sugar industry, faltered in the early 1930s. The economic turmoil weakened the political hold of President Gerardo Machado on the country, and when a general strike in 1933, sparked by a bus drivers' strike in Havana, escalated into widespread revolt, Machado was driven from office. Cuban nationalists subsequently forced the United States to abandon the Platt Amendment and ensure Cuba's full independence and sovereignty. The ensuing constitution was remarkably inclusive, providing for "free elections, universal adult suffrage, and the freedom of association, speech, religion, and the press" (Skwiot 2010, 145). Greater political stability was accompanied by economic growth as the demand for sugar in World War II spurred economic prosperity in the early 1940s. The Cuban government also renewed its strong support of the tourism industry and placed special emphasis on attracting tourists from the United States.

While migration from Cuba to the United States was not as pronounced as Mexican and Puerto Rican migration to the United States in the 1930s and early 1940s, the relationship between Cuba and the United States continued to develop and expand after 1930. African Americans, for instance, and Afro-Cubans (Cubans of African descent) formed new and important bonds in the 1930s and 1940s. One bond developed around arts and literature, and was aided greatly by the work of noted African American literary figure Langston Hughes. Hughes, already a cultural star by 1930, traveled to Cuba and was thrilled at the vibrancy of Cuban, especially Afro-Cuban, intellectual and artistic life. Determined to showcase the rich intersections between African American and Afro-Cuban culture, Hughes and collaborators like famed Mexican muralist Miguel Covarrubias sponsored travel for artists between Havana and New York City, literary engagements, and lectures to mixed African American and Afro-Cuban audiences. Another link between the two countries was forged by women's groups, such as the National Council of Negro Women (NCNW) in the United States and the Asociación Cultural Feminina (Women's Cultural Association) in Cuba. The latter group was founded in 1935 and focused on the political involvement and civic engagement of Afro-Cuban women, an aim that paralleled the goals of the NCNW.

Although political unrest and the effects of the Great Depression in the United States initially dampened tourism to Cuba, the lull was short-lived and the Cuban tourism industry soon rebounded. Travel between Cuba and the United States, in general, continued at a brisk pace after 1930. In addition to the Ward Line, also known as the New York and Cuba Mail Steamship Company, which had dominated transportation earlier in the century, new companies started service in the 1930s. The United Fruit Company expanded their fleet, according to one historian, "of 44 ships that could transport 350 passengers to one of 90 ships that carried 2,500 passengers throughout the region" (Guridy 2010, 8). Travelers also journeyed by air between the two countries, as Pan American airlines launched its first flight between Key West, Florida, and Havana in 1927 and expanded its routes in years to come.

Like so many Latina/o immigrants over the course of U.S. history, the largest Dominican community in the United States developed in New York City. According to Jorge Duany, "the first known Dominican-owned bodega (grocery store) in the city was established in 1933 on West 100th Street in Upper Manhattan" (Duany 2011, 55). Nearby the bodega, on West 109th Street, according to the 1940 U.S. census, lived Petra Moreno, a widowed, 42-year-old housekeeper who had been born in Spain but whose three children had all been born in the Dominican Republic. Next to the Moreno family lived Carlos and Emilia Acosta, who had been in the city since at least 1930 (see chapter 6). Carlos, born in the Dominican Republic, worked as a musician, while Emilia, a Venezuelan, listed no occupation. Dominicans in New York also lived in the Bronx. Forty-three-year-old Mary Burgos headed a household of Dominicans in the Bronx that included her son and daughter and two cousins, both seamstresses. The Burgos's neighbors were largely working-class Puerto Ricans, as well as a Panamanian woman, Marcelina Moreno, who worked in a box factory and was married to a Puerto Rican man, and Clara Negron, who was a 23-year-old "wigmaker" for theatrical productions and had been born in Santiago, Cuba.

Though most Dominicans continued to live in New York City in the 1930s and 1940s, a small number made homes outside the New York area. Juanita Basham (see chapter 6), who was identified as "White" in the U.S. census, was born in the Dominican Republic, spoke Spanish, and lived with her husband and family in Jumping Branch, West Virginia, in both 1930 and 1940. In the census of 1940, Basham was listed as a naturalized alien resident of the United States. Other Dominicans resided in bigger cities and within a broader community of both Latina/o and non-Latina/o immigrants. In Chicago lived Stella Abreu, a 30-year-old native of the Dominican Republic who had recently moved to the city from New York City's Washington Heights neighborhood. Abreu lived with her mother and two brothers, who were all also born in the Dominican Republic, as well as her Puerto Rican husband (Angel Ramirez, who was interestingly listed as a "motion picture technician" in the census) and their three children (Angel, presumably named after his father, Adam, and Shirley). Nearby the Abreu family were the homes of native-born neighbors, as well as immigrants from Germany, Poland, Russia, and Sweden.

Like the Dominican American community, the population of Central and South Americans in the United States was relatively small in the 1930s and 1940s, and tended to be more dispersed throughout the country. Census records offer a more detailed glance at the lives of some of these Latina/o immigrants. Panamanian Maria Abignon, for instance, lived in Los Angeles in 1940. Abignon worked as a housekeeper in the home of a Filipino man, who was in the U.S. Navy, and his Colombian wife. In New Orleans lived Alvaro Acuna, a 21-year-old furniture upholster who had been born in San José, Costa Rica. In Galveston, Texas, in 1940 lived a community of sailors and fishermen that included Agapito Alveal, a Chilean, Carlos Diaz and Joe

Carasco, both born in unspecified countries in "South America," as well as several Puerto Ricans and Spaniards.

One of the best-known mid-century South American immigrants, and, in fact, one of the best-known Latina/os in the twentieth century, was singer and movie star Carmen Miranda. Born in Portugal and raised in Rio de Janeiro, Brazil, the prodigiously talented Miranda became the country's biggest singing star of the 1930s and in 1939 starred in her first Broadway show. With her characteristic headdress filled with tropical fruit (the "tutti-frutti" hat), Miranda starred in a series of hit films in the early 1940s, including *Down Argentine Way* (1940), *That Night in Rio* (1941), and *Week-End in Havana* (1941). By 1945, Miranda had an income of $200,000 and was the highest-paid woman in the United States.

Miranda, who died tragically of a heart attack in 1955 at the age of 46, helped popularize Latin music in the United States and has remained

Singer and actress Carmen Miranda was one of the most recognized Latina/os in the United States in the mid-twentieth century. (AP Photo)

popular among a great many Latina/os ("her shows in the Mexican theaters of downtown Los Angeles," notes historian Brian O'Neil, "were always standing-room-only events at which Mexican and Mexican-American crowds often referred to Miranda as 'our star' " [O'Neil 2005, 206]). Yet Miranda's performances also reinforced harmful stereotypes about Latinas and Latin American women as exotic "bombshells" with thick accents, a stereotype that has haunted generation after generation of Latina performers through the rest of the twentieth and into the twenty-first century.

That Carmen Miranda would perform for capacity crowds of Mexican concertgoers in Los Angeles points to the presence of substantial Mexican communities across the Southwest in the early twentieth century. The booming agricultural economy in the region had depended heavily on imported Mexican labor, and the ethnic Mexican population in the region grew steadily during the period. At the same time, during the 1920s anti-immigrant activists had increasingly targeted Mexicans and Mexican communities, arguing that Mexican immigration should be severely limited. This strong anti-Mexican sentiment metastasized when the stock market crashed in 1929 and the U.S. and global economy collapsed. Mexicans, regardless of their citizenship status, were blamed for supposedly taking "American" jobs and straining government efforts to support needy families. Local repatriation efforts received help from Mexican government officials, who often sought ways to shield Mexican citizens from harsh treatment in the United States.

Compounding the misery of the Great Depression for Mexicans, therefore, was a widespread effort to deport Mexicans from large cities throughout the West and Midwest. With rising unemployment in the 1930s (unemployment in the United States rose to 6 million by the end of 1930 and to 11 million by 1932), Mexicans were portrayed as taking scarce jobs from Anglos and supposedly overusing local relief support. Anti-Mexican activists began major campaigns across the Southwest and in midwestern cities like Chicago, Detroit, and Gary, Indiana, to coerce Mexicans, whether U.S. citizens or not, to leave the United States and relocate across the border in Mexico. These repatriation campaigns beginning in the early 1930s and stretching throughout the decade had disastrous effects on Mexican individuals, families, and communities. Scores of Mexicans were herded onto railroad cars and forcibly deported while many thousands of others fled their homes and sought to rebuild their lives in Mexico. Historians estimate that between 350,000 and 600,000 people of Mexican descent returned to Mexico during the decade. The repatriation campaigns were one of the most traumatic and troubling events in the history of Mexican communities in the United States. Those Mexicans who managed to endure the attacks and remain in their homes and communities in the United States, however, formed a new and lasting commitment to their rights as U.S. citizens.

Los Angeles, home to one of the nation's largest Mexican populations, was the scene of both heightened anti-immigrant measures and concerted efforts by Mexicans to defend themselves and their communities. In 1930, nearly 100,000 Mexicans lived in Los Angeles, with another 70,000 in broader Los Angeles County, and Mexicans represented about 10 percent of the city's population. As economic turmoil spread throughout the country in the early 1930s, Anglo city leaders shifted from a relatively tolerant attitude toward Mexicans, viewing them as capable of assimilating to U.S. culture, to a more rigid sense of Mexicans as incapable of assimilation, prone to disease, and dangerous to the broader public. This emerging "image of the diseased Mexican who infected his or her family and larger social networks," in the words of historian Natalia Molina, became widespread during the period and was often perpetuated by LA's public health officials (Molina 2006, 125).

Los Angeles was also the site of two of the biggest events in World War II-era Mexican American history: the Sleepy Lagoon trial and the "zoot suit riots." Sleepy Lagoon was the name of a reservoir used to irrigate crops in what was, at the time, a rural location in Los Angeles. The reservoir was a popular destination for many young people in the area and was frequently used by Mexicans, who were often denied access to city-owned recreation facilities like swimming pools. One night in August 1942, a fight broke out near the reservoir during a party. In the aftermath of the fight, the body of José Diaz, a Mexican immigrant who had grown up in LA, was found. He had been beaten and stabbed to death. In response, Los Angeles police rounded up more than 500 young people and indicted nearly two dozen for the murder of Diaz. The trial, riddled with legal errors, captured the city's attention for several months, and the young men were eventually convicted and sentenced to long prison terms. Determined family and community members helped organize appeals of the convictions, however, and the case was finally overturned by a California higher court.

World War II Los Angeles was also the site of the infamous "zoot suit riots." In the summer of 1943, Anglo sailors and other servicemen on leave rampaged through downtown LA, targeting young men wearing "zoot suits," a fashion style associated with Mexican youth culture. LA police officials refused to intervene and the rioting continued for days, often with the enthusiastic support of Anglo residents of the city, before officers finally stepped in to halt the violence and the terrorizing of Mexican young men and women. Events like the Sleepy Lagoon trial and the "zoot suit riots" reinforced Mexicans' subordinate and relatively powerless position in World War II Los Angeles.

Mexicans responded to these difficult times in multiple ways. Many turned to political activism and formed new political organizations committed to defending Mexican communities. In Los Angeles, a collection of high school and college students helped to establish a group known as the Mexican American Movement. The Mexican American Movement was most notable for its focus on Mexican youth and the importance of education. Organizers emphasized the need to integrate into U.S. society by adopting proper behavior and activities and avoiding crime and juvenile delinquency while retaining a pride in Mexican culture and history. Membership in the Mexican American Movement included both Mexican young men and women, and the group produced a periodical, *The Mexican Voice*, that showcased the writing of young Mexicans in the Southwest. The group also organized regular youth conferences, events that would continue into the 1960s. Although the Mexican American Movement's influence would begin to fade after several decades, their commitment to educational reform and serving the needs of vulnerable, and often demonized, Mexican young people set the group apart.

Another important group was the League of United Latin American Citizens (LULAC), which was officially founded in 1929 in Corpus Christi, Texas. LULAC leaders were typically attorneys, restaurant owners, teachers, and small-business people. Unlike some groups, which based their organizations on mutual cooperation between Mexican immigrants and Mexican Americans, LULAC excluded all non-U.S. citizens from membership. Though proud of their heritage, LULAC members believed strongly that newcomers to the United States should assimilate as quickly as possible to the country's mainstream. LULAC conducted its meetings in English, displayed a U.S. flag on its stationery and in all group ceremonies, sang songs celebrating the United States, and even opened their meetings with a recitation of the "George Washington Prayer." Members also campaigned for voter registration, desegregation of public facilities ("No blacks or Mexicans" was sadly a common sign in Texas well into the twentieth century), and more representation of Mexican Americans on Texas juries.

As the economy turned sour during the Great Depression and the repatriation movement gained momentum, LULAC began to argue that their work for ethnic Mexicans in the United States accomplished little if the border remained open, and the organization therefore began to advocate for the restriction of immigration from Mexico. The legacy of LULAC is thus mixed. LULAC was an early and important civil rights organization, yet the group's decision to exclude non-U.S. citizens from membership during an especially perilous time for all Mexicans in the United States, regardless of citizenship status, remains controversial.

Mexicans were also active in other traditional political endeavors, such as electoral politics and government service. Senator Dennis Chávez of New Mexico, the only U.S. senator of Mexican descent for many years, provided important support to efforts to fight anti-Mexican discrimination. Senator Chávez was a vocal supporter of the Fair Employment Practices Commission, which was established in 1941 and sought to combat employment discrimination against African Americans, Mexican Americans, and other racial minorities in the United States. Chávez was instrumental in encouraging Mexicans with employer-related grievances to turn to the Fair Employment Practices Commission for assistance. His leadership also aided in the appointment of ethnic Mexicans to leadership positions in the agency. Dr. Carlos Castañeda, a prominent Tejano educator and scholar, for instance, was appointed to a regional directorship position covering portions of the Southwest.

The legal arena was another important site of Mexican political activism and resistance in the 1930s and 1940s. Two school desegregation cases, one from California and one from Texas, were especially significant. In 1930, Mexican parents of children in Lemon Grove, California, took the school district to court to force it to halt its practice of segregating Mexican girls and boys from Anglo children. The parents, in alliance with government officials from Mexico and Anglo allies, won their suit. Also notable in 1930 was a lawsuit against the Del Rio, Texas, school district, which similarly sought to ban the segregation of Mexican schoolchildren from their Anglo counterparts. While broader forms of racial segregation and anti-Mexican sentiment persisted in the 1930s and 1940s (and neither case directly challenged segregation targeting African American schoolchildren), the cases were early legal victories that made important contributions to the later civil rights movements.

Mexican women and men challenged their second-class citizenship and subordination through other channels as well in the 1930s and 1940s. Mexican workers, of course, have a long history of labor activism in the United States. In California, the first strike in which Mexicans played a major role was in 1903, when Mexican workers joined Japanese American workers in attempting to gain concessions from beet farm owners. In the next 30 years, labor activism continued, including the major Imperial Valley Cantaloupe Strike of 1928, a strike organized by La Unión Trabajadores del Valle Imperial (the Imperial Valley Workers Union). The 1930s saw increasing labor activism, once again centering on California agriculture. During the 1930s, 1933 was an especially turbulent year, with nearly 40 strikes involving almost 50,000 workers. The El Monte Berry Strike and a strike by San Joaquin Valley cotton pickers were the biggest of these strikes.

In forming unions and turning to labor activism, Mexicans confronted both internal challenges and a series of powerful external opponents. Agricultural work, in the first place, paid some of the lowest wages in the nation

Mexican workers helped lead labor organizing movements across the Southwest in the 1930s (California workers' strike, 1933). (Library of Congress)

and workers often could not afford to pay large union fees. Such fees would have paid for hiring experienced and skilled organizers, printing signs and leaflets, and providing clothes and living expenses for families participating in strikes. Workers were also often undereducated—many could not read or write in either Spanish or English—making it harder to develop a group of organizers from within the workforce. In addition, some workers had entered the country without documentation and understandably sought to keep out of the public eye and avoid deportation. Most importantly, Mexicans were forced to confront the full power of agribusiness throughout this period. These enormous companies were wealthy enough to endure long strikes and work stoppages, and business leaders often had the support of national and state governments and militias.

Another significant aspect of these labor struggles was the important role of the Mexican government in protecting the rights of its citizens and former citizens. During the prolabor government of Mexican president Lázaro Cárdenas of the mid-1930s, for instance, Mexican consulates in the United States were very active in defending the rights of Mexican workers. Enrique Bravo, a consul in Monterey, was involved in the 1933 San Joaquin Valley strike, while Joaquín Terrazas, another consul, supported Mexican strikers in the Imperial Valley in 1934, and Ricardo Hill, consul of Los Angeles, supported strikers battling the Southern California citrus industry in the mid-1930s.

Also notable in these labor struggles before World War II was the prominent role of Latinas in the movement. Latinas, especially in working-class families, often worked long hours outside the home. They also formed the bulk of rank-and-file union membership in many industries, including in cannery factories and apparel making. In the 1930s, several Latinas assumed leadership roles in unions and labor organizations. Emma Tenayuca, for instance, was born in San Antonio and started organizing immediately after graduating from high school. Tenayuca's biggest success was in leading a major strike of pecan shellers, most of them Mexicanas, in 1938. Josefina Fierro de Bright was born in Mexico and raised in Southern California. As a young woman, she worked as a farm laborer in the fields of the San Joaquin Valley and eventually enrolled at the University of California, Los Angeles, before beginning her career as an activist.

Like labor unions, the military offered some Mexicans an opportunity to claim rights as full citizens of the nation. In sharp contrast to images of Mexicans as un-American and hesitant to join U.S. society, large numbers of Mexicans served in active duty during World War II, many in fact volunteering for military service. According to one estimate, between 250,000 and 500,000 Mexicans served during the war, accounting for as much as 18 percent of the 2.7 million ethnic Mexicans in the United States in the early 1940s. Mexican communities throughout the country sent young people to war, including the small town of Silvis, Illinois, where 110 Mexicans joined the military. Mexican soldiers served with distinction and won many honors, including 12 who were awarded the Congressional Medal of Honor. Mexican women also supported the war effort, both through military service and by their labor on the home front, where "they sold war bonds," according to one historian, "and set up numerous organizations to assist servicemen and servicewomen" (Gonzales 2005, 167).

To the north, Latina/os in the Midwest faced a new series of challenges as the U.S. economy faltered in the 1930s. Chicago, already the site of significant Mexican migration, remained the hub of Latina/o life in the region. In 1920, there had been more than 1,000 Mexicans in the city. That population grew significantly in the next decade, rising to more than 20,000 by 1930. Despite the serious impact of repatriation and deportation campaigns in the 1930s (according to historian Gabriela Arredondo, "as a result of the Depression, repatriations, and deportations, at least one-quarter of the population of Mexicans in Chicago in 1930 had left by 1939"), there were still an estimated 16,000 Mexicans in Chicago by the beginning of the 1940s (Arredondo 2008, 29).

Chicago, however, was not alone as an important midwestern city for Latina/os. In Lorain, Ohio, for instance, Mexicans represented a significant portion of the population in 1930. In one neighborhood, there were well over 400 individuals of Spanish or Latin American descent. Most (85%) were ethnic Mexicans, while about 70 individuals were born in Spain and a handful of others were born in Puerto Rico, Cuba, Peru, or other countries in Latin America. This intermingling of predominantly working-class Latina/os was especially evident in the neighborhood near Lorain's massive steel mills. In 1930, households along Lorain's Pearl Avenue included residents of Mexican, Cuban, and Spanish ancestry. In one home, Mary and Eduardo Sánchez lived with their three children, one each born in Spain, New York, and Ohio, and six roomers (two born in Spain and the other four natives of Mexico). Next door lived the Pérez family, parents born in Spain, two eldest children born in Cuba, a daughter born in Ohio, and three Spanish men renting rooms from the family. Nearby were the Arredondo and Nieto families, all born in Mexico except Refugia Nieto, who was born in Texas. Like so many of their neighbors, Latina/o residents of Pearl Avenue depended on the steel factories for employment (most of the men worked as "Laborers" in Lorain steel mills according to the U.S. census), and many of the women and men had immigrated to the U.S. mainland in the past two decades.

As elsewhere in Latina/o America, social service organizations provided important community support in Lorain. By the 1940s there were several Mexican organizations in the city. Besides the "Mexican Mutual Club" and the "Club Ideal," separate clubs were formed for young Mexicanas and young Mexicanos. Both clubs seemed to have strong weekly attendance and the Mexicana group apparently went so far as to make their own uniforms for the club. Mexicans also gathered to celebrate important holidays, such as Cinco de Mayo, in Lorain. One observer described more than 200 Mexicans gathered at a local Cinco de Mayo celebration in the early 1940s. The social hall was decorated in the colors of the Mexican flag and partygoers enjoyed both traditional Mexican and American foods.

Few periods in American history had as deep or as lasting an effect on the nation as the era from the Great Depression to the end of World War II. For Latina/os, these years would be transformative as well, altering Latina/o lives from the U.S. Southwest to midwestern cities like Chicago and Lorain to the East Coast. Latina/os managed to endure widespread poverty and virulent anti-immigrant attacks like the repatriation campaigns that plagued the nation during the Depression and form durable and sustainable communities.

Latinas, of course, were pivotal to this community success, working both inside and outside the home, and many Latinas rose to national prominence as labor leaders. Latina/os also served in the military during World War II, many gaining recognition for their bravery, and civil rights groups often pointed to military service as evidence of Latina/os' commitment to the nation and fitness for full citizenship. Having overcome considerable adversity since the onset of the Great Depression, Latina/os entered the second half of the twentieth century with newly resilient communities and a newfound desire for full inclusion in the American nation.

PROFILE: PURA BÉLPRE

In 1920, at the age of 21, Pura Bélpre migrated from Puerto Rico to New York City. Bélpre, living in Harlem, was drawn to work in the city's public library system and by the 1930s had established a reputation as a gifted storyteller, often writing and performing her own work, and as an activist for bilingual education. During the 1930s, Bélpre rotated from library to library throughout various Spanish-speaking communities in New York and was determined to recognize not just the diversity of Latina/os in the city, especially in the mixing of Puerto Rican and Cuban communities, but the range of cultural influences on Latina/o lives. Most notably, she highlighted the strong influence of African, Native, and Spanish traditions. Bélpre is credited with organizing scores of events for the Latina/o community and with establishing bilingual story hours and young adult reading groups in the New York public library system.

In addition to her performances for children and her duties as a bilingual librarian and educator, Bélpre was a widely published author of children's books. She was inspired to write, she recalled later, by the absence of books of Puerto Rican folktales and children's books. In 1932, Bélpre's "Pérez and Martina," a tale perfected during her storytelling performances from the 1920s, became what may have been, according to one literary scholar, "the first Puerto Rican folktale published in the mainland United States" (González 2005, 153). The main characters of "Pérez and Martina," Pérez the Mouse and Martina the Cockroach, pursue an ill-fated romance, and the book touches on themes that Bélpre would follow throughout her long literary career, such as animal fables, the use of trickster figures, and concern with poverty and unhealthy living conditions. In 1946, Bélpre published *The Tiger and the Rabbit and Other Tales*, a collection of animal fables with roots in Puerto Rican, African, Spanish, and other traditions, and would continue to publish for decades to come.

Bélpre's accomplishments as a writer, librarian, and community activist were recognized with a children's book award named in her honor and lifetime achievement awards from groups like the New York Public Library. Bélpre died in 1982 at the age of 83.

PROFILE: JOVITA GONZÁLEZ

In 1930, after taking a leave from her job teaching Spanish at a small college in San Antonio, Texas, 26-year-old Jovita González submitted her thesis for a master's degree in history at the University of Texas. The thesis, "Social Life in Cameron, Starr, and Zapata Counties," directly challenged dominant views of Mexicans in South Texas as intellectually and culturally inferior to Anglos. González, who was born in 1904 in Starr County, Texas, and died in 1983, was raised in the midst of increasing Anglo political and economic dominance of South Texas. Her family moved to San Antonio in 1910, and González struggled to finance her higher education, often taking teaching jobs to pay for her course work. In the 1920s, González began collecting local Mexican folktales, and by the end of the decade she had risen to a leadership position in the Texas Folklore Society. Though Anglo men dominated the organization, González was elected its president in 1930 and 1931. Over the next decade, González solidified her standing as one of the nation's most respected scholarly experts on Mexican Americans.

In 1934, González completed a book-length manuscript, *Dew on the Thorn*, exploring the lives of Mexicans in South Texas at the turn of the twentieth century. Like her master's thesis, *Dew on the Thorn*, which was recently rediscovered and published in book form, balanced an appreciation of Mexican folklore and culture along the border with a sharp critique of U.S. imperialism and the dispossession and denigration of Mexican communities at the hands of Anglo newcomers.

PROFILE: LUISA MORENO

During one of the most vibrant periods in the history of the U.S. labor movement, Luisa Moreno stands out as an extraordinary organizer and labor leader. Blanca Rosa Rodríguez López was born to a wealthy family in Guatemala in 1907. At the age of nine, she was sent by her parents to a convent in Oakland, California. Unhappy, facing racial discrimination, and disenchanted with Catholicism and organized religion, she convinced her parents after several years to allow her to return home to Guatemala. Prohibitions against higher education for women, though, soon forced her to flee from her family and, at the age of 19, to move to Mexico City. A talented writer, she worked as a journalist and published a book of poetry, *El Vendedor de Cocuyos (Seller of Fireflies)*, in 1927.

Marrying a fellow Guatemalan from an elite family, she moved to New York City with her husband in 1928. Motivated by the poverty and despair she witnessed in the city, she joined the Communist Party and began full-time work as a union organizer. After several years working for the International Ladies Garment Workers Union, she accepted a job with the American Federation of Labor in Florida organizing tobacco workers. In Florida, she changed her name from Blanca Rosa Rodríguez López to Luisa Moreno, perhaps to signal her identification with dark-skinned workers ("moreno" means dark in Spanish) and as a tribute to Luisa Capetillo, who years earlier had also been a labor organizer in Florida.

Moreno left the AFL in the late 1930s and joined the United Cannery, Agricultural, Packing, and Allied Workers of America. She moved to Texas to support Mexican workers like pecan shellers in San Antonio and migrant laborers in the Rio Grande Valley. Moreno also helped lead the planning of *El Congreso de Pueblos de Hablan Española*. *El Congreso* was "the first national civil rights assembly for Latinos in the United States," according to historian Vicki Ruiz, and included "approximately 1,000 and 1,500 delegates representing over 120 organizations assembled in Los Angeles to address issues of jobs, housing, education, health, and immigrant rights" (Ruiz 2005, 182). After the success of *El Congreso*, Moreno continued her work with United Cannery, Agricultural, Packing, and Allied Workers of America, rising to the rank of vice president in 1941, the highest-ranking position a Latina had yet achieved in a national labor union.

In the post–World War II era, Moreno's prominence as a labor leader and her membership in the Communist Party in the early 1930s (she left the party in 1935) placed her in danger from rabid anticommunists in the U.S. government. Facing deportation charges based on her political beliefs and activism, Moreno left the United States in 1950 and returned to her native Guatemala. She lived the rest of her life in Guatemala and died in 1992.

REFERENCES

Arredondo, Gabriela F. *Mexican Chicago: Race Identity and Nation, 1916–39*. Champaign: University of Illinois Press, 2008.

Briggs, Laura. *Reproducing Empire: Race, Sex, Science, and U.S. Imperialism in Puerto Rico*. Berkeley: University of California Press, 2002.

Duany, Jorge. *Blurred Borders: Transnational Migration between the Hispanic Caribbean and the United States*. Chapel Hill: University of North Carolina Press, 2011.

Gonzales, Manuel G. *Mexicanos: A History of Mexicans in the United States*. New York: Houghton Mifflin, 2005.

González, Lisa Sánchez. "Pura Bélpre: The Children's Ambassador." In *Latina Legacies: Identity, Biography, and Community*, edited by Vicki L. Ruiz and Virginia Sánchez-Korrol, 148–57. New York: Oxford University Press, 2005.

Guridy, Frank Andre. *Forging Diaspora: Afro-Cubans and African Americans in a World of Empire and Jim Crow*. Chapel Hill: University of North Carolina, 2010.

Molina, Natalia. *Fit to Be Citizens?: Public Health and Race in Los Angeles, 1879–1939*. Berkeley: University of California Press, 2006.

O'Neil, Brian. "Carmen Miranda: The High Price of Fame and Bananas." In *Latina Legacies: Identity, Biography, and Community*, edited by Vicki L. Ruiz and

Virginia Sánchez-Korrol, 193–208. New York: Oxford University Press, 2005.

Ruiz, Vicki L. "Luisa Moreno and Latina Labor Activism." In *Latina Legacies: Identity, Biography, and Community*, edited by Vicki L. Ruiz and Virginia Sánchez-Korrol, 175–92. New York: Oxford University Press, 2005.

Sánchez-Korrol, Virginia. *From Colonia to Community: The History of Puerto Ricans in New York City*. Berkeley: University of California Press, 1994.

Skwiot, Christine. *The Purposes of Paradise: U.S. Tourism and Empire in Cuba and Hawai'i*. Philadelphia: University of Pennsylvania Press, 2010.

_____ *Chapter 8* _____

Latina/os in Mid-Twentieth-Century America, 1945–1965

Migration and the creation of new homes and communities in unfamiliar lands are at the heart of Latina/o history. For Puerto Ricans and Cubans, the two decades following World War II were pivotal periods of migration to the U.S. mainland. After 1945, the Puerto Rican populations of major American cities like New York, Philadelphia, and Chicago blossomed, as did communities in smaller cities like Lorain, Ohio; Dover, New Jersey; and Hartford, Connecticut. For Cubans, the 1959 revolution sparked the first of several periods of significant migration to the United States, particularly to Florida and the city of Miami.

The post–World War II era also saw the continued growth of the nation's Mexican population. The federal government embarked on major efforts to support the labor needs of American agribusiness, most notably the Bracero Program, a contract labor agreement between the United States and Mexico, and Mexican communities expanded in both urban and rural areas. So too did Mexican civil rights organizing grow during the period, including major legal efforts to ensure school desegregation and the equal participation of Mexicans on juries.

Challenges abounded for Latina/os in the mid-twentieth century, including anti-immigrant attacks, limited employment and educational opportunities, and lack of political representation. Nonetheless, Latina/os, including Latina labor leaders and political activists, responded with typical determination and creativity and adopted a range of strategies to defend their communities and their citizenship rights in post–World War II U.S. society.

One of the defining features of the United States in the post–World War II era was the rise in the size and the scope of the federal government. Latina/os experienced this expansion in multiple ways, but one of the most dramatic forms was in the creation of the Bracero Program. Just as occurred during

World War I, the Second World War created labor shortages in agribusiness, one of the pillars of the economy in the Southwest and the nation. In addition to labor shortages caused by enlistment in the military during wartime, employers found that farmworkers jumped at opportunities to leave agricultural work in favor of better-paying and less onerous jobs (not to mention ones perceived as more patriotic) in factories in war-related production. Agribusiness thus found itself in need of reliable workers that would demand reasonable wages (or, at least what employers wanted to pay) and turned to the federal government for help.

As a result, Mexico and the United States agreed to a system to allow labor contracts for Mexican farmworkers to come to the Southwest to work, and in August 1942, the two governments instituted the Bracero Program. Under the program, which would last long after the war and into the 1960s, hundreds of thousands of impoverished Mexican men hoping to earn a significant amount of money on the U.S. side of the border would eventually abandon their rural communities and head north to work as contract laborers, also known as "braceros."

The majority of the braceros were experienced farm laborers who came from important agricultural regions of Mexico and arrived by train to cities

The Bracero Program (1942–1964) brought millions of Mexican workers to the U.S. as contract laborers (Mexican migrant workers employed under the Bracero Program). (AP Photo)

along Mexico's northern border with the hope that they would be accepted into the program. Once accepted, the men were expected to sign work contracts, often in English, under the control of government officials and agribusiness employers. These contracts required the men to return to Mexico once the contracts had expired.

Over the course of the program, more than 2 million Mexicans entered the United States to labor in the nation's agricultural fields. Workers could return to their homes in Mexico only in case of an emergency and only with written permission from their employer. When the contracts expired, the braceros were required to return to Mexico. Abuses in the program, especially in terms of the poor work and living conditions provided by employers, were widespread; however, the program was extended for more than two decades until it was finally terminated in 1964.

Another federal program, the U.S. Border Patrol, also expanded significantly after World War II. The Border Patrol, founded in 1924, grew during the war from 773 officers and a budget of $1.7 million in 1939 to 1,500 officers and a $3.8 million budget in 1941 and even higher after the war ended in 1945. The focus of the Border Patrol activities also shifted to concentrate almost exclusively on the United States-Mexico border region in the 1940s. According to historian Kelly Lytle Hernández, "by the mid-1940s, removing Mexicans from the United States had emerged as the central project of the U.S. Border Patrol" (Hernández 2010, 148). The expansion of the agency continued in the 1950s as well, with an overall budget jumping from $7.1 million in 1954 to $11.5 million in 1955 and $12.1 million in 1956.

The U.S. government also played a major role in Puerto Rican migration to the U.S. mainland in the postwar era. Operation Bootstrap, or Operación Manos a La Obra, was a broad, dual-focused plan to lure North American manufacturers and other industries to relocate to the island and to stimulate migration out of Puerto Rico to the mainland (an aim justified by supposed "overpopulation" on the island). Under the plan, U.S. businesses were encouraged to recruit Puerto Rican contract laborers to supply their employment needs.

Operation Bootstrap was initiated by Luis Muñoz Marín, one of twentieth-century Puerto Rico's major political figures. As a young man in the 1920s and 1930s, Muñoz Marín had been a socialist and a strong supporter of Puerto Rican independence. He had also been deeply influenced by the presidency of Franklin Delano Roosevelt and the programs of the New Deal. Following the lead of New Deal policies, Muñoz Marín founded the Popular Democratic Party in Puerto Rico and became a champion of commonwealth status for the island. Throughout the 1940s, labor activists and independence leaders in Puerto Rico had been demanding the right to vote on the island's status. In 1952, in response to these protests, the U.S.

Congress authorized such a vote. The subsequent vote, however, allowed Puerto Ricans to choose only between remaining a direct colony of the United States or becoming a commonwealth. Neither the opportunity to become a U.S. state nor independence for Puerto Rico were ever presented on the ballot. As a result, in 1952 Puerto Rico became a commonwealth of the United States.

Operation Bootstrap, another of Luis Muñoz Marín's major initiatives, was established in 1947 and was, in essence, a plan to industrialize and "modernize" Puerto Rico. The program sought to attract U.S. companies to the island with tax incentives and the lure of cheaper labor costs (U.S. minimum wage laws were not applied to Puerto Rico). As in other modernizing efforts, however, the benefits of Operation Bootstrap were not evenly distributed. The program, by focusing on heavy industry and manufacturing and away from subsistence agriculture, helped undermine rural, agricultural communities on the island and contributed to large-scale displacement and unemployment among ordinary Puerto Ricans. As a result, a great many Puerto Ricans turned to migration to the U.S. mainland.

In 1947, the Puerto Rican government established the Migration Division, with offices in New York, Chicago, and elsewhere in the Midwest and Northeast. The Migration Division sought to place workers both in agricultural jobs, where they harvested fruits, vegetables, and tobacco, and in heavy industry like railroads and steel factories. Puerto Rican women were also actively recruited as domestic workers. In 1946, for instance, nearly 400 Puerto Rican women arrived in Chicago under contracts for live-in domestic service. They joined 200 Puerto Rican men that year in Chicago who were contracted to work in steel manufacturing.

Abuses of the sort documented during the Bracero program were less common (though hardly absent) for Puerto Rican contract laborers, in part due to Puerto Ricans' status as U.S. citizens and their insistence on exercising their citizenship rights. In one case, recounted by historian Lilia Fernández, 1,000 Puerto Rican men were hired for temporary summer employment by the Pennsylvania Railroad in 1953. The following summer, however, the railroad refused to rehire the men, and they filed for unemployment compensation. Their initial claims were denied, yet the men persisted in their legal struggle and, according to Fernández, "were ultimately successful in securing sixteen weeks of compensation." This "remarkable achievement," Fernández continues, "was made possible because they were US citizens and thus eligible under unemployment compensation laws" (Fernández 2012, 24).

Puerto Rican contract laborers represented a small but significant component of a much larger migration of Puerto Ricans to the U.S. mainland after World War II. Historian Carmen Whalen has identified three major periods of Puerto Rican migration in the second half of the twentieth century. According to Whalen, the first era lasted from the late 1940s to the 1960s and consisted of a massive out-migration of working-class Puerto Rican men and women moving from the island to the industrial cities of the East Coast and Midwest, including places like New York, Philadelphia, and Chicago. During this period, the Puerto Rican population on the U.S. mainland rose from about 70,000 to 887,000. In New York City, the primary destination for Puerto Rican migrants, the population grew to 612,000. Whalen notes that a second era of migration occurred between the 1960s and 1970s and was characterized by broader geographic dispersion and a stagnant American economy that did not allow many Puerto Ricans to escape poor work conditions and low wages. For Whalen, a third period of migration stretches from the 1970s to the present and includes a higher number of return migrations. In some years, she notes that the number of Puerto Ricans returning to live on the island outnumbered those leaving it for the mainland.

While the overall Latina/o population in the United States tended to be geographically dispersed in the post–World War II era, with Mexicans generally in the Southwest, Puerto Ricans and Dominicans in the urban Northeast, and Cubans in Florida (especially after the Cuban revolution in 1959), some regions of the country were the home to more heterogeneous Latina/o communities. In Chicago, where Mexicans had arrived in significant numbers in the 1910s and 1920s, a new Puerto Rican population arrived in the 1940s and 1950s. The Near West Side of Chicago became the home of one of the city's largest Latina/o populations in the mid-twentieth century. In 1940, the Mexican-born population of the neighborhood was 3,000 and constituted the second-largest foreign-born group, after Italians, in the area. The Mexican community grew rapidly in the next decade throughout Chicago, reaching more than 60,000 by one estimate in 1950.

Puerto Rican communities also grew during the period. In 1940, according to the U.S. census, fewer than 300 Puerto Ricans lived in Chicago. Seven years later, the Puerto Rican population had grown to 6,000 and was approximately 20,000 by the mid-1950s. In 1960, more than 30,000 Puerto Ricans lived in Chicago. As did Mexicans, Puerto Ricans moved in large numbers to the Near West Side neighborhood. The Near West Side, according to historian Lilia Fernández, was home to "an estimated twenty-eight thousand 'Spanish-speaking' people" and by 1960, "housed nearly 20 percent of all Mexicans and Puerto Ricans in Chicago, the largest concentration in the city" (Fernández 2012, 59).

Although Chicago was the main destination of Puerto Rican migrants to the Midwest in the postwar period, Puerto Ricans were drawn to other midwestern locations as well. The Puerto Rican population of Lorain, Ohio, grew rapidly in the late 1940s and early 1950s. According to historian Eugenio Rivera, 100 Puerto Ricans arrived per week to Lorain by 1951. Rivera estimates that the Puerto Rican community reached nearly 4,000, or about 10 percent of Lorain's total population, by the middle of the decade.

As elsewhere in the nation, most Puerto Rican men in Lorain worked in industrial settings like steel mills and for local railroad companies, and the neighborhood south of the steel factories became the center of the Puerto Rican community, housing over 60 percent of the city's Puerto Ricans. Social service organizations were soon founded in South Lorain, including El Hogar Puertorriqueño, which hosted, according to Rivera, a wide range of celebrations, including "baptism parties, quinceañeras, weddings, and wakes" (Rivera 2005, 18). Churches also offered much needed support to Puerto Rican newcomers to Lorain. La Capilla del Sagrado Corazón de Jesús was founded in 1952 and a Pentecostal church, El Templo Bethel, also served Puerto Ricans in South Lorain.

As did Puerto Ricans and Mexicans in the Midwest, Latina/os across the United States responded in many ways to persistent forms of discrimination and poverty in the mid-twentieth century. As in the broader postwar nation, struggles for civil rights were a critical feature of Mexican American life during the period. Like the African American freedom struggle of the post–World War II era, the legal realm was an important arena for activists and community leaders. In the 1940s, Mexican legal strategists developed new approaches to combat legally sanctioned discrimination in housing, jury selection, and the segregation of Mexican children in public schools. In one landmark case from Southern California (*Mendez v. Westminster*) in 1946, Mexican parents and civil rights attorneys forced the local school district to abandon its policy of requiring separate schools for Anglo and Mexican children.

In another landmark case, *Hernández v. Texas*, which was eventually decided by the U.S. Supreme Court, Pete Hernández, who was convicted of murder by an all-Anglo jury in Jackson County, Texas, challenged his conviction on the grounds that Mexicans had been intentionally excluded from juries in the county for decades. Hernández's legal team presented a remarkable record of jury discrimination in Jackson County. No Mexicans, for instance, had served on a jury for more than a quarter century, despite the fact that 14 percent of the county's population, and a significant portion of those eligible to serve on juries, had Spanish surnames. Carlos Cadena, Hernández's lawyer, also described systematic discrimination against Mexicans in pools and restaurants, and added, according to legal historian Clare Sheridan, that the Jackson County courthouse, where the original trial had been held, "had one bathroom for whites and one for 'Colored Men' that was also labeled 'Hombres Aquí' ('Men Here')" (Sheridan 2003, 124). After

Hernández's original conviction, the Texas Court of Criminal Appeals refused to consider his appeal and the legal team decided to turn to the U.S. Supreme Court. In 1954, the Supreme Court ruled in favor of Hernández and ordered a new trial.

Mexicans were also critical participants in another significant legal case. In 1947, the case of *Perez v. Sharp* reached the California Supreme Court. Andrea Perez, of Mexican descent but labeled "White" according to the government, and Sylvester Davis, an African American, had applied for a marriage license in Los Angeles but were turned down by the Los Angeles County marriage clerk's office. The couple was denied the right to marry on the grounds that their marriage would violate the state's law against intermarriage (also known as an antimiscegenation law).

Perez and Davis challenged the constitutionality of the law and appealed to the California Supreme Court. During the case, both sides agreed that Andrea Perez, despite her Spanish surname, was "White" according to California law and that Sylvester Davis was "a Negro male." Since both Perez and Davis were Catholics, the lawyer defending the couple tried to make a religious argument. Because the Catholic Church did not prohibit intermarriage, according to the lawyer's reasoning, laws prohibiting them from marrying were a violation of their freedom of religion. The state of California, on the other hand, argued that there was a long precedent in California law prohibiting whites from marrying blacks, a precedent based on supposedly clear, and scientifically verifiable, racial differences.

During the trial, one of the higher court judges challenged the notion that racial differences could be grounded in science and biology. Sensing an opportunity, the couple's legal team quickly shifted their strategy from focusing on the freedom of religion to arguing that the concept of race was biological nonsense. Relying on social scientists like anthropologists, the lawyer claimed that experts had determined that "race, as popularly understood, is a myth" and that laws based on such "irrational prejudices" were based on "myth, folk belief, and superstition" (Pascoe 2009, 218). He even compared the biological arguments of racial difference to Adolf Hitler's *Mein Kampf*. In 1948, the California Supreme Court ruled in favor of Perez and Davis and ruled the California antimiscegenation law unconstitutional.

This decision was significant in several respects. First, this was the first time since the Reconstruction period in U.S. history in the late nineteenth century that a state court had ruled that a state antimiscegenation law was unconstitutional. Second, this ruling was not simply about a racial misclassification (that a couple should be allowed to marry because, for instance, both the man and the woman were biologically black, or that both were biologically white). Instead, this ruling called the entire system of racial classification into question. Ultimately, *Perez v. Sharp* is important because it helped lead to a point when American courts would abandon their reliance on racial categories in marriage law. Twenty years later, in the case *Loving v. Virginia* (1967), the U.S. Supreme Court ruled that laws banning intermarriage were unconstitutional across the nation.

Increasingly repressive border enforcement also sparked legal action by Latina/os in the post–World War II era. In July 1954, Sara Harb Quiroz, born in Mexico and 20 years old, requested and received status as a permanent resident of the United States. Six years later, Quiroz, who lived in El Paso, Texas, and worked as a domestic servant in the city, was detained by U.S. immigration officials as she crossed into El Paso from Juarez, Mexico, in a taxicab. When she was stopped for questioning, Quiroz was likely returning from visiting her parents and nine-year-old daughter, who lived in Juarez. Quiroz was apparently held at the border because, in the view of her lawyer, the border agent "had a thing for people, especially women ... who were lesbian, or in his mind were deviates" (Luibhéid 2002, 81). According to her employer, Quiroz often "wore trousers and a shirt when she came to work and her hair was cut shorter than some women's" (Luibhéid 2002, 81).

As a result of her appearance, Quiroz was interrogated and subsequently "confessed" that she had engaged in sexual activity with women and even "enjoyed sexual relations more with women than with men" (Luibhéid 2002, 90). Based on provisions in immigration law that were not repealed until 1990 where, as scholar Eithne Luibhéid writes, "lesbian immigrants were excludable and deportable from the United States," Quiroz was deported to Mexico (Luibhéid 2002, 77). Sustaining a long and important tradition of Latinas turning to U.S. courts to protect and defend their rights, Quiroz refused simply to accept the deportation order and remove herself from her home and employment in the United States. Instead, she appealed the deportation order. Unable to overcome the U.S. government's animosity toward women who engaged in sexual relations with other women, Quiroz ultimately lost her legal case and appears to have been deported. Though unsuccessful, Quiroz's legal case points to the homophobia that for decades pervaded U.S. immigration law. The case also points to her determination to exercise her legal rights, a determination displayed by countless ordinary Latinas, and Latinos, in U.S. history.

Latina/os also responded to discrimination and unequal treatment in the post–World War II era through union organizing. In the early 1950s, ethnic Mexicans in southwestern New Mexico led a strike at the Empire Zinc mine. At the mine, the vast majority of the miners were Mexican men, who were forced to work in the most backbreaking, dangerous underground jobs at lower wages, while Anglos worked at safer, better-paying surface jobs. Mine owners also segregated workers into separate, and unequal, facilities and housing. When the largely Mexican union made demands for better pay and work conditions, the mine management refused to negotiate, hoping simply to break the union and install nonunion workers. In response, a strike was called and the overwhelmingly Mexican miners walked off the job. The New Mexico National Guard was called in and a judge issued an injunction prohibiting the workers from picketing the mine.

The injunction, however, did not cover women and children, and the families of the miners immediately took over the picket lines and manned (or woman-ned!) the pickets at the mine entrance. Several clashes between the female picketers and the mine guards, including the New Mexico National Guard, soon followed, leading to the arrest of 45 women and 18 children. Finally, the governor of New Mexico ordered state troopers into the area to force the end of the picket line and the opening of the road to the mine. The governor's actions, and the alliance between the forces of the New Mexico state government and the Empire Zinc mine owners, did not result in the breaking of the strike and subsequent negotiations led to gains for workers. The Empire Zinc strike subsequently became the subject of the movie *Salt of the Earth*, which was banned for a period in the United States during the early 1950s but received huge international acclaim elsewhere and showcased the courage and dignity of Mexican men and women involved in the strike.

Mexican families led a strike against the Empire Zinc Mine in New Mexico in the 1950s, which was the subject of the pro-labor film, *Salt of the Earth* (Empire Zinc Company during strike). (Time & Life Pictures/Getty Images)

Latina/o labor activism, of course, was not limited to the American Southwest. Puerto Rican women and men in the Northeast were active union members in multiple industries. For decades, the garment industry in New York City had provided one of the main sources of employment for Puerto Rican women, and this trend continued in the post–World War II era in the city. The main union for garment workers, the International Ladies Garment Workers Union (ILGWU), for example, listed 7,500 Puerto Rican women among its membership in the late 1940s. In the next decade, half of the membership in certain ILGWU local affiliates was Puerto Rican, such as Local 23, which focused on skirtmakers. Another ILGWU local, Dressmakers Union Local 22, also experienced growth in its Puerto Rican membership in mid-century New York City. Between 1945 and 1953, the percentage of Puerto Rican members, the vast majority of whom were women, rose from 8 percent to 16 percent.

Local groups with sizable Puerto Rican membership often attended closely to their members' needs, appointing Spanish-speaking union officials and organizing classes and events specifically oriented toward the Puerto Rican community, such as trips to Puerto Rico, holiday parties, and community celebrations. Local 22 even took a leadership role in combating civil rights violations and housing discrimination facing the broader Puerto Rican community in New York.

In addition to serving as rank-and-file union members, Puerto Rican women at times assumed leadership roles in unions like the ILGWU. Linda Delgado, for instance, became a full employee of the union in 1957 after serving as a member of Local 22 for 15 years. Delgado had arrived in New York in 1923 from Puerto Rico at the age of eight and in the mid-1930s began work in a factory sewing children's dresses. In a relocation that would soon become common, the dress factory closed its New York shop several years later and began manufacturing in Puerto Rico. Delgado and her sister turned to a nonunion garment job but soon left in favor of a unionized employer in their own, largely Puerto Rican neighborhood. At the union shop, Delgado experienced far better work conditions and wages, eventually earning between $150 and $250 per week. Delgado's decision to begin work as an ILGWU organizer was inspired by a union-sponsored organizing trip to Puerto Rico and the encouragement of union leaders searching for talented Spanish-speaking organizers.

In 1958, thousands of Puerto Rican women like Linda Delgado participated in a massive ILGWU strike. The union, representing workers from New York, New Jersey, and five other states, called for wage increases, improved overtime pay and work conditions, and limits on companies' ability to relocate and hire contract workers rather than full-time employees. The strike began in early March 1958 and included 100,000 dressmakers throughout the East Coast. Union leaders went to considerable lengths to welcome their Spanish-speaking members during the strike. In a major rally in New York's Madison Square Garden, prominent speakers addressed the crowd in Spanish, and one of the speeches was given by an Afro-Panamanian ILGWU activist. The strike ultimately proved successful and the support of Puerto Rican women was critical to the victory.

While defenders of Latina/o communities largely disavowed violence and focused on legal challenges and nonviolent protest, the 1954 armed attack on the U.S. Congress in Washington, D.C., by Puerto Rican independence leaders was an important exception. On March 4, 1954, four Puerto Rican activists, including their leader, Lolita Lebron, walked into the gallery of the U.S. Congress. The group was following the instructions of Pedro Albizu Campos, the Harvard-educated nationalist leader who considered the United States a rogue occupier of his homeland. The four fired their weapons down upon the members of Congress below. As they displayed the Puerto Rican flag, Lolita Lebron shouted, "Free Puerto Rico now!" Five members of Congress were hurt, some severely, but no one was killed. The four Puerto Ricans, including Lebron, were captured and received long prison sentences. Though the vast majority of Puerto Ricans, and Latina/os, undoubtedly condemned the violent attack, champions of Puerto Rican independence, and critics of U.S. imperialism, drew wide support among mid-century Latina/o communities.

Unlike Puerto Ricans and Mexicans, Cuban migration to the United States was relatively small in the immediate post–World War II era. In the 1940s, 26,000 Cubans immigrated while nearly 80,000 did so in the following decade. Although migration between the two countries was limited, cultural ties remained strong. U.S. tourism to the island accelerated, aided by a dramatic expansion in air travel between the two countries. In the 1950s, nearly 30 daily flights aboard Pan American airline linked Miami and Havana. The two countries were bound in cultural and consumer ways as well, as Cubans imported Hollywood movies and other U.S. consumer goods and North Americans danced to widely popular Cuban music and watched Desi Arnaz, the Cuban costar of *I Love Lucy*, one of the most popular television shows of the era. As historian María Cristina García notes, "Vacationing in Miami Beach or New York City was as popular for middle-class Cubans before the Castro revolution as vacationing in Havana was for middle-class Americans" (García 2004, 148). Working-class Cubans, such as cigar workers, in Cuba and in the United States also maintained strong links during the period, often supporting each other in their labor activism.

Another critical form of exchange between Cuba and the United States built upon the links established decades earlier between African Americans in the United States and Cubans of African descent, or Afro-Cubans. Women's groups took a leading role in these exchanges, including the National Council of Negro Women in the United States and the Asociación Cultural Feminina (Women's Cultural Association; ACF) in Cuba. One of the leaders of the ACF was Ana Echegoyen de Cañizares, who was a feminist leader and the first Afro-Cuban woman to serve on the faculty at the University of Havana. One highlight of the developing relationship between the two groups was a visit to Cuba organized jointly by the ACF and the NCNW. In addition to attending lectures on topics such as the history of Afro-Cubans on the island and "The Social Life of Cuba and the Negro Woman," visitors gathered at the homes of ACF members, dined on Cuban food, and even attended a wedding.

The NCNW and ACF were not alone in sponsoring travel between the two countries. Two important Afro-Cuban organizations, the Unión Fraternal and the Club Atenas, offered regular tourist excursions to the United States in the 1940s and 1950s. One, nearly three-week visit included a flight from Havana to Miami and a Greyhound bus ride through the South to Washington, D.C. (carefully planned to protect tourists from potential racist attacks along the journey) and New York City. The itinerary included visits to well-established African American churches, Howard University (one of the nation's most prominent African American universities), and the national headquarters of the NCNW. Tourists also met with members of the Comité Cubano de Washington, which represented the small Afro-Cuban community in the nation's capital.

These links between the two countries were largely severed by the 1959 Cuban revolution, when Fidel Castro led the overthrow of U.S. backed Cuban president Fulgencio Batista. Diplomatic, commercial, and cultural ties were broken and the once vibrant transnational exchange dissolved into a largely one-way flow of Cuban migrants, including significant numbers of anti-Castro political exiles, fleeing to the United States. Between 1959 and 1962, nearly a quarter million Cubans left the island for the United States. Many had deep ties with the deposed Batista regime and hoped that a quick overthrow of the Castro government would lead to their rapid return to Cuba.

This first era of large-scale Cuban migration to the United States included what would come to be known as the Peter Pan, or Pedro Pan, flights, where Cuban children were flown to the United States and placed in new homes with relatives or sponsor families. While some Cubans were relocated throughout the United States, including the famous artist Ana Mendieta, who moved to Iowa as a child, the vast majority of migrants made their homes in Miami, Florida. Miami would become the heart of the Cuban

American community in the United States. By 1965, the city was the home of tens of thousands of Cuban Americans.

As in the case of Cuban migrants, immigration from the Dominican Republic to the United States was relatively small before 1965. In the 1950s, the dictatorship of President Rafael Trujillo maintained a tight grip on out-migration. By one estimate a total of only 10,000 people left the country for the United States during that decade. Though mid-century Dominican migration to the United States was relatively small compared to Puerto Ricans and Mexicans, Dominican communities began to form in cities like New York City and Washington, D.C. In the nation's capital, former Dominican domestic servants who had worked for families of the Dominican Republic's diplomatic staff assigned to the city and who decided to remain in the United States formed a critical component of the Dominican American presence in the city. "In the 1940s and 1950s, these Latin American service workers lived alongside African Americans," according to sociologist Ginetta Candelario, "in the Adams Morgan neighborhood where much of the international community had settled due to its proximity to embassies" (Candelario 2007, 140). Primarily "poor, female, and black," in Candelario's words, these migrants managed to navigate the complicated racial dynamics of the city, including the marked discrimination against African Americans. One of the early members of the Dominican community in Washington, D.C., was Juana Campos, who originally worked as a seamstress for a Dominican diplomatic family and decided to remain in the United States after the family departed.

As Dominicans carved new lives for themselves in the United States in the 1950s and 1960s, in their native land President Rafael Trujillo's tyrannical grip on the country, often with the support of the U.S. government, began to crumble. Trujillo was assassinated in 1961 and two years later, Juan Bosch, a populist reformer who had spent more than two decades in exile for his opposition to Trujillo, was elected president. Bosch's efforts at land reform and his refusal to deal harshly with the nation's expanding Communist Party led to conflict with a range of powerful groups, including merchants, wealthy landowners, factory owners, and the Catholic Church, and Bosch was forced to resign after a military coup less than a year into his presidency.

Two years later, another coup attempted to reinstall the popularly elected Bosch to the presidency. As this pro-Bosch revolt grew, the Dominican military seemed on the verge of defeat, and the U.S. government, fearing that another left-leaning nation would emerge in the Caribbean after the Cuban revolution and the rise of Fidel Castro to power, sent 40,000 U.S. troops to the Dominican Republic. Although U.S. officials claimed neutrality, the result was a government victory and a crushing blow to pro-Bosch, and pro-democracy, forces in the country. By one count, 3,000 pro-Bosch activists were killed by the government of the Dominican Republic between 1966 and 1974.

Like migrants from the Dominican Republic, the Central American and South American population in the United States was relatively small in the mid-twentieth century. By 1960, the number of Central Americans was nearly 50,000. Panamanians were the largest group, with a population of 13,000, and Nicaraguans were second in size, at 9,400. The next largest groups were Costa Ricans, Guatemalans, Hondurans, and Salvadorans, all with populations in the United States of between 5,000 and 6,000 in 1960. There were also 90,000 South Americans in the United States in 1960, with relatively even numbers of Argentinians (17,000), Brazilians (14,000), and Colombians (13,000) as the largest immigrant groups from the region.

Although the visibility of Latina/os in broader U.S. popular culture was limited in the post–World War II era, one of the most influential images of Latina/os appeared in the 1961 film *West Side Story*. Based on a hit Broadway production, the movie musical retold the story of Romeo and Juliet through the lens of rival gangs in New York City. Reinforcing increasingly prominent images of Puerto Rican young men as violent and prone to criminal behavior, the film also perpetuated a stereotypical depiction of Puerto Rican women as either meek and submissive or fiery "sexpots."

One of the positive results of the tremendous popularity of *West Side Story* (the film won 10 Oscars, including Best Picture) was the newfound fame of one of its stars, Puerto Rican singer and dancer Rita Moreno. Moreno was born in Humacao, Puerto Rico. When she was 5 years old, she and her mother moved to New York City and she soon began dancing lessons, making her Broadway debut at the age of 13. A veteran of many films by the early 1960s, Moreno won an Oscar for *West Side Story* (she portrayed the character "Anita"). She has gone on to be the only Latina, and one of very few women or men, to win an Oscar, an Emmy, a Grammy, and a Tony award.

Professional baseball offered another important area of visibility for Latina/os. For much of the first half of the twentieth century, major league baseball prohibited African American players, a barrier that often excluded dark-skinned Latinos as well. At the same time, according to historian Adrian Burgos Jr., there was "a Latino presence on either side of baseball's racial barrier," and Burgos points to more than two dozen Latinos in major leagues in the decade before 1947 (Burgos 2007, 162).

When baseball took the final step in a long process of racial integration and African American Jackie Robinson joined the Brooklyn Dodgers in 1947, darker-skinned Latinos also officially entered the major leagues. In fact, according to Burgos, between 1947 and 1959, of the 16 "integration pioneers" (the first player of color on a major league team) 4 were Latinos: Minnie Miñoso (Chicago White Sox, 1951), Nino Escalera (Cincinnati Reds, 1954), Carlos Paula (Washington Senators, 1954), and Ozzie Virgil Sr. (Detroit Tigers, 1958) (Burgos 2007, 180–81). In coming decades, the number of Latino stars in baseball would grow rapidly, with legends like Roberto Clemente, Luis Aparicio, Orlando Cepeda, and Juan Marichal.

Less visible was the Latino heritage of other prominent baseball players. Boston Red Sox star Ted Williams, for instance, often regarded as one of the best hitters in baseball history, was of mixed Anglo and Mexican descent. Williams's mother, May Venzor, was born in El Paso, Texas, and later moved to San Diego. She worked for the Salvation Army and would on occasion bring her son on trips to visit poor communities in Tijuana, across the United States-Mexico border. Although he only publically acknowledged his Mexican heritage later in life, noting in his autobiography that he would have experienced prejudice in Southern California if his surname had been Venzor, his mother's name, rather than Williams, Ted Williams has more recently been claimed as one of many Latino-heritage professional athletes in mid-century U.S. sports.

Twenty years after the end of World War II, Puerto Rican and Cuban populations had grown substantially and Latina/os had begun to appear more prominently in American popular culture, most notably in films like *West Side Story* and television shows like *I Love Lucy*. At the same time, faced with persistent forms of poverty and discrimination, Latina/os defended their communities in multiple ways, from civil rights organizations to religious groups to labor activism. As had occurred throughout Latina/o history, Latinas helped drive many of these organizing efforts. Though separate Latina/o groups tended to focus on their own, individual communities, certain spaces drew Latina/os together and became sites of cooperation, shared activism, and intimacy. These new Latina/o coalitions and alliances would prove especially important as the nation entered one of its most tumultuous and challenging periods, the era of the Vietnam War and the American counterculture.

PROFILE: LOLITA LEBRON

Lolita Lebron was born in 1919 in Lares, a town in the interior of Puerto Rico. Her father was a coffee plantation foreman. As a young woman, Lebron became a single mother but decided to leave her daughter with her mother in Puerto Rico in order to sail for the United States and seek a better life. Lebron joined a large group of Puerto Ricans in the 1940s hoping for improved work and living conditions in New York City. Most Puerto Rican newcomers, like Lebron, were grindingly poor and lived in what she would later describe as ghetto-like conditions. Discrimination toward Puerto Ricans was common, according to Lebron, who remembered shopkeepers displaying signs that said, "No blacks, no dogs, no Puerto Ricans."

In New York, Lebron took night classes and worked as a seamstress, even sewing insignias onto U.S. military uniforms despite her increasing critiques of U.S. imperial actions in Puerto Rico and elsewhere in Latin America. In New York, Lebron also met Puerto Rican nationalist leader Pedro Albizu Campos and joined Campos's movement calling for the independence of Puerto Rico from the United States. Campos reportedly had such faith in Lebron that he chose her to lead the 1954 attack on Congress.

After the attack, Lebron was arrested and sentenced to a long prison term. She was eventually pardoned by President Jimmy Carter in 1979. Lolita Lebron continued to be an activist for Puerto Rican independence and against U.S. imperial control of the island, and was one of the protesters arrested in a 2001 demonstration denouncing the U.S. occupation of the Puerto Rican island of Vieques.

PROFILE: TITO PUENTE

Ernest "Tito" Puente was born in East Harlem, New York, in 1923. His parents were natives of Puerto Rico who moved to New York City in the early twentieth century. Musically talented as a child, Puente was also an accomplished dancer as a child. He attended the New York School of Music, and his mother used precious family resources to pay for piano lessons for the boy. Puente also sang and learned to play the saxophone and drums. In his teens, Puente took a job as a drummer in a band that played Latin music. His talent as a drummer soon attracted the attention of famous bandleaders like Machito (Frank Grillo) and Johnny Rodríguez, and Puente began to be featured as a soloist during nightly performances.

In 1942, at the age of 19, Puente was drafted into the U.S. Navy. Aboard the USS *Santee*, he and his crewmates faced numerous battles and Puente, in addition to his job loading artillery, played in the ship's band. After being discharged in 1945, he studied at the Julliard School of Music using funds provided by the GI Bill; and in 1949 he formed his own band, the Tito Puente Orchestra.

Puente's fame spread in the 1950s and he broke new ground as a composer and popular artist. He released the album *Dance Mania* in 1957, which contained the hit song "Cayuco," and by the mid-1990s, it had sold over 500,000 copies. In the 1960s, Puente was the host of his own television program, *El Mundo de Tito Puente*, served as the grand marshal of New York's Puerto Rican Day parade, and was awarded a key to the city of New York by the mayor.

Puente maintained his popularity and critical acclaim in the 1970s as a new generation of Latina/o salsa and rock musicians rose to prominence such as Johnny Pacheco, Willie Colón, and Carlos Santana, who recorded a version of Puente's song "Oye Como Va." In 1979, Puente won his first of four Grammy awards for the album *Homanaje a Beny*, which was dedicated to the legendary Cuban singer Beny Moré.

In 1991, Puente released his 100th album, and in 1997, his half century of music was celebrated in the record *50 Years of Swing*. Tito Puente died in New York City in the summer of 2000.

PROFILE: DESI ARNAZ

Desi Arnaz, the only son of a prominent family in Santiago de Cuba, was born in 1917. Arnaz and his family came to the United States in 1934 after the overthrow of Cuban leader Gerardo Machado. Arnaz's father, who had been the mayor of Santiago de Cuba, was a supporter of Machado, and the family fled to Miami, where Arnaz attended St. Patrick's High School and played on the football team. After graduating from high school, the young man worked at several odd jobs before getting a job singing at a small Miami nightclub. Xavier Cugat, the famous Cuban bandleader, spotted Arnaz and hired him to sing for his band.

Arnaz soon formed his own band and began touring the American nightclub circuit. A Broadway director saw his nightclub act and cast him in a musical that soon became a hit. Arnaz was invited to star in the movie version of the musical, and on the set of the film he met an actress named Lucille Ball. Arnaz and Ball fell in love and married in 1940. In 1951, Arnaz and Ball starred together in the sitcom *I Love Lucy*. The show was a major hit, becoming one of the most popular television shows of the 1950s, and lasted six seasons, until 1957.

Arnaz's character, Ricky Ricardo, was undoubtedly one of the most recognizable Latina/os in the country through much of the second half of the twentieth century. Arnaz died in 1986 at the age of 69.

REFERENCES

Burgos, Adrian, Jr. *Playing America's Game: Baseball, Latinos, and the Color Line*. Berkeley: University of California Press, 2007.

Candelario, Ginetta E. B. *Black Behind the Ears: Dominican Racial Identity from Museums to Beauty Shops*. Durham, NC: Duke University Press, 2007.

Fernández, Lilia. *Brown in the Windy City: Mexicans and Puerto Ricans in Postwar Chicago*. Chicago: University of Chicago Press, 2012.

García, María Cristina. "Exiles, Immigrants, and Transnationals: The Cuban Communities in the United States." In *The Columbia History of Latinos in the*

United States since 1960, edited by David G. Gutiérrez, 146–86. New York: Columbia University Press, 2004.

Hernández, Kelly Lytle. *Migra!: A History of the U.S. Border Patrol.* Berkeley: University of California Press, 2010.

Luibhéid, Eithne. *Entry Denied: Policing Sexuality at the Border.* Minneapolis: University of Minnesota Press, 2002.

Pascoe, Peggy. *What Comes Naturally: Miscegenation Law and the Making of Race in America.* New York: Oxford University Press, 2009.

Rivera, Eugenio. "La Colonia de Lorain, Ohio." In *The Puerto Rican Diaspora: Historical Perspectives*, edited by Carmen Teresa Whalen and Víctor Vázquez Hernández, 68–87. Philadelphia: Temple University Press, 2005.

Sheridan, Clare. " 'Another White Race': Mexican Americans and the Paradox of Whiteness in Jury Selection." *Law and History Review* 21, no. 1 (Spring 2003): 109–44.

_____ *Chapter 9* _____

New Worlds, New Homes, 1965–1986

For Latina/os, as for the rest of the country, the 1960s and 1970s were decades of turbulence and transformation. New groups and activist energies surged through established Latina/o communities in the East Coast, Midwest, and Southwest, while immigrants from Cuba, Dominican Republic, and Central America established new homes and new lives across the country.

The 1960s began with a series of events, both within and outside the United States, that would have lasting effects on the country's Latina/o population. The Cuban revolution led by Fidel Castro in 1959 and the assassination of the Dominican Republic's dictator Rafael Trujillo in 1961 sparked multiple and lasting changes, including unprecedented levels of Cuban and Dominican immigration. Latina/os also played active roles in many of the key events (the Vietnam War, the civil rights movement, the counterculture, the rise of the conservative movement, transformations in the U.S. manufacturing and service economy) that shook the country in the next two decades.

For decades, the major Latina/o groups in the United States were ethnic Mexicans and Puerto Ricans. The dominance of these two groups in broader American perceptions of Latina/os, and the actual composition of the Latina/o population, began to shift in the 1960s and would continue to do so for the remainder of the twentieth century—and continue to shift in the twenty-first century as well. One of the driving forces in this change was the passage of a new immigration law, the Hart-Celler Act.

While legal battles and new federal civil rights laws are rightly regarded as hallmarks of the 1960s, other legal arenas had similarly profound effects on the lives of Latina/os in the United States. In 1965, the United States passed the Hart-Celler Act. The law continued a trend in the mid-twentieth century of liberalizing immigration law and, in a sense, accompanied two other very important laws, the 1964 Civil Rights Act and the 1965 Voting Rights Act. The Hart-Celler Act abolished national origins quotas, which had been established 40 years earlier in the National Origins Act of 1924, and dramatically revised the visa system to give preference in admissions to families and relatives.

After the Hart-Celler Act, immigration to the United States in general began to rise steadily and assume a much different profile than in the past. European immigration, once the dominant source of immigrants to the United States, became less of a factor in the late twentieth century. By the 1980s, only 11 percent of total foreign immigrants came from Europe (compared to 90% in 1900), while Latin Americans and Asians formed the large majority of new, post-1965 immigrants. Annual immigration rose steadily during this period, averaging 450,000 annually in the 1970s and rising to more than 700,000 annually in 1980s. In a certain respect, this trend continued a pattern that had existed prior to 1965 in the relatively large proportions of white-collar workers, women, and whole families immigrating to the United States. One reason for this trend toward larger numbers of female immigrants was that employment opportunities for women increased (such as in service jobs) while heavy manual labor jobs, which had historically drawn predominantly male immigrant workers, continued to dwindle.

From the 1960s to the 1980s, the Latina/o population of the United States began a remarkable period of growth. Seven million Latina/os lived in the United States in 1960, constituting about 4 percent of the country's population. In 1970, the Latina/o population was 9 million, also about 4 percent of the country. In the next decade, the Latina/o population jumped to nearly 15 million and was more than 22 million in 1990, rising from less than 7 percent of the U.S. population in 1980 to 9 percent in 1990.

The increasing Latina/o population in the 1960s and 1970s help produce and sustain a wide range of popular culture in the post-1965 era. Latina/o writers, for instance, achieved newfound success during the period. Poets like Miguel Piñero and Pedro Pietri in New York, and the establishment of the Nuyorican Poet's Café in 1975, and the Chicano poet Alurista in the Southwest blended literary innovation with activist politics. Building on the continued popularity of Latin music, a new generation of Latina/o musicians also pioneered the development of salsa music in the United States. At the center of this "salsa revolution" was a pan-Latina/o group of emerging stars, such as Puerto Rican Hector Lavoe, Cuban Celia Cruz, and Panamanian Rubén Blades. While the East Coast was a home for salsa, Carlos Santana, a Mexican immigrant from Jalisco, Mexico, helped revolutionize rock music in California's Bay Area.

U.S. born and immigrant Mexicans like Carlos Santana represented by far the largest Latina/o group in the United States. In 1960, the U.S. population

Latina/o writers like Marvin Felix Camillo and Miguel Piñero gained new visibility in the 1960s and 1970s. (AP Photo/Jerry T. Mosey)

of Mexican descent was 3.5 million, or about half of all Latina/os in the United States. The population had grown at a rate of over 70 percent in the 1940s and over 50 percent in the 1950s. A large number of Mexicans in 1960 had been born in the United States and were thus U.S. citizens. At the same time, a great many Mexicans in the United States maintained strong ties with Mexico. In fact, a third of U.S. born Mexicans in 1960 had at least one parent who was born in Mexico. In the following decade, the Mexican population grew to more than 5 million and by 1980 had reached nearly 9 million. In 1990, there were 14.5 million Mexicans living in the United States.

Economic transformations in both the United States and Mexico played a major role in increased Mexican immigration and the growth of Mexican communities in the United States. In the United States, declines in manufacturing and industry in the 1970s and 1980s led to a jump in demand for laborers in service-sector jobs. Meanwhile, in Mexico, rapid economic expansion in the post–World War II era, as historian David Gutiérrez states, "never came close to creating the number of jobs necessary to meet the needs of a population that grew from just 19 million in 1940 to 48 million in 1970" (Gutiérrez 2004, 63). Thus, when a major economic crisis struck in Mexico in the 1980s (unemployment reached 25% in the early 1980s and inflation skyrocketed to nearly 160% in 1987), hundreds of thousands of desperate Mexicans were drawn to available and relatively higher-paying jobs in the United States.

At the same time, "it would be a mistake," Gutiérrez cautions, "to view these developments simply in terms of the classic 'push-pull' model of immigration" (Gutiérrez 2004, 63). Heightened levels of post-1965 Mexican immigration, in fact, were only the latest feature of a long-standing pattern of transnational labor migration that had been developing for decades across the United States-Mexico border. Mexican immigrants had been displaced by shifting economic and political developments in Mexico since at least the late nineteenth century, and demands on the U.S. side of the border for manual laborers had a similar long history in the region, stretching from railroad construction and agricultural jobs at the turn of the twentieth century to the Bracero program of the post–World War II era. While large-scale Mexican immigration to the United States may have seemed new to many, untrained eyes, movements in both directions across the United States-Mexico border have a long tradition in Latina/o history.

For Cuban Americans, the 1960s and 1970s were marked by continued migration to the United States and the creation of a vibrant Cuban community in Miami and broader South Florida. Between 1965 and 1973, nearly 300,000 Cubans arrived on American shores. By the late 1970s, a total of more than 650,000 Cubans had relocated to the United States. The Latina/o population of the city of Miami, which was overwhelmingly of Cuban descent, grew dramatically during that period. There were 150,000 Latina/os in Miami in 1970, representing 45 percent of the city's total population. A decade later, the Latina/o population was nearly 200,000, and in 1990 it was 225,000, rising from 55 percent to over 60 percent of the city's total inhabitants. In broader Dade-Miami County, growth in Cuban communities led to an increase in the Latina/o population from only 50,000 in 1960 to 300,000 in 1970 and 580,000 in 1980. Cubans were even more predominant in cities like Hialeah, where the Latina/o population jumped from 45,000 in 1970 to 107,000 in 1980 to 165,000 in 1990, increasing from 45 percent of the population in 1970 to nearly 75 percent in 1980 to 88 percent in 1990.

A second major period of Cuban immigration, one whose scale and significance would rival that of the immediate post-1959 period, occurred in 1980 in what would come to be known as the Mariel boatlift. In early 1980, Fidel Castro announced to the Cuban nation that all those interested in leaving the island could depart from the port city of Mariel. Tens of thousands soon raced to the coast, eager to leave the island and make a new home outside of Cuba. As a result, between April and October 1980, 125,000 Cubans, mostly in boats and rafts, some of them barely seaworthy, migrated to the United States, mainly to South Florida.

Among the Cuban newcomers arriving during the Mariel period was a significant number of gay men (there is less evidence of the presence of Cuban women among the Mariel migrants who engaged in same-sex sexual activity). Reinaldo Arenas, the author of *Before Night Falls*, would eventually become one of the best known of these Cubans. Like many others in postrevolutionary Cuba, Arenas suffered from the increasing persecution and targeting of gay men. Although the Cuban government would eventually ease its attack on those who engaged in same-sex sexual practices, Arenas was one of a considerable number of gay men fleeing to the United States in 1980. The U.S. government faced a bind in their approach to these newcomers. U.S. immigration policy, like many segments of the government, treated gay men and lesbians with hostility, and entry to the United States was often denied based on sexuality (see the story of Sara Quiroz in chapter 8). At the same time, driven by anticommunism, the U.S. government was determined to welcome new arrivals from Cuba, celebrating and supporting them as refugees from a dictatorial, communist Cuba under the grips of Fidel Castro.

Like the majority of Cuban immigrants to the United States in the post-1959 era, many Cuban gay men during the Mariel period made new homes in Miami and the broader South Florida area. These gay men had a significant impact on the sexual culture, especially the gay male sexual culture of 1980s South Florida. Fleeing persecution in Cuba and perceiving the United States to be a place of greater sexual freedom, some men challenged the strict gender norms that even many gay men in Miami refused to transgress. "Drag and transvestitism," sociologist Susana Peña writes, "were reinvented by young, poor immigrants who grew out their hair and then peroxided it and wore housedresses out on the street at night" (Peña 2005, 139). "Concentrated in neighborhoods like South Miami Beach and Southwest Miami," Peña continues, these men, often described as "locas" or "Marielenas," helped fashion a newly dynamic and "visible gay Mariel culture in Miami in the 1980s" (Peña 2005, 139). As Cuban immigrants during the Mariel period remade Latina/o life in South Florida, gay Cuban men played a vital role in that transformation.

Unlike Cuban refugees, who received substantial federal assistance upon migrating to the United States in the 1960s, Dominican migrants received no such comparable federal assistance when they arrived on U.S. shores. The U.S. occupation of the Dominican Republic in the mid-1960s, in fact, enabled the reimposition of conservatism in the country and the onset of 12 years of repressive political rule under Joaquín Balaguer, a leading official under the previous dictatorship of Rafael Trujillo. Under Balaguer, the Dominican Republic embarked on a development project that prioritized industry and commerce. Not unlike Operation Bootstrap in nearby Puerto

Rico, the government offered huge incentives to both foreign and domestic businesses, including low taxes, or no taxes at all, and provisions for government-financed building of infrastructure for industrial developments.

Balaguer was also an heir to Trujillo's legacy of state-sponsored terror and the promotion of white supremacy. In response, an influential cohort of Dominican intellectuals in the 1960s and 1970s developed an approach toward Dominican culture and politics that celebrated, rather than denigrated, the contribution of Afro-Dominicans to the nation's history and culture and challenged the legitimacy of U.S. intervention and imperial influence.

Dominican migration to the United States grew steadily after 1965. Government policies favored industrial development and the concentration of agricultural land into the control of small groups of individuals and corporations. As a result, agrarian jobs dwindled and increasing numbers of Dominicans moved to urban spaces. In the two decades between 1965 and 1984, the country's rural population decreased from 65 percent of the total population to 45 percent. Though Dominican cities offered more job opportunities than the countryside, unemployment in the capital city of Santo Domingo was estimated at 20 percent in the early 1970s and by 1988 had risen to 30 percent.

As occurred in Puerto Rico during the Operation Bootstrap era, industrialization and the consolidation of wealth in the Dominican Republic encouraged out-migration from the island (and may have also served government interests in eliminating a possible source of domestic political opposition and activism). Sixteen thousand Dominicans migrated to the United States in 1966, 9,000 in 1968, and 14,000 in 1973, many of them from urban areas and the working class. In all, between 1961 and 1986 more than 400,000 Dominicans immigrated to the U.S. mainland (another 44,000 Dominicans moved to Puerto Rico during the same period). According to one study, between 1968 and 1978, "nearly two-thirds of all Dominicans in the United States were described as laborers, operatives, or service workers" (Levitt 2004, 238). New York City and New Jersey were primary destinations for Dominican migrants, with smaller communities in the Miami and Boston areas.

For recently arrived Dominicans in the United States, political activism in the 1960s and 1970s often focused on events in the Dominican Republic rather than in the United States or in more local arenas. With the return to a conservative government under President Joaquín Balaguer, Dominican exiles tended to support progressive, left-wing organizations. Dominicans, for instance, were leaders in the Marxist group Linea Roja, and others helped found organizations and political clubs in New York City like Asociación Dominicana and the Dominican Committee for Human Rights.

While local politics drew some attention, activists focused on promoting transformations in the Dominican Republic and, like Cuban immigrants during the same period, hoped for a prompt return to their homeland.

During the 1980s, Dominicans in New York began to focus closer to home in their political organizing. According to anthropologist Ana Aparicio, "the shift from organizing almost exclusively for 'homeland' politics to organizing to empower Dominicans locally spanned the better part of the 1980s" (Aparicio 2010, 260). Aparicio points to several factors contributing to this political reorientation, including the recognition that, after two decades of forced exile, a mass movement of Dominicans back to the Dominican Republic was increasingly unlikely. The emergence of a new generation of Dominican activists who had been raised in New York City and assumed leadership roles in the community in the 1980s also had an important effect, as did new relationships that developed between Dominican groups and other political organizations and agencies in the city. Developments in the Dominican Republic, of course, continued to draw special attention from Dominicans in the United States; however, as the end of the century drew near, Dominican political activists increasingly turned to their own local communities in their efforts to improve lives and battle poverty and discrimination.

Like so many other Latina/o groups, Central Americans have been arriving in the United States since the nineteenth century. Central American immigration grew somewhat during the 1960s, as more than 100,000 Central Americans were admitted to the United States. In the 1970s, the number increased to 175,000. In 1970, Panamanians were the largest group; however, by 1980 Salvadorans had become the largest group of the 300,000 Central Americans in the United States.

One of the largest Central American communities lived in San Francisco. Increased immigration to Northern California in the 1960s and 1970s led to a Latina/o population in the city of more than 80,000 by 1980. While there were small percentages of Puerto Ricans and Cubans, and a larger of number Mexicans (approaching 40% of all Latina/os), Central Americans, especially those from El Salvador and Nicaragua, were the biggest segment of the Latina/o population. The Mission District was the heart of San Francisco's Central American community. Nicaraguans, for instance, had lived in the neighborhood for decades. According to historian Cary Cordova, "a large influx of Nicaraguans came to the city just prior to, or in the wake of, the 1934 assassination of revolutionary leader Augusto Sandino" (Cordova 2010, 214). With the rise to power of right-wing leader Anastasio Somoza, Cordova adds, Nicaraguans were often "unable to return to their home country for the next forty years" (Cordova 2010, 214). Like Cubans in Florida and Dominicans in New York City, Nicaraguans in San Francisco were often deeply involved in exile politics throughout the second half of the twentieth century.

While Latina/o activists in San Francisco joined the civil rights movement, including support for gay rights, and anti-Vietnam War protests during the era, events in Nicaragua in the 1970s animated the organizing efforts of many Latina/os. A devastating earthquake in Managua, Nicaragua's capital city, which killed 20,000 people and leveled much of the city, led to the formation of groups to raise money to aid the rebuilding of the country. The intensification of anti-Somoza activity in Nicaragua further inspired a pan-Latina/o collection of activists. These activist, including poets, filmmakers, and muralists, supported the Frente Sandinista Liberación Nacional through fund-raising, public demonstrations, and even joining the battle as soldiers. Organizers founded the Spanish-language *Gaceta Sandinista* in 1974, which was the only newspaper in the United States specifically supporting the Sandinista movement, and the Mission Cultural Center, which devoted a week of films, music, and poetry in their "Week of Solidarity with the People of Nicaragua" in 1978. Poet Nina Serrano and filmmaker Lourdes Portillo produced the film *Después del Terremoto (After the Earthquake)*, which explored gender inequalities and Nicaraguan exile politics in San Francisco in the 1970s.

The triumph of the Frente Sandinista Liberación Nacional in 1979 was celebrated by many Latina/o activists in San Francisco and elsewhere. The new Sandinista government, however, faced a hostile U.S. government that was committed to overthrowing the Nicaraguan government. Over the course of the 1980s, the United States under President Ronald Regan supported a military force, the Contras, dedicated to toppling the Sandinista government. By one count, the Contra War led to the death of 30,000 Nicaraguans and cost billions of dollars. The Sandinista government eventually collapsed in 1990. As in many Latina/o communities, Central American political activists drew from a pan-Latina/o group of supporters and balanced organizing for change in their homelands with attention to events and issues close to home.

While the Central American population rose rapidly in the 1970s and 1980s, the number of immigrants from South America also grew significantly during the period. The U.S. census of 1960 counted almost 90,000 South Americans living in the nation, with Argentina (17,000) and Colombia (13,000) representing the largest Spanish-speaking countries of origin (Brazil was the second-largest country with a U.S. population of 14,000). In 1970, the South American population had jumped to more than 250,000, as the Colombian community grew to more than 60,000 and Argentinian (45,000) and Ecuadorian (37,000) populations more than tripled in size. A decade later, in 1980, there were more than 500,000 South

Americans in the United States, with Colombians (144,000), Argentinians (68,000), and Peruvians (55,000) representing the largest portion of immigrants from predominantly Spanish-speaking countries.

Of the many transformations in the United States in the 1960s and 1970s, changes in the broader U.S. economy weighed heavily on all Americans, including Latina/os. One of the groups hit especially hard by this shift away from manufacturing and heavy industry was the nation's Puerto Rican community. In 1960, the Puerto Rican population on the U.S. mainland was nearly 900,000 (by contrast, the population of Puerto Rico itself was 2.3 million). Two-thirds of Puerto Ricans on the mainland, more than 600,000 people, had been born on the island, while approximately 300,000 had parents born in Puerto Rico. A decade later, in 1970, there were nearly 1.4 million Puerto Ricans on the mainland, and the population of Puerto Rico was 2.7 million. The East Coast of the United States, especially New York City, continued to be the home of the largest Puerto Rican communities in the country, with more than 1 million in living in the states of New York and New Jersey. In 1980, the Puerto Rican population grew to 1.9 million, with 990,000 Puerto Ricans living in New York State and nearly 250,000 in New Jersey.

At the same time, Puerto Ricans began to live elsewhere in the nation in larger numbers in the 1960s and 1970s. The percentage of mainland Puerto Ricans living in New York City, for instance, dropped from over 80 percent in 1950 to 60 percent in 1970. By 1970, the Midwest was the home of 10 percent of the mainland Puerto Rican population, with 80,000 Puerto Ricans living in Chicago. Another 10,000 Puerto Ricans lived in Los Angeles in 1970, with nearly 7,000 more in Miami and 5,000 in San Francisco. A decade later, Puerto Rican communities in Illinois (130,000), Florida (95,000), and California (93,000) had grown even larger. Whereas nearly 80 percent of all Puerto Ricans on the U.S. mainland had lived in New York and New Jersey in 1960, by 1980 that percentage had dropped to just above 60 percent.

As manufacturing and factory jobs steadily decreased in the United States (while lower-paid, less reliable service employment increased), Puerto Ricans found fewer opportunities to escape poverty and difficult living conditions. The percentage of Puerto Rican men and women in factory jobs fell from 50 percent in 1960 to 36 percent in 1970 and 31 percent in 1980, while the percentage in professional jobs grew only slightly over the same period (from 6% in 1960 to 9% in 1970 to 12% in 1980). The unemployment rate among Puerto Ricans also grew, rising from 9.7 percent in 1960 to 12.6 percent in 1972 to 14 percent by the mid-1980s. More pointedly, Puerto Ricans suffered much higher rates of unemployment than the rest of the country. According to one study, Puerto Ricans on the U.S. mainland experienced

"1.8 times (1960) and 2.0 times (1972) the general levels of unemployment across the United States" (Santiago-Valles and Jiménez-Muñoz 2004, 96), a disparity that would persist for several decades. Average Puerto Rican household income, though rising during the period, also did not keep pace with the wider U.S. growth, declining from 71 percent of the U.S. average in 1959 to 69 percent of the average by 1974.

As would occur in the Mexican Southwest, Puerto Rican political activism in the 1960s and 1970s was wide ranging, involving both well-established social service organizations and a new, younger generation of activists. Political activism took multiple forms in Puerto Rican communities. The Puerto Rican Forum, for instance, was composed of Puerto Rican young professionals and argued that poverty resulted from discriminatory practices by Anglo employers as well as inferior educational opportunities that led to poor jobs and little hope for progress. The group dismissed the notion, which was increasingly prevalent among Anglo politicians and policy makers during the era, that a "culture of poverty" existed in Puerto Rican communities that led to economic inequality. Members also disputed the notion that Puerto Ricans would eventually, without strong government efforts to combat poverty, educational inequality, and the effects of a rapidly deindustrializing American economy, be allowed to assimilate into U.S. culture and rise out of poverty.

Another visible and influential activist group was the Young Lords Party (YLP). Initially formed as the Young Lords Organization in Chicago in 1968, the organization spread rapidly, with branches soon established in other major midwestern and eastern cities. The New York City chapter, renamed the Young Lords Party, became one of the most prominent YLP groups and was characterized by its commitment to Puerto Rican civil rights on the mainland and for its support for the Puerto Rican independence movement on the island. The YLP was also multiracial, with membership open to Puerto Ricans and non-Puerto Ricans alike (in fact, one of its early leaders was Denise Oliver, an African American who was not of Puerto Rican descent). The YLP reasoned that its multiracial membership reflected the diverse backgrounds of Puerto Rican people. Feminist concerns were also primary in the YLP from nearly its beginning as an organization. The YLP linked efforts to allow women reproductive freedom, that is, the right to choose safely whether to have children or not, with questions of civil rights and broader political goals like battling poverty and discrimination.

In their support for Puerto Rican independence, the YLP shared with the wider Puerto Rican community a focus on political developments on the island. Puerto Rican island residents, recall, occupied a unique position in the United States over the twentieth century. During the 1960s, newly independent Asian and African states pressured the United States to allow a vote

Young Lords Party spokesman addresses crowd in New York City, 1978. (AP Photo)

on the status of Puerto Rico. In theory, this vote would be the first time Puerto Ricans would have the chance to vote between independence, statehood, and the current commonwealth status that had been in effect since the 1950s. The voting process, however, had several flaws. The U.S. Congress refused to commit itself to accepting the decision of the Puerto Rican people and insisted that Congress, not Puerto Ricans, had the ultimate authority over the island's status. Congress also refused to clarify before the election what changes would occur if Puerto Rico chose to become either independent or a U.S. state. In protest of these ambiguities, proindependence forces boycotted the vote, as did many prostatehood Puerto Ricans. As a result, the commonwealth option received a 60 percent share of the vote; however, the outcome was hardly a mandate for commonwealth status among Puerto Ricans. Despite this setback for independence leaders, calls for Puerto Rico's independence among groups like the YLP continued throughout the late twentieth century.

Though less well known than the YLP, another important Latina/o activist group during the 1960s and 1970s was GALA, the Gay Latino Alliance, which was founded in the San Francisco Bay Area in the early 1970s. At that time, an estimated 80,000 Latina/os lived in the Bay Area, most in the Mission District in San Francisco but others spread throughout the region. For gay and lesbian Latina/os, there were no gay and predominantly Latina/o spaces in which to gather and socialize. The bars and clubs in the Bay Area were overwhelmingly white, leading Latina/o activists to search for a space, both literal and figurative, to link their gay activism with their Latina/o political activism.

Diana Felix, one of the early members of GALA, recalled the importance of discovering, or in truth creating, a location for both her activism on Latina/o issues and her activism as a Chicana lesbian. Another early member of GALA was Jesús Barragán. Like other GALA founders, Barragán recalled that his gay awareness and his racial consciousness took shape simultaneously. The youngest of seven children, Barragán and his family migrated from Arizona to California in 1955. He served in the Vietnam War and returned to San Jose in 1969. While attending college by day, Jesús socialized at night in San Jose's gay bars, which sparked his interest in meeting formally with fellow gay Latinos. With members like Felix and Barragán, GALA became one of the first Latina/o gay organizations to gain national visibility, and members marched in events like Gay Freedom Day in San Francisco. In addition to political activism, the group sponsored social events like dances and parades. GALA lasted for several years and then dissolved as an organization in the mid-1980s.

In Boston, Puerto Rican activists mobilized around a similar set of issues. The Puerto Rican population had grown steadily after World War II and reached more than 7,000 in 1970 and nearly 20,000 a decade later. By 1984, according to one estimate, almost 40,000 Puerto Ricans lived in Boston. The South End neighborhood was home to the largest Puerto Rican community, and significant numbers of Puerto Ricans lived in areas like Jamaica Plain and Roxbury. Political activism by Puerto Ricans in Boston ranged from supporting gay and lesbian rights and anti-AIDS organizing to struggles for bilingual education and voter rights and against gentrification in traditional Puerto Rican neighborhoods. In 1978, El Comité de Homosexuales y Lesbianas de Boston was founded, and Lesbianas Latinas was established in 1986. Like GALA in the Bay Area, LGBTQ activists were critical members of Boston's Puerto Rican political-organizing community of the 1970s and 1980s.

Another influential group during the period was the Brown Berets, founded in Los Angeles in the late 1960s. As LA, following broader national trends, suffered through the disappearance of manufacturing and industrial jobs in the central city and regional governments drew middle-class residents and government spending to new suburbs, young Mexicans, like African Americans, faced dwindling job opportunities and an underfunded public education system that was often hostile to their educational growth. Mexican high school students adopted a range of strategies to challenge their subordinate status, including joining forces with older Mexican youth in forming the Brown Berets. The Brown Berets led protests against the inferior state of public schools for Mexican children, the lack of political response among civic leaders, and more national concerns such as the Vietnam War.

Community activists in midwestern cities like Chicago also mobilized beginning in the late 1960s to combat poverty and neglect by civic leaders. In Chicago's Pilsen area, the Latina/o population, which was largely Mexican, had grown rapidly, and by 1970, an estimated 80 percent of the neighborhood (about 25,000 people) were of Mexican descent. Poverty, however, was widespread, schools were overcrowded and in poor condition, and unemployment rates for Latina/os were over 25 percent. The Pilsen neighborhood, also known as Eighteenth Street, became, in the words of historian Lilia Fernández, "the physical center of the local Chicano movement" (Fernández 2012, 225). Community activists, at times allied with Anglo social workers and scholars, established important community centers like Casa Aztlán and El Centro de la Causa and organizations like Mujeres Latinas en Acción (MLEA).

Led by Mexican women such as María Mangual, who had arrived in Chicago from El Paso in the early 1970s, MLEA consciously formed itself as a panethnic group, bringing together Mexicans, Puerto Ricans, and other Latin American women. The group soon provided services such as day care, health care, and legal assistance. According to Fernández, MLEA also "started teaching classes for women: an English class, a GED class, and nutrition and health workshops" (Fernández 2012, 251). Most notably, MLEA joined with another women's organization in 1981 to establish the first battered women's shelter in Chicago to serve primarily Spanish-speaking women. Unlike many similar groups founded in the late 1960s and 1970s, MLEA continued to remain a viable and thriving organization well into the twenty-first century and is a cornerstone of Chicago's Latina/o community.

Other individual Latina/o activists rose to national prominence during the 1960s. One of the most charismatic leaders was Reies López Tijerina. Although he is most often identified with New Mexico, Tijerina was born in Texas in 1926 to a family of farmworkers. Tijerina became an itinerant preacher and in northern New Mexico witnessed some of the most debilitating poverty in the country in the small mountain villages there. Interested in land rights and the Treaty of Guadalupe Hidalgo (which ended the Mexican-American War in 1848), Tijerina became convinced that U.S. national forest land in Tierra Amarilla County in northern New Mexico had been illegally taken from the townspeople of the village of Chama. In 1963, Tijerina organized La Alianza Federal de Mercedes (Federal Alliance of Land Grants), which demanded the return of large chunks of federal forest land to *Nuevomexicana/os*. In the fall of 1966, 350 La Alianza members occupied the national forest campgrounds around Echo Amphitheater and asserted the rights of the village of Chama to 1,400 acres of national forest land surrounding the campground. La Alianza was eventually forced out of Echo Amphitheater and Tijerina and others were arrested.

Another major player in the post–World War II Chicana/o movement was Rodolfo "Corky" Gonzales. Gonzales was born in Denver in 1928, the child of migrant sugar beet workers. Early in his life, he was best known as a champion Golden Gloves boxer and between 1947 and 1955 was considered one of the better featherweights in the country before he turned to political activism. In 1957, Gonzales became the first Chicano district captain of the Democratic Party in Colorado and in 1963 formed a group that demonstrated against police brutality called Los Voluntarios. In 1966, Gonzales founded the Crusade for Justice, a major social justice organization, which began a K–12 school in Denver, opened a social center, and started its own newspaper. One of the most important legacies of Gonzales's leadership was his poem "Yo Soy Joaquín," which celebrates the endurance of Mexican people under U.S. colonial rule.

Latina/o activists also turned to more formal electoral politics during the period, rejecting the largely unresponsive Republican and Democratic parties and forming third-party alternatives for Latina/o voters. One such case occurred in South Texas in the 1970s with the formation of La Raza Unida Party (LRUP). Dissatisfied with the traditional party structure in Crystal City and the seven-county region known as Winter Garden along the United

Rodolfo "Corky" Gonzales was one of the most prominent leaders of the Chicano movement in the 1960s and 1970s. (Bettmann/Corbis)

States-Mexico border, activists adopted, in the words of historian Ernesto Chávez, "a low-keyed, pragmatic strategy that avoided confrontation and inflexible ideological views" (Chávez 2002, 82). Focusing on immediate results, LRUP began to register voters in several counties and within a few months had managed to win all the seats on the Crystal City school board and to elect two of the five members of the city council. LRUP candidates were also elected mayors in two other Texas towns.

LRUP groups made similar efforts to organize third parties elsewhere in the Southwest. In Southern California, multiple chapters of LRUP led extensive voter registration drives; however, these groups, due in part to continued allegiances to the Democratic Party among older Mexican Americans, proved less successful in electing representatives to local offices. Despite some electoral successes, LRUP was ultimately unable to create a sustainable third party in the Southwest.

From a broader perspective, Latina/os steadily came to represent a growing portion of national voters. There were more than 2 million Latina/o voters in the 1976 presidential election, representing 2.4 percent of the total electorate. That proportion grew to 2.6 percent in 1980, with 2.5 million Latina/o voters, and to 3 percent and more than 3 million voters in 1984. By the presidential election of 1988, there were 3.7 million Latina/o voters, approaching 4 percent of the total national vote. In states with large Latina/o populations, of course, the share of the total vote was much higher. In 1988, for instance, Latina/o voters claimed major shares of the vote in states like Texas (14%), California (8%), Florida (7%), New York (6%), Arizona (9%), Colorado (9%), and New Mexico (28%).

An important factor in the expansion of the Latina/o voting power was the extension of the Voting Rights Act of 1965 to cover Latina/os. The original act, passed in order to protect the ability of African Americans to vote without intimidation, was broadened in 1975 to cover Latina/os, as well as Asian Americans and Native Americans, and also provided for the distribution of bilingual voting materials. The extension of the Voting Rights Act eventually helped ensure the existence of majority Latina/o voting districts. In the following decades, the number of Latina/o elected officials rose dramatically across the country, from fewer than 1,500 Latina/o officials, both elected and appointed, in 1973 to nearly 4,000 by the late 1980s.

Two decades after the 1965 Hart-Celler Act, the U.S. government once again passed major immigration legislation in the mid-1980s. The Immigration and Reform Control Act of 1986 was framed by its supporters as a response to supposedly out-of-control Mexican immigration. Observers have refuted this belief that large-scale Mexican immigration, even undocumented immigration, was a threat to the nation. "Rather than being out of control," one set of scholars argues, "Mexican-U.S. migration functioned during the period 1965 to 1985 according to measurable parameters that were stable over time and produced regular, structured patterns of movement within the system" (Massey, Durand, and Malone 2002, 4). Nonetheless, opportunistic politicians and the media flamed a national hysteria targeting Mexican immigrants.

One of the primary components of the Immigration and Reform Control Act was increasing the budget for the Border Patrol, which received hundreds of millions of dollars in new funding to hire additional officers. The law also required that employers ensure that their workers had entered the country with proper documentation. Employers who continued to hire undocumented workers could receive large fines and even face criminal charges. To gain the support of immigrant rights supporters and members of immigrant communities, the law also contained an amnesty program that offered permanent residency status in the United States to undocumented immigrants who could prove that they had lived in the country continuously since 1982 and had taken required English-language and civics classes. Another provision, which had the strong support of major agricultural industries, similarly allowed permanent resident status to agricultural workers employed in the United States. Under the Immigration and Reform Control Act, an estimated 3 million people received permanent residence documents, and ethnic Mexicans represented 75 percent of the newly authorized U.S. residents. The amnesty program had its biggest impact in the U.S. Southwest, where hundreds of thousands of Mexicans, including more than 800,000 in Los Angeles County alone, claimed new rights as permanent members of the nation.

The civil rights era transformed both the broader United States and the lives of Latina/os across the nation. For Latina/os, the most dramatic changes occurred as a result of changes in immigration laws and the resulting rapid growth of new Dominican and Central American communities, and a newfound political activism among Latina/o communities. Latinas were at the forefront of many of these changes, leading the way as political activists, community organizers, and feminist intellectuals. Existing bonds between Latina/o groups were also strengthened and new coalitions developed, especially among a younger generation of activists.

Throughout the era, Latina/os faced the perils of an increasingly stagnant American economy, especially in manufacturing, and periodic anti-immigrant attacks, not to mention the consequences of the Vietnam War and other American military interventions, including in Latin America. As they had managed throughout their nearly 500-year history in North America, Latina/os rose to such challenges with courage, creativity, and determination.

PROFILE: DOLORES HUERTA

Dolores Huerta was born in 1930 in a mining town in northern New Mexico, where her father was a miner and a union activist. Her parents divorced when she was three years old, and her mother raised Huerta, along with her two brothers and two sisters. The family moved to the central San Joaquin Valley farmworker community of Stockton, California, where her mother owned and operated a restaurant and a 70-room hotel, which often allowed farmworker families to reside in for free.

In 1955, Huerta was a founding member of the Stockton chapter of the Community Service Organization (CSO), a grassroots community organization. It was through her work with the CSO that Dolores met Cesar Chavez. In 1962, after the CSO turned down their request to organize farmworkers, Chavez and Huerta resigned from the CSO. They formed the National Farm Workers Association, the predecessor to the more well-known United Farm Workers of America union.

Huerta and Chavez worked closely together on the Delano grape workers strike, and Huerta coordinated the hugely successful movement to boycott table grapes in support of striking workers. Moving to New York City in the late 1960s, she led a boycott of grapes that eventually drew the support of nearly 20 million consumers. In 1970, Huerta led the negotiations between grape growers and the United Farm Workers of America that resulted in significant pay raises for workers as well as important other labor provisions.

Huerta was also a prominent feminist leader in the late twentieth century. She was on the board of the Feminist Majority Foundation and cofounded the Coalition of Labor Union Women in 1974. In 1998 she was selected by *Ms.* magazine as one of its "Women of the Year," and the *Ladies Home Journal* listed her on its "100 Most Important Women of the 20th Century."

Huerta's storied career as a union activist and feminist has made her one of the nation's most prominent Latinas and a role model for a wide range of Latina/o (and non-Latina/o) community organizers.

PROFILE: ANTONIA PANTOJA

Antonia Pantoja, one of the most successful and influential Latina/o leaders of the twentieth century, was born in a poor neighborhood of San Juan, Puerto Rico, in 1921. Struggling against grinding poverty, Pantoja's family, including her unwed mother, her aunt and grandmother, and her grandfather who had worked as a labor organizer, offered her a strong and nurturing home life. An intelligent student, though often sick with chronic asthma, Pantoja managed to convince her family to allow her to stay in school after eighth grade rather than dropping out to help support the family financially. She graduated from high school and entered the University of Puerto Rico with a scholarship and the help of her family, who had managed to contribute a small amount of hard-earned savings to her education. Graduating from college in 1942, Pantoja began a teaching career in an isolated mountain community in Puerto Rico. Though she enjoyed teaching, Pantoja soon decided to leave the island, like so many other Puerto Ricans, for the U.S. mainland.

In 1944, Antonia Pantoja moved to New York City. Working first in a series of factory jobs, she soon found employment at a Puerto Rican social service organization. In the 1950s, she helped create several important community groups, as well as earned a master's degree in social work from Columbia University (two decades later, she would receive a PhD in sociology from Union Graduate School). In 1961, Pantoja founded ASPIRA, which focused on improving educational opportunities for Puerto Rican youth. An unequaled organizer, Pantoja established chapters, according to historian Virginia Sánchez Korrol, in "schools, churches, storefronts, and wherever Spanish-speaking young people congregated" (Sánchez Korrol 2005, 219). "Classes in Puerto Rican history and culture," Sánchez Korrol continues, "became cornerstones for developing knowledge, pride, and confidence" (Sánchez Korrol 2005, 219). Among the many triumphs of ASPIRA was a legal victory in 1974 that supported bilingual education in New York City.

Pantoja moved to Southern California in the 1970s. In San Diego, she met a fellow activist, Dr. Wilhelmina Perry, and the two founded what would eventually become the Graduate School for Community Development. In the mid-1980s, Pantoja and Perry moved to Puerto Rico, where they continued to be involved in local politics, helping to build, among other initiatives, a Head Start program. Pantoja returned to New York City with Perry in the late 1990s. Still politically active well into her seventies, Antonia Pantoja died of cancer in 2002 at the age of 80.

PROFILE: CESAR CHAVEZ

Cesar Chavez was born in Yuma, Arizona, in 1927. As a child, he worked as a migrant laborer with his family. He eventually moved to San Jose, California, and became involved in union organizing. Chavez's first major organizing experience was with the CSO in California, where he learned basic grassroots organizing strategies and eventually rose to the position of general director of the CSO. In 1962, Chavez resigned from the CSO and began organizing a union of farmworkers in California. He focused on the San Joaquin Valley, where farmworkers lived and worked year-round. In 1965, the union formed by Chavez and Dolores Huerta, the National Farm

Workers Association, had grown to 1,700 members and was receiving support from Protestant and Catholic groups, civil rights volunteers, and Anglo-led labor groups.

One of the triumphs of Chavez's organizing efforts emerged from a strike involving Filipino and Mexican farmworkers in Delano, California. After Filipino workers, led by prominent labor organizers such as Larry Itliong, initiated a strike against grape growers in Delano in 1965, Chavez and the National Farm Workers Association joined the strike. Chavez helped lead the strike, which included a boycott of table grapes that spread throughout the nation and eventually forced grape field owners to negotiate with their workers. Chavez also embarked on a number of lengthy "hunger strikes" to publicize the union and its organizing campaigns. Chavez died in 1993 as one of the most celebrated and beloved figures in Latina/o history.

REFERENCES

Aparicio, Ana. "Translocal Barrio Politics: Dominican American Organizing in New York City." In *Beyond El Barrio: Everyday Life in Latina/o America*, edited by Gina M. Pérez, Frank A. Gurdy, and Adrian Burgos Jr., 253–71. New York: New York University Press, 2010.

Chávez, Ernesto. *Mi Raza Primero!: Nationalism, Identity, and Insurgency in the Chicano Movement in Los Angeles, 1966–1978*. Berkeley: University of California Press, 2002.

Cordova, Cary. "The Mission in Nicaragua: San Francisco Poets Go to War." In *Beyond El Barrio: Everyday Life in Latina/o America*, edited by Gina M. Pérez, Frank A. Gurdy, and Adrian Burgos Jr., 211–32. New York: New York University Press, 2010.

Fernández, Lilia. *Brown in the Windy City: Mexicans and Puerto Ricans in Postwar Chicago*. Chicago: University of Chicago Press, 2012.

Gutiérrez, David G. "Globalization, Labor Migration, and the Demographic Revolution: Ethnic Mexicans in the Late Twentieth Century." In *The Columbia History of Latinos in the United States since 1960*, edited by David G. Gutiérrez, 43–86. New York: Columbia University Press, 2004.

Levitt, Peggy. "Transnational Ties and Incorporation: The Case of Dominicans in the United States." In *The Columbia History of Latinos in the United States since 1960*, edited by David G. Gutiérrez, 229–56. New York: Columbia University Press, 2004.

Massey, Douglas S., Jorge Durand, and Nolan J. Malone. *Beyond Smoke and Mirrors: Mexican Immigration in an Era of Economic Integration*. New York: Russell Sage Foundation, 2002.

Peña, Susana. "Visibility and Silence: Mariel and Cuban American Gay Male Experience and Representation." In *Queer Migrations: Sexuality, U.S. Citizenship, and Border Crossings*, edited by Eithne Luibhéid and Lionel Cantú Jr., 125–45. Minneapolis: University of Minnesota Press, 2005.

Sánchez Korrol, Virginia. "Antonia Pantoja and the Power of Community Action."
     In *Latina Legacies: Identity, Biography, and Community, edited by Vicki L.
     Ruiz and Virginia Sánchez-Korrol*, 209–24. New York: Oxford University
     Press, 2005.
Santiago-Valles, Kelvin A., and Gladys M. Jiménez-Muñoz. "Social Polarization and
     Colonized Labor: Puerto Ricans in the United States, 1945–2000." In *The
     Columbia History of Latinos in the United States since 1960*, edited by David
     G. Gutiérrez, 87–145. New York: Columbia University Press, 2004.

_____ *Chapter 10* _____

Latina/os in a New Century, 1986–Present

In the last quarter century, Latina/os have risen to a new prominence in mainstream American society. The Latina/o population has grown from 14.6 million in 1980 to 22.4 million in 1990 to 35.3 million in 2000, and reached 50.5 million in 2010. By the end of the first decade of the twenty-first century, there were an estimated 31.8 million ethnic Mexicans, 4 million Central Americans, and 1.4 million Dominicans in the United States, with an additional 1.8 million Cuban Americans and 4.6 million Puerto Ricans in the country's mainland.

Latina/os were far more visible in U.S. popular culture as well, with well-known celebrities in film, music, television, and professional sports, especially baseball. On the political front, Latina/os organized massive rallies and campaigns for immigrant rights and refused to give ground to periodic waves of anti-immigrant fervor, while the appointment of the first Latina/o, Sonia Sotomayor, to the U.S. Supreme Court was a legal and cultural milestone.

The increasing presence and visibility of Latina/os in the United States, however, did little to ease the considerable economic and political challenges facing Latina/o communities across the nation. Latina/os continued to experience high rates of poverty, unemployment, and incarceration in the early twenty-first century as well as low percentages of high school graduation and economic mobility. Anti-immigrant attacks, moreover, continued to target the Latina/o, especially the Mexican, community. These attacks frequently sought to humiliate and punish severely the most vulnerable individuals and families, who were often sentenced to detention and deportation. Latina/os thus entered the twenty-first century with both great hope and promise and a significant set of persistent challenges.

The Latina/o population continued to grow rapidly in the first decade of the twenty-first century. The total percentage of Latina/os in the United States went from 12 percent to 16 percent. There were nearly as many Latina/os in the United States in 2010 as there were, combined, African Americans (38 million) and Asian Americans (14 million). The rate of Latina/o population growth (44%) was matched only by the percentage increase of the Asian American population (also 44%). By contrast, Anglo and African American populations grew far more slowly, at 1 percent and 12 percent change, respectively. The significant majority of Latina/os remained Catholic at the turn of the twenty-first century, despite a noticeable rise in the Latina/o evangelical population. One study, from 2003, reported that 70 percent of Latina/os identified as Catholic and 23 percent as Protestant, with a majority of Latina/o Protestants claiming evangelical identity. Another study, from 2001, noted that 57 percent of Latina/os were Catholics, a drop from 66 percent in 1990, but added that the percentage of Pentecostal Latina/os, a major group within Protestant evangelicals, had risen slightly, from 3 percent to 4 percent, during the same period.

Although Latina/o migrants made new homes throughout America, from small towns to sprawling metropolises, cities remained the primary destination and home for Latina/os at the turn of the twenty-first century. By 1990, the Latina/o population of Los Angeles had reached 3.3 million, or approaching 40 percent of the 8.8 million people living in the county. In the broader Los Angeles metropolitan area, another 560,000 Latina/os lived in Orange County and more than 300,000 in Riverside County. Ten years later, there were 4.2 million Latina/os in Los Angeles, or 45 percent of the county's total population, and 875,000 in Orange County and 560,000 in Riverside County. By 2010, nearly half of the population of Los Angeles (48%) was Latina/o, with the considerable majority, 3.5 million of the total of 4.7 million, of ethnic Mexicans. In Orange County, one-third of the county (1 million of the total population of 3 million) was Latina/o in 2010, while there were 995,000 Latina/os in Riverside, accounting for 45 percent of the population.

Los Angeles's diverse Latina/o population included, by the turn of the twenty-first century, a significant indigenous Mexican population. Anthropologist Lourdes Gutiérrez Nájera notes that Mexican migration to the United States in the 1990s contained a new pattern, "that of migration from new regions within México, primarily from southern states like Guerrero, Oaxaca, Veracruz, and Chiapas" (Gutiérrez Nájera 2010, 66). According to Gutiérrez, this new set of migrants has increasingly been of indigenous background. In Los Angeles, one of the most prominent Mexican indigenous groups are Zapotecs from the Mexican state of Oaxaca. In the early twenty-first century, Los Angeles County was the home of between "fifty and

Migrants of indigenous Mexican descent formed significant communities in Los Angeles at the turn of the twenty-first century (Traditional Oaxacan celebration, Los Angeles, California, 2003). (Hector Mata/AFP/Getty Images)

seventy thousand Zapotecs" (Gutiérrez Nájera 2010, 64). In Los Angeles, Zapotec women and men worked as day laborers and in low-paying service jobs. Many women were employed as nannies and in other forms of domestic service.

Other cities with large Latina/o populations were New York City and Houston. In the combined New York and New Jersey metropolitan area, there were 4.3 million Latina/os in 2011. Latina/os represented nearly a quarter of the entire region's total population. Twenty-eight percent of the New York/New Jersey region's Latina/os were Puerto Ricans, over 20 percent Dominicans, and 12 percent Mexicans. More than 2 million Latina/os also lived in Houston, Texas, in 2011, where they constituted 37 percent of the city's total population. The overwhelming majority of Latina/os in Houston were Mexicans, while a smaller, but also significant, percentage was Salvadoran (7%) and Honduran (3%).

Chicago also retained its place as one of the centers of Latina/o life in the late twentieth century, and even came to rival cities like Los Angeles, New York, and Miami as the home of large and varied Latina/o communities. Two of the areas in Chicago with the largest Latina/o populations were the West Town and Pilsen neighborhoods. In West Town, half of the population was Latina/o in 2000 (a drop from 60% a decade earlier due largely to rising rents caused by gentrification) with a Latina/o population that was 50 percent Mexican and one-third Puerto Rican. In Pilsen, the population in 2000 was nearly 90 percent Latina/o and overwhelmingly of Mexican descent. In both neighborhoods, the median household income for Latina/os was less than $30,000.

Latina/os of Mexican ancestry, whether foreign-born or born in the United States, continued to represent the overwhelming majority of the nation's Latina/o population in 2010. The 32 million ethnic Mexicans accounted for nearly two-thirds of the entire Latina/o population. Besides Mexicans, none of the other Latina/o groups topped more than 10 percent of the total Latina/o population. Sixty-five percent of Mexicans in the United States, as of 2011, were born in the United States, while 35 percent were born in Mexico. The more than 11 million Mexican immigrants in the United States represented more than a quarter of all immigrants (40 million) in the country and far outdistanced the second-largest immigrant group, the 2 million Chinese immigrants. Regionally, the largest Mexican population lived in the western U.S. states (52%), and predominantly in California, while about a quarter of the Mexican population lived in Texas. In the early twentieth century, significant Mexican communities also developed in southern states. Between 2000 and 2011, the Latina/o population of South Carolina grew over 150 percent to more than 240,000, while North Carolina experienced a 120 percent growth of its Latina/o population to reach nearly 830,000. The Latina/o populations in Arkansas (123%) and Kentucky (132%) also increased significantly, to 190,000 and 132,000, respectively. In all four cases, Mexicans represented a major share of this rapid growth.

Like the ethnic Mexican communities in the United States, one of the most striking trends in the recent history of Puerto Ricans on the U.S. mainland has been the rapid growth of communities outside traditional population centers. The mainland Puerto Rican population in 2011 was nearly 5 million, with nearly 25 percent, or more than 1 million people, living in the New York area. At the same time, in the 1990s the Puerto Rican population in Florida almost doubled. By the end of the first decade of the twenty-first century, there were more than 800,000 Puerto Ricans in the state, making Florida the home of the second-largest Puerto Rican population in the country, trailing only New York. In 2007, Puerto Ricans in Florida, according to anthropologist Jorge Duany, "owned 42,418 businesses in the state," and in terms of electoral politics, "the Puerto Rican electorate in Florida could influence local, state, and even presidential elections" (Duany 2011, 108).

Latina/o communities in central Florida, especially the Orlando metropolitan region, have experienced one of the fastest growth rates in the nation. In Orange County, Florida, encompassing much of Orlando, the Latina/o population grew from 65,000 in 1990 to more than 260,000 in 2009. Puerto Ricans were the largest group, constituting close to half (122,000) of the Latina/o population. Beyond Orange County, in the broader Orlando region, there were nearly 250,000 Puerto Ricans in 2009 and half a million Latina/os. Puerto Ricans owned more than 6,000 businesses and, according to Duany, had "higher income, occupational, and educational levels" than Puerto Ricans in New York City (Duany 2011, 108). Orlando's Puerto Rican community, in fact, grew faster in the 1990s than any other mainland Puerto Rican community in the United States.

One of the fastest-growing Latina/o immigrant groups at the turn of the twentieth century were Central Americans. According to the 1980 census, there were 331,000 people of Central American descent in the United States. Ten years later, in the 1990 census, that number would grow to more than 1.3 million. The majority of those 1.3 million had been born outside the United States, and well over half had arrived in the United States in the past decade. By 2000, the Central American population had risen to 1.7 million and would more than double in the next decade, to 4 million in 2010.

The largest group of Central American immigrants was from El Salvador. In 1990, more than half of those of Central American descent in the United States were Salvadorans, followed by Guatemalans, Nicaraguans, and Hondurans. Smaller numbers of Central Americans were of Costa Rican, Panamanian and Belizian descent. In 2000, while the number of Guatemalans and Hondurans had increased substantially, Salvadorans were again the largest group. The biggest concentration of Salvadorans lived in Los Angeles, and there were also significant Salvadoran communities in Houston, Dallas, San Francisco, and Washington, D.C.

One of the major reasons that the 1980s saw such a major growth in Central American migration to the United States was political instability in countries like El Salvador and Nicaragua. This political turmoil affected the entire region, convincing a great many to abandon their homelands and seek safety elsewhere, including in the United States. In Nicaragua, the conservative regime of Anastasio Somoza was overthrown in 1979 after 40 years in power, after an uprising by the Nicaraguan people, and the left-leaning Sandinista party took control. In the 1980s, the U.S. government funded a military opposition in Nicaragua, known as the contras, against the Sandinista-led Nicaraguan government. The United States also provided major support for the right-wing military government in El Salvador.

In the 1990s, political instability did not necessarily cease in many Central American countries, and large numbers of Central Americans who had originally planned to stay in the United States only temporarily decided to become permanent residents. In one study of 300 Salvadorans and

Guatemalans in Los Angeles, the individuals were asked when they arrived in the 1980s if they planned to stay in the United States. Half of the individuals said they planned to stay in the United States temporarily and only 14 percent said they planned to remain permanently. By the mid-1990s, half of those same 300 individuals said that they planned to stay permanently in the United States.

Among the Central American newcomers to the United States in the late twentieth century were children who were adopted by American parents. One of the major countries of origin of American adoptees was Guatemala, which was "the largest exporter of children per capita (the fifth largest by nation), with 90 percent of the infants adopted internationally going to the United States" (Briggs 2006, 356). Adoption in Guatemala constituted a major portion of the country's economy, accounting in 2001 for $50 million. Mexico, Brazil, and Argentina were also major sources of adopted children for American families. Like many other Latina/o immigrants, adoptees often hailed from regions with a long history of U.S. involvement and even military intervention. In Guatemala, for instance, the United States had for decades been complicit in human rights abuses in the support of violent political regimes.

The majority of Central American immigrants settled in urban areas, with major concentrations in Los Angeles, Houston, Miami, New York, San Francisco, and Washington, D.C. In 1990, about one-third of all people of Central American descent, nearly 500,000 people, lived in Los Angeles. LA also had the biggest population of Guatemalans, Hondurans, and Costa Ricans. Miami had the second-largest population of Central Americans with 120,000 and boasted a large Nicaraguan community that mixed with the more established Cuban American community. New York was third in Central American population with 110,000, and Washington, D.C., was fourth with 79,000. In San Francisco, the Mission District became a center of the Central American community in California. By the 1990s, Central Americans constituted 35 percent of the Latino population and were the largest Latino group in San Francisco. Salvadorans, as elsewhere, made up the majority of Central Americans in San Francisco.

One of the challenges facing Central Americans in the Bay Area, and which continues to threaten Latina/os throughout the nation, is rapid gentrification. Faced with skyrocketing rents and largely confined to low-wage service jobs, Central Americans struggle to afford to live in newly expensive neighborhoods like the Mission District. Gentrification has also had a major effect on the Central American community in the Washington, D.C., area. Large numbers of Central Americans initially lived in the Mount Pleasant and Adams Morgan areas, but rising rents have led many to move to suburban Virginia and Maryland communities.

Though the rapid growth of the Central American population in the United States drew considerable attention around the turn of the twenty-first century, South American immigrants also arrived in large numbers during the period. In 1990, there were more than 1 million residents of the United States who had been born in South America. In that year, the Colombian-born population was 286,000, and Peru (144,000) and Ecuador (143,000) were the second- and third-largest nationalities, respectively. By 2000, Colombians numbered nearly half a million (470,000), with about a quarter of a million Ecuadorians (260,000) and Peruvians (233,000), and the total population that identified as South American origin in the country was 1.3 million. In the most recent decennial census, that of 2010, the South American population was 2.8 million, with Colombians (908,000), Ecuadorians (565,000), and Peruvians (531,000) once again representing the largest communities.

Like Central and South Americans, Dominican American communities have grown considerably in recent decades. In 1990, 500,000 Dominicans were living as permanent residents in the United States. Of those, over 65 percent lived in the state of New York, and of those, 93 percent lived in New York City. Ten years later, in 2000, according to U.S. census figures, there were more than 750,000 Dominicans in the United States. Other studies place the population even higher, estimating the Dominican population at between 1 million and 1.2 million. In 2000, Dominicans were highly concentrated in the New York and New Jersey metropolitan area (accounting for about two-thirds of the total Dominican population) with important concentrations in the Miami-Ft. Lauderdale area (7.7%) and in Massachusetts (4.1%).

New York City, specifically Washington Heights, was the main destination for Dominican immigrants to the United States. The largest concentration of Dominicans in the United States, in fact, was in the Washington Heights/Inwood area of New York City. During the 1980s, Dominicans accounted for nearly 80 percent of all immigrants to the neighborhood, and by 1990, according to one scholar, "almost one out of every two persons in Washington Heights/Inwood was of Dominican descent" (Hernández 2002, 112).

As in the Puerto Rican community, the disappearance of manufacturing jobs in major East Coast cities in the final decades of the century had a devastating effect on Dominican Americans. Dominicans had the misfortune to arrive in New York during a period of large-scale job loss in areas like manufacturing. Between 1969 and 1985, for example, the city lost more than 450,000 jobs in manufacturing. The garment industry was especially hard hit, but major job loss occurred in other areas such as employment in warehouses and trucking companies. Moreover, hundreds of thousands of jobs were lost in New York in fields that required fewer than 12 years of education. These losses had an especially damaging effect on recent immigrants like Dominicans who predominantly worked in manufacturing jobs and had lower levels of formal education. In New York, between 1980 and 2000, the percentage of Dominican workers in manufacturing jobs plummeted from nearly 50 percent to just over 10 percent. This rapid decline created, according to one scholar, "economic distress in the city, particularly among Dominican women" (Candelario 2007, 183).

Like Dominicans across New York and across the nation, Dominicans in Washington Heights/Inwood faced daunting economic challenges. Although a significant number of Dominicans had resided in the United States for many years by the end of the twentieth century, prosperity or even financial stability continued to elude a large percentage of the community. In 1990, the Washington Heights/Inwood neighborhood was the third poorest in the borough of Manhattan, with high unemployment rates, high rates of families living in poverty (28%), and disproportionate numbers of births covered by Medicaid (estimated at 70% in 1990 compared to 30–40% in New York City overall). Within the neighborhood, Dominicans had the lowest per capita income, significantly less than Puerto Ricans and more than half as much as African Americans (Hernández 2002, 113). The poverty rate of Dominicans in Washington Heights/Inwood was over 40 percent, also significantly higher than the rate of other groups.

At the same time, Dominicans in New York and elsewhere have shown considerable resilience in the face of such economic hardships. Second-generation Dominicans, those born in the United States, tended to have higher incomes and more education than the first generation of immigrants. One study compared U.S.-born Dominicans with those arriving in the country prior to 1990. The study showed that 91 percent of U.S.-born Dominicans had completed high school, compared to only 47 percent of pre-1990 migrants. The same study showed that 22 percent of U.S. born Dominicans had a college degree, compared to 7 percent of pre-1990 arrivals. U.S.-born Dominicans also had higher median income ($26,000 compared to $20,000) and were nearly twice as likely to work as professionals and managers as pre-1990 arrivals (18% to 10%).

In Dominican New York, small businesses were key institutions in the community, and Dominicans in New York showed considerable success as entrepreneurs and small-business owners. Dominican-owned hair salons, as scholar Ginetta Candelario has demonstrated, were often financially successful and became cornerstones of the community, as did grocery stores, or bodegas, and travel agencies. According to one study, 70 percent of all bodega or small-grocery store owners in New York City were Dominicans. These stores had annual combined sales of $1.8 billion.

Like other Latina/o groups, Dominican Americans maintained deep and sustained ties with their home country. Both those living abroad and those moving back to live in the Dominican Republic were a key factor in the country's economy. In 1984, for instance, Dominican return migrants accounted for 60 percent of home sales in the Dominican Republic. In 1995, moreover, nearly $800 million in remittances were sent to the Dominican Republic from migrants. In 1999, that number was nearly $1.4 billion.

Evidence of this sustained link between Dominican migrants and their home country appears in the migration pattern linking the city of Boston and the small community of Miraflores in the Dominican Republic. In the late 1960s, commercialization of agriculture made it increasingly difficult for those living in Miraflores to make a living by farming, a difficulty that was mirrored in other countries in Latin America. Many villagers from Miraflores moved to the United States and eventually settled in the Boston area. In 1994, 65 percent of the 545 households in Miraflores had relatives in Boston, mainly in and around the Jamaica Plain neighborhood. That year, 60 percent of Miraflores households said they relied for at least some of their monthly income on remittances from those in United States. For 40 percent of those households, remittances accounted for between 75 percent and 100 percent of their income. Other villages and cities in the Dominican Republic have similar relationships with U.S. cities. New arrivals from Tenares, for instance, have largely settled in Lawrence, Massachusetts, while natives of Sabana Iglesias have moved to Queens, New York, and many migrants from Santiago have found new homes in Washington Heights in New York City.

Although Cuban migration to the United States in the last 25 years did not approach the level of Dominican or Central American migration, Cuban Americans remained one of the most politically powerful Latina/o groups in the nation. In the mid-1980s, the two governments signed an agreement whereby the Cuban government would accept nearly 3,000 return migrants with criminal backgrounds who fled to the United States in 1980 during the Mariel era and the United States agreed to permit entry to 20,000 Cubans per year. The establishment, however, of Radio Martí in South Florida, named after the famed Cuban independence leader José Martí and designed to broadcast anti-Castro programming into Cuba, angered the Cuban government and stalled the program for several years.

A more recent flashpoint in the relationship between Cuba, Cuban Americans, and the broader United States occurred in the late 1990s. On Thanksgiving Day 1999, the U.S. Coast Guard rescued two people from a shipwreck off the Florida coast. One of those rescued was six-year-old Elián González, who had been on a small ship with his mother and several others

The controversy over Elián González strained relations between Cuban Americans, and the U.S. and Cuban governments in 2000. (AFP/Getty Images)

who were attempting to flee Cuba by boat to the United States. Elián's mother was 1 of 11 people who died in the shipwreck. According to U.S. immigration policy, Elián was supposed to have been returned to Cuba. The policy stated that those fleeing Cuba who managed to reach U.S. soil could request permission to remain in the United States. Those, like Elián, who did not yet reach U.S. soil, however, were to be returned to Cuba. While Elián's father and grandfather still lived in Cuba and wanted him to return to his home country, relatives in the United States, and many in the broader Cuban American community, pressured the U.S. government to allow Elián to remain in the United States with family members in Miami.

A battle ensued between the United States and Cuba, as well as between family members on both sides of the Florida Straits. Elián's father traveled to Washington, D.C., to make his case to federal officials, while Elián's relatives in Miami argued that his mother had died trying to reach the United States and that Elián should be allowed to live with them. In April 2000, the Immigration and Naturalization Service (INS) raided the house where Elián lived with relatives in Miami and took him to Washington, D.C., to stay with his father while the U.S. courts decided the case. In June 2000, the U.S. Supreme Court ruled that Elián had to be returned to his father. Elián González and his father returned to Havana to live and were given a hero's welcome in Cuba. Although there has been no equivalent of the Mariel boat-lift or the Peter Pan flights in recent years, the controversy surrounding Elián González points to the highly charged relationship that for many Cuban Americans continues to exist between Cuba under Fidel Castro and the United States.

Despite efforts by the U.S. government, most notably the administration of President George W. Bush, to limit contact between the two countries, Cubans in the United States proved persistent in maintaining critical links with the island. Many Cubans, of course, had relatives still living in Cuba (by one count, over 75% of Cubans in Miami had family members in Cuba) and, despite U.S. opposition, exchanges of several forms continued. Improved telecommunication technology in the 1990s and 2000s, for instance, enabled a huge rise in telephone communication between the countries (the number of telephone messages jumped from 11 million in 2000 to more than 59 million in 2008). Family visits similarly drew together Cubans from both nations. The number of Cuban Americans visiting Cuba began to grow in the early 1990s, exceeding 125,000 per year by 2002, and by 2007, a third of Miami's Cuban population had traveled to the island. The number of parcel packages delivered to Cuba has also risen in recent years (there were more than 50,000 parcels delivered per month to Cuba in 2002) as did individual transfers of money (remittances) to family and friends. In the first decades of the twenty-first century, Cubans, as well as Latina/os more broadly, increasingly hoped that the vibrant exchange of ideas, culture, and people that for decades had enriched both countries could once again flourish between Cuba and the United States.

Though Latina/os were not unknown to wider America by the 1980s, the end of the twentieth century commenced a new period of visibility and a wider public presence. This broader view of Latina/os was especially evident in the realm of politics, as groups across the political spectrum seemed newly eager to attract Latina/o voters. Efforts by both the Democratic and Republican parties to draw Latina/o votes accelerated after the 2004 presidential election when incumbent president George W. Bush seemed to amass a significantly higher percentage of Latina/o votes than had previous Republican presidential candidates, including Bush himself four years earlier in 2000. Estimates of the percentage of the Latina/o vote claimed by Republicans varied considerably, often hovering around 40 percent; however, observers across the political spectrum quickly concluded that Latina/os offered a newfound conservative voting bloc, one capable of swinging a generation of elections toward the Republican Party.

Accompanying the increased attention to Latina/o voters was a heightened interest in Latina/o consumers and Latina/o purchasing power. The money spent by U.S. companies advertising to Latina/o communities, for instance, ballooned in the early twenty-first century, rising from $2.3 billion in 2000 to $3.6 billion in 2007. According to another study, the Latina/o consumer market exceeded $850 million by 2007. "The growing realization that Latinos buy products, that they contribute to the economy, not only as producers but as consumers," according to anthropologist Arlene Dávila, "has been an important political gain" (Dávila 2008, 90). Yet Dávila is careful to note the limits of such gains. Latina/os were consistently portrayed by business marketers and advertisers as recent immigrants and monolingual Spanish speakers with traditional cultures and lifeways, a characterization that drastically oversimplified the country's Latina/o population and masked the severe underrepresentation of Latinas and Latinos among the nation's political and economic leaders.

While many mainstream media outlets vacillated between ignoring the presence of Latina/os entirely and ridiculing or harshly criticizing Latina/os in the United States, Spanish-language radio programming offered public recognition for Latina/os in the form of on-air "shout-outs" and valuable community information as well as reliable entertainment and a break from the tedium of often grueling, backbreaking work. Spanish-language radio, in fact, held a critical place in expanding Latina/o communities in the Southwest. The number of Spanish-language radio stations in the United States grew from fewer than 70 in 1980 to nearly 400 in 1990 and almost 600 in 2000, experiencing a much higher rate of growth than English-language radio programming. According to one report, Latina/os listened to the radio, on average, three more hours a week than their Anglo, English-speaking counterparts.

Latina/o communities across the United States in the late twentieth and early twenty-first centuries achieved some important political and economic gains during the period; however, persistent inequalities remained between Latina/os and the broader nation. The disparities were especially stark in terms of education. As historian Rudolfo Acuña points out, "21 percent of Latina/os between the ages of sixteen and twenty-four dropped out of school in 2000, compared to 7 percent of white students and 12 percent of blacks" (Acuña 2011, 189). The graduation rate of Latina/os (53%) was also well below the national average of 68 percent. Latina/os also consistently faced higher unemployment rates than the broader U.S. population. In 2000, the unemployment rate for Latina/os was 8 percent, or about twice the rate of Anglo Americans. Latina/o employment also tended to be confined in low-wage work and underrepresented in professional work. In 2000, for instance, only 16 percent of Latina/os worked in professional or managerial positions, compared to 34 percent of Anglos and 42 percent of Asian American workers.

Similarly, Latina/o disenfranchisement remained a critical problem. While there were more than 5,000 Latina/o elected officials nationwide in 2005, those representatives remained clustered in predominantly municipal posts and local school boards. At higher, more powerful levels of government, Latina/os were far less common. More troubling was the low level of Latina/o voter participation. Despite significant population gains in the early twenty-first century, less than 40 percent of the Latina/o population was eligible to vote in 2004 (compared to 75% of Anglos and 65% of African Americans). Moreover, a far smaller percentage of Latina/os (18%) actually voted in 2004 in comparison with nearly 40 percent of African Americans and over 50 percent of Anglos

Critiques leveled against Latina/o communities took on many forms at the turn of the twenty-first century. One of the most pointed attacks was that the sexual lives of Latina/os, especially Latina teenagers, was improper and excessive, and put young women at risk of pregnancy and sexually transmitted infections. Scholars and mainstream media alike highlighted both the growth of the Latina/o population and its relative youth, with Latina/os in the first decade of the century accounting for nearly 20 percent of the nation's 16- to 25-year-olds. Commentators also pointed to the comparatively higher teen pregnancy rates among Latinas, despite the overall decline of such rates during the same time period.

Latina/o immigrants, especially immigrants from Mexico, also drew widespread criticism during the period. Anti-immigrant fervor and deep racism toward Latina/os led political leaders to pass additional laws targeting unauthorized immigration, such as the Immigration Act of 1990 and the Illegal Immigration Reform and Immigrant Responsibility Act of 1996. Heightened border enforcement was a main feature of these laws, and both the U.S. Border Patrol and the INS grew rapidly in both size and scope of activity. In mid-1990s California, anti-immigrant attacks generated Proposition 187, which sought to deny public services, including public education for children, to undocumented immigrants in the state. The new law would also have required educators and medical professionals to report to immigration officials those individuals that they discovered to be in the country illegally. Protests against Proposition 187 were widespread, including one march in fall 1994 in Los Angeles of more than 70,000 people.

The same anti-immigrant and anti-Latina/o climate that enabled the passage of Proposition 187 in California led to the launching in October 1994 of Operation Gatekeeper. Operation Gatekeeper was an unprecedented escalation and militarization of federal enforcement of the United States-Mexico boundary. According to one scholar, "Gatekeeper aims at significantly increasing the ability of U.S. authorities to control the flow of unauthorized people and goods across the U.S.-Mexico boundary" (Nevins 2002, 4). In the following years, border enforcement near urban areas like San Diego and Tijuana, Mexico, expanded dramatically, as did funding for the INS. The number of Border Patrol agents grew from 4,200 in 1994 to 9,200 in 2000, and the INS budget doubled from $400 million in 1993 to $800 million in 2000.

Two years after Operation Gatekeeper was instituted, the nation passed legislation imposing harsh penalties on both unauthorized and authorized immigrants. Before 1996, authorized immigrants could lose their residency status and be deported for major felonies like murder and rape. The new laws included many more, smaller offenses that could result in deportation, leading one writer to conclude that, similar to the wider U.S. prison population, "the largest group of deportees are most probably nonviolent drug offenders" (Nevins 2002, 143). The new law sparked operations like the INS raids in Texas in 1998 that led to the deportation of more than 500 immigrants, many of them in the United States legally, for drunken driving convictions. In one especially poignant example, a legal resident of the United States was deported for selling $10 of marijuana and was denied even the right to visit the United States to attend the funeral of his son when the teenager committed suicide two months after his father's deportation.

Latina/os responded in a variety of ways to the challenges facing their communities at the turn of the twenty-first century. Like generations of Latina/os before them, some young Latinos and Latinas found in the U.S. military an opportunity to display their commitment to the nation and their qualities as respectable U.S. citizens, not to mention the chance to afford college and receive training and job skills. As anthropologist Gina Pérez notes, U.S. military recruiters have developed increasingly sophisticated campaigns to attract Latina/o youth to careers in the armed forces. Recruitment officials, according to Pérez, sought to "understand and navigate the transnational, bilingual, and bicultural lives of many Latina/o residents" (Pérez 2010, 170). Exemplifying this trend is the army's "Yo Soy el Army" advertising campaign. When the new "Army of One" slogan was introduced in 2000, officials quickly realized that the phrase did not translate easily into Spanish and thus commissioned a new slogan. The resulting catchphrase, "Yo Soy el Army," captured both the bicultural and bilingual nature of the lives of many young Latinas and Latinos and spoke to the strong personal attachment that significant numbers of Latina/o youth held for the military specifically and the U.S. nation in general.

In the legal realm, Latina/os took an active role in challenging inequities in American immigration laws. This activism is especially notable in laws related to sexuality and immigration. In one precedent-setting case,

Armando Toboso-Alfonso, a gay Cuban man who had been forced by the Cuban government in 1980 (the year of the Mariel boatlift) to either flee the country or face a long prison term, requested asylum in the United States and protection from deportation. Although the original immigration court ruled in Toboso-Alfonso's favor, the INS appealed the ruling, criticizing Toboso-Alfonso for supposedly engaging in "sexually deviant behavior" (Randazzo 2005, 33). In 1991, the appeals court upheld the original judgment, handing a defeat to the INS and preventing Toboso-Alfonso's deportation. Four years later, the case came to serve as a precedent for other cases involving asylum for gay and lesbian refugees.

Another important case was initiated by Marcelo Tenorio, a Brazilian gay man who sought asylum in the United States after being beaten and stabbed in an antigay attack in his home country. In 1993, Tenorio was initially granted asylum in the United States. Once again, the INS appealed the decision, and once again the INS appeal was turned down, permitting Tenorio in 1999 to remain in the country. A third significant case involving immigrants and sexuality was decided in 2000 after Geovanni Hernandez-Montiel asked for asylum "to escape beatings and rape that he suffered at the hands of Mexican police for adopting female dress and mannerisms" (Randazzo 2005, 37). Though initially denied asylum in the United States by the Board of Immigration Appeals, Hernandez-Montiel appealed the decision and the U.S. Ninth Circuit Court of Appeals eventually ruled in his favor.

Latina/os filing asylum claims related to sexuality joined a broader array of Latin American immigrants seeking asylum in the United States in the late twentieth century. According to Lionel Cantú, "during the late 1980s and 1990s, Latin Americans filed the majority of asylum petitions" (Cantú 2005, 63). Central Americans were especially prominent among asylum seekers, accounting for more than half of all applications in the decade between 1986 and 1996. In more recent years, the number of applicants from Mexico has risen, as have applications from South America. Between 2000 and 2001, for instance, Mexican asylum seekers doubled in number, jumping from 3,900 to 9,100, constituting the largest single group from any country in that year.

In terms of education, as in previous generations, Latina/o students across the country took the lead in challenging educational inequities. At the college and university level, Latina/o students repeatedly called upon their institutions to establish Latina/o Studies programs and to follow through on commitments to diversity and multiculturalism. From hunger strikes in Minnesota, Colorado, and Massachusetts to the occupation of administration offices and mass demonstrations in Los Angeles and the Bay Area to lawsuits in Texas and California, activists adopted a range of strategies in confronting institutional neglect and ignorance. At times, as in Fullerton,

California, in the early 1990s, college students allied with high school students in joint protests. After police fired pepper spray on students calling for a celebration of Mexican Independence Day at Fullerton Community College in Los Angeles, nearly 300 students at several nearby high schools staged demonstrations of support and called for more inclusive curriculum at their own schools.

Latinas played pivotal roles in many of these organizing efforts. The persistence of poverty and neglect by political leaders in Los Angeles, for instance, drew Mexican women once again into community organization and activism. In 1984, the group Mothers of East Los Angeles formed to protest the construction of a prison in their neighborhood in East LA. Mothers of East Los Angeles gathered support from community members as well as local politicians. One Chicana state assemblywoman noted that "the new prison would be built 'within a four mile radius' of four correctional facilities and 'within two miles of twenty-six schools' " (Ruiz 1998, 143). Through large rallies (one protest attracted some 3,000 demonstrators) and lobbying pressure directed toward elected officials, the group managed to stop construction of the prison. Mothers of East Los Angeles also focused on a range of environmental justice issues, including plans to construct an incinerator in East LA, graffiti cleanup, and raising financial aid support for college-bound local youth.

In rural areas, Mexicanas staged similar protests, battling against the placement of an incinerator near their homes in a small town in California's Central Valley and forming the group Mujeres Mexicanas in the Coachella Valley, a farming region east of Los Angeles. Mujeres Mexicanas engaged in traditional electoral politics, conducting voter registration drives and supporting candidates for local offices, as well as starting AIDS education and outreach programs.

The turn of the twenty-first century was a period of profound transformation in the history of Latina/os in the United States. The rapid expansion of the Latina/o population (from 35 million in 2000 to 50 million in 2010, and from 12% of the nation's population to 16%) was the most dramatic change and was accompanied by a newfound visibility in popular culture and politics. Despite the persistence of high levels of poverty, unemployment, and rates of incarceration, Latina/os managed to maintain thriving communities throughout the nation.

The establishment and maintenance of new communities in what would become, or what is now, the United States is one of the enduring themes in Latina/o history. So too have Latinas continued in recent decades to resist attempts to diminish their status or marginalize their experiences, either within broader U.S. society or within their own Latina/o communities. Shared affinities and coalitions across Latina/o groups have also proved durable in recent decades and have even expanded beyond traditional alliances between, for instance, Puerto Ricans and Cubans in nineteenth-century New York City or Mexicans and Puerto Ricans in the mid-twentieth-century Midwest to include new groups like Dominicans and Central Americans.

Though many of the same challenges continue to face Latina/os in the twenty-first century, Latina/os enter the new era on the brink of making an unprecedented impact on U.S. politics, economy, and culture.

PROFILE: GLORIA ANZALDÚA

In recent decades, few Latinas or Latinos have achieved as widespread scholarly and intellectual influence as Gloria Anzaldúa. Anzaldúa's best-known work, her book *Borderlands/La Frontera: The New Mestiza*, was published in 1987 and has become a classic in the fields of Chicana/o Studies, Queer Studies, Ethnic Studies, and Women's Studies, as has *This Bridge Called My Back: Writing by Radical Women of Color* (1981), which she coedited with another prominent Chicana intellectual, the poet and playwright Cherríe Moraga.

Gloria Anzaldúa was born in South Texas in 1942 and attended segregated schools until she reached high school. As a child, she suffered from the sharp anti-Mexican racism of Texas as well as a lack of family support for her interest in school and her obvious academic talent. Smaller than other children, Anzaldúa was a prodigious reader. She remembered herself as a "eighty pound kid who carried around the complete works of Aristotle" (Quiñonez 2006, 51). The death of her father when she was a teenager forced the family, including the children, to turn to migrant farmwork. Anzaldúa continued working in the fields during both high school and college.

After graduating from Pan American University in Edinburg, Texas, in 1969, Anzaldúa received a master's degree in English from the University of Texas at Austin in 1972. Frustrated that traditional academic departments refused to recognize the validity of Chicana literature, Anzaldúa left Texas and moved to the San Francisco Bay Area in the mid-1970s. Inspired by the vibrant feminist and lesbian intellectual and political life of the Bay Area, Anzaldúa embarked on her remarkable writing career. She was living in Santa Cruz, California, when she wrote *Borderlands/La Frontera*.

In addition to *Borderlands/La Frontera* and *This Bridge Called My Back*, Anzaldúa was an editor of important collections of feminist and queer writings like *Making Face, Making Soul/Haciendo Caras: Creative and Critical Perspectives by Feminists of Color* (1990) and *This Bridge Called Home: Radical Visions for Transformation* (2002). Over her career, Anzaldúa also taught creative writing classes and courses in Chicana studies and feminist studies at various universities. Gloria Anzaldúa suffered from diabetes from an early age and in 2004 died in Santa Cruz at the age of 62.

PROFILE: SONIA SOTOMAYOR

Sonia Sotomayor was born in 1954 in a South Bronx neighborhood of New York City. Like so many other Puerto Ricans, her parents had moved to New York from Puerto Rico in the 1940s. Sotomayor's father died when she was nine years old and she was raised by her single mother, who worked long hours as a nurse, and a devoted grandmother. Diagnosed with diabetes as a girl, Sotomayor was a superb student who managed to excel in her studies while working at after-school jobs to help support her family.

Sotomayor graduated from Princeton University in 1976 and Yale Law School in 1979. At Princeton, she continued to be an excellent student and was involved in Latino student groups, such as Acción Puertorriqueña, which pressured the university administration to create a diverse student body, faculty, and staff (Sotomayor remembers in her memoir that in the mid-1970s, "there was not one Hispanic on the faculty or the administrative staff" [Sotomayor 2013, 147]). At law school, Sotomayor continued to be a standout student and published an essay on mineral and oil rights in Puerto Rico in the prestigious *Yale Law Journal*.

After graduation, Sotomayor began her career as an assistant district attorney in New York City and joined the board of the Puerto Rican Legal Defense and Education Fund, which battled against discrimination in voting rights, education, and employment. She became a U.S. district court judge in 1992 and a U.S. Court of Appeals judge in 1998. She was nominated to be on the U.S. Supreme Court in May 2009 by President Barack Obama. On August 8, 2009, Sonia Sotomayor became the first Latina/o to serve on the U.S. Supreme Court.

PROFILE: JUNOT DÍAZ

A highly acclaimed author and professor of writing, Junot Díaz was born in the Dominican Republic in 1968. His father migrated to New Jersey when he was a young child, and in 1975, the rest of the family moved to New Jersey. Díaz graduated from high school in New Jersey and received a bachelor's degree from Rutgers University. He earned a master of fine arts degree from Cornell University and taught writing at Syracuse University in the 1990s. In 1996, Díaz published *Drown*, a short story collection that was widely praised and has been translated into 12 languages. In 2000, he became a professor of writing at the Massachusetts Institute of Technology.

In 2008, Díaz received the Pulitzer Prize for his novel *The Brief Wondrous Life of Oscar Wao*. In addition to his characteristic virtuosity in blending Spanish and English, Díaz offers a biting critique of Rafael Trujillo's presidency of the Dominican Republic and wonderfully mixes science fiction (the favorite genre of the main character, Oscar Wao) with rich and moving accounts of Dominican immigrant life. In 2012, Díaz published another collection of short stories, *This Is How You Lose Her*, and was also awarded the prestigious MacArthur Fellowship.

REFERENCES

Acuña, Rodolfo F. *The Making of Chicana/o Studies: In the Trenches of Academe.* New Brunswick, NJ: Rutgers University Press, 2011.

Briggs, Laura. "Making 'American' Families: Transnational Adoption and U.S. Latin American Policy." In *Haunted by Empire: Geographies of Intimacy in North American History*, edited by Ann Laura Stoler, 344–65. Durham, NC: Duke University Press, 2006.

Candelario, Ginetta E. B. *Black Behind the Ears: Dominican Racial Identity from Museums to Beauty Shops.* Durham, NC: Duke University Press, 2007.

Cantú, Lionel, Jr. (with Eithne Luibhéid and Alexandra Minna Stern). "Well-Founded Fear: Political Asylum and the Boundaries of Sexual Identity in the U.S.-Mexico Borderlands." In *Queer Migrations: Sexuality, U.S. Citizenship, and Border Crossings*, edited by Eithne Luibhéid and Lionel Cantú Jr., 61–74. Minneapolis: University of Minnesota Press, 2005.

Dávila, Arlene. *Latino Spin: Public Image and the Whitewashing of Race.* New York: New York University Press, 2008.

Duany, Jorge. *Blurred Borders: Transnational Migration between the Hispanic Caribbean and the United States.* Chapel Hill: University of North Carolina Press, 2011.

Gutiérrez Nájera, Lourdes. "Hayandose: Zapotec Migrant Expressions of Membership and Belonging." In *Beyond El Barrio: Everyday Life in Latina/o America*, edited by Gina M. Pérez, Frank A. Gurdy, and Adrian Burgos Jr., 63–80. New York: New York University Press, 2010.

Hernández, Ramona. *The Mobility of Workers under Advanced Capitalism: Dominican Migration to the United States.* New York: Columbia University Press, 2002.

Nevins, Joseph. *Operation Gatekeeper: The Rise of the "Illegal Alien" and the Making of the U.S. Mexico Boundary.* New York: Routledge, 2002.

Pérez, Gina M. "Hispanic Value, Military Values: Gender, Culture, and the Militarization of Latina/o Youth." In *Beyond El Barrio: Everyday Life in Latina/o America*, edited by Gina M. Pérez, Frank A. Gurdy, and Adrian Burgos Jr., 168–88. New York: New York University Press, 2010.

Quiñonez, Naomi H. "Gloria Anzaldúa." *In Latinas in the United States: A Historical Encyclopedia*, edited by Vicki L. Ruiz and Virginia Sánchez-Korrol, 51–52. Bloomington: Indiana University Press, 2006.

Randazzo, Timothy J. "Social and Legal Barriers: Sexual Orientation and Asylum in the United States." In *Queer Migrations: Sexuality, U.S. Citizenship, and Border Crossings*, edited by Eithne Luibhéid and Lionel Cantú Jr., 30–60. Minneapolis: University of Minnesota Press, 2005.

Ruiz, Vicki L. *From Out of the Shadows: Mexican Women in Twentieth-Century America.* New York: Oxford University Press, 1998.

Sotomayor, Sonia. *My Beloved World.* New York: Knopf Doubleday Publishing Group, 2013.

Bibliography

Acuña, Rodolfo F. *The Making of Chicana/o Studies: In the Trenches of Academe.* New Brunswick, NJ: Rutgers University Press, 2011.

Alamillo, José M. *Making Lemonade Out of Lemons: Mexican American Labor and Leisure in a California Town 1880–1960.* Champaign: University of Illinois Press, 2006.

Almaguer, Tomás. *Racial Fault Lines: The Historical Origins of White Supremacy in California.* Berkeley: University of California Press, 1994.

Anzaldúa, Gloria. *Borderlands/La Frontera: The New Mestiza.* San Francisco: Spinsters/Aunt Lute, 1987.

Aparicio, Ana. "Translocal Barrio Politics: Dominican American Organizing in New York City." In *Beyond El Barrio: Everyday Life in Latina/o America*, edited by Gina M. Pérez, Frank A. Gurdy, and Adrian Burgos Jr., 253–71. New York: New York University Press, 2010.

Aparicio, Frances R. *Listening to Salsa: Gender, Latin Popular Music, and Puerto Rican Cultures.* Middletown, CT: Wesleyan University, 1998.

Arredondo, Gabriela F. *Mexican Chicago: Race Identity and Nation, 1916–39.* Champaign: University of Illinois Press, 2008.

Barr, Juliana. *Peace Came in the Form of a Woman: Indians and Spaniards in the Texas Borderlands.* Chapel Hill: University of North Carolina Press, 2007.

Benton-Cohen, Katherine. *Borderline Americans: Racial Division and Labor War in the Arizona Borderlands.* Cambridge, MA: Harvard University Press, 2009.

Blackhawk, Ned. *Violence over the Land: Indians and Empires in the Early American West.* Cambridge, MA: Harvard University Press, 2006.

Briggs, Laura. "Making 'American' Families: Transnational Adoption and U.S. Latin American Policy." In *Haunted by Empire: Geographies of Intimacy in North American History*, edited by Ann Laura Stoler, 344–65. Durham, NC: Duke University Press, 2006.

Briggs, Laura. 2002. *Reproducing Empire: Race, Sex, Science, and U.S. Imperialism in Puerto Rico.* Berkeley: University of California Press.

Brooks, James. *Captives and Cousins: Slavery, Kinship, and Community in the Southwest Borderlands*. Chapel Hill: University of North Carolina Press, 2002.

Burgos, Adrian, Jr. *Playing America's Game: Baseball, Latinos, and the Color Line*. Berkeley: University of California Press, 2007.

Candelario, Ginetta E. B. *Black Behind the Ears: Dominican Racial Identity from Museums to Beauty Shops*. Durham, NC: Duke University Press, 2007.

Cantú, Lionel, Jr. (with Eithne Luibhéid and Alexandra Minna Stern). "Well-Founded Fear: Political Asylum and the Boundaries of Sexual Identity in the U.S. Mexico Borderlands." In *Queer Migrations: Sexuality, U.S. Citizenship, and Border Crossings*, edited by Eithne Luibhéid and Lionel Cantú Jr., 61–74. Minneapolis: University of Minnesota Press, 2005.

Carroll, Mark M. *Homesteads Ungovernable: Families, Sex, Race, and the Law in Frontier Texas, 1823–1860*. Austin: University of Texas Press, 2001.

Casas, María Raquel. *Married to a Daughter of the Land: Spanish-Mexican Women and Interethnic Marriage in California, 1820–80*. Reno: University of Nevada Press, 2007.

Casas, María Raquel. "Victoria Reid and the Politics of Identity." In *Latina Legacies: Identity, Biography, and Community*, edited by Vicki L. Ruiz and Virginia Sánchez-Korrol, 19–38. New York: Oxford University Press, 2005.

Castañeda, Antonia. "Sexual Violence in the Politics and Policies of Conquest: Amerindian Women and the Spanish Conquest of Alta California." In *Building with Our Hands: New Directions in Chicana Studies*, edited by Adela de le Torre and Beatriz Pesquera, 15–33. Berkeley: University of California Press, 1993.

Chávez, Ernesto. *Mi Raza Primero!: Nationalism, Identity, and Insurgency in the Chicano Movement in Los Angeles, 1966–1978*. Berkeley: University of California Press, 2002.

Chávez-García, Miroslava. *Negotiating Conquest: Gender and Power in California, 1770s to 1880s*. Tucson: University of Arizona Press, 2004.

Chávez-García, Miroslava. *States of Delinquency: Race and Science in the Making of California's Juvenile Justice System*. Berkeley: University of California Press, 2012.

Cohen, Deborah. *Braceros: Migrant Citizens and Transnational Subjects in the Postwar United States and Mexico*. Chapel Hill: University of North Carolina Press, 2011.

Cordova, Cary. "The Mission in Nicaragua: San Francisco Poets Go to War." In *Beyond El Barrio: Everyday Life in Latina/o America*, edited by Gina M. Pérez, Frank A. Gurdy, and Adrian Burgos Jr., 211–32. New York: New York University Press, 2010.

Dávila, Arlene. *Latino Spin: Public Image and the Whitewashing of Race*. New York: New York University Press, 2008.

de la Teja, Jesús F., ed. *Tejano Leadership in Mexican and Revolutionary Texas*. College Station: Texas A&M University Press, 2010.

De Leon, Arnoldo. *The Tejano Community, 1836–1900*. Albuquerque: University of New Mexico Press, 1982.

Delgado, Linda C. "Jesús Colón and the Making of a New York City Community, 1917 to 1974." In *The Puerto Rican Diaspora: Historical Perspectives*, edited by Carmen Teresa Whalen and Víctor Vázquez Hernández, 68–87. Philadelphia: Temple University Press, 2005.

Deutsch, Sarah. *No Separate Refuge: Culture, Class, and Gender on an Anglo-Hispanic Frontier in the American Southwest, 1880–1940*. New York: Oxford University Press, 1987.

Duany, Jorge. *Blurred Borders: Transnational Migration between the Hispanic Caribbean and the United States*. Chapel Hill: University of North Carolina Press, 2011.

Estrada, William David. *The Los Angeles Plaza: Sacred and Contested Space*. Austin: University of Texas Press, 2008.

Fernández, Lilia. *Brown in the Windy City: Mexicans and Puerto Ricans in Postwar Chicago*. Chicago: University of Chicago Press, 2012.

Fernández, Lilia. "Of Immigrants and Migrants: Mexican and Puerto Rican Labor Migration in Comparative Perspective, 1942–1964." *Journal of American Ethnic History* 29, no. 3 (Spring 2010): 6–39.

Findlay, Eileen Suárez. *Imposing Decency: The Politics of Sexuality and Race in Puerto Rico, 1870–1920*. Durham, NC: Duke University Press, 1999.

Firmat, Gustavo Pérez. *Life on the Hyphen: The Cuban-American Way*. Austin: University of Texas Press, 1994.

Flores, Lisa Pierce. *The History of Puerto Rico*. Santa Barbara, CA: Greenwood Press, 2010.

Foley, Neil. *The White Scourge: Mexicans, Blacks, and Poor Whites in Texas Cotton Culture*. Berkeley: University of California Press, 1997.

Fregoso, Rosa Linda. *MeXicana Encounters: The Making of Social Identities on the Borderlands*. Berkeley: University of California Press, 2003.

García, Ignacio M. *White but Not Equal: Mexican Americans, Jury Discrimination, and the Supreme Court*. Tucson: University of Arizona Press, 2008.

Garcia, Lorena. *Respect Yourself, Protect Yourself: Latina Girls and Sexual Identity*. New York: New York University Press, 2012.

García, María Cristina. "Exiles, Immigrants, and Transnationals: The Cuban Communities in the United States." In *The Columbia History of Latinos in the United States since 1960*, edited by David G. Gutiérrez, 146–86 New York: Columbia University Press, 2004.

García, María Cristina. Havana USA: *Cuban Exiles and Cuban Americans in South Florida, 1959–1994*. Berkeley: University of California Press, 1996.

García, Mario T. *Católicos: Resistance and Affirmation in Chicano Catholic History*. Austin: University of Texas Press, 2012.

Glasser, Ruth. "From 'Richport' to Bridgeport: Puerto Ricans in Connecticut." In *The Puerto Rican Diaspora: Historical Perspectives*, edited by Carmen Teresa Whalen and Víctor Vázquez Hernández, 174–99. Philadelphia: Temple University Press, 2005.

Glasser, Ruth. *My Music Is My Flag: Puerto Rican Musicians and Their New York Communities 1917–1940*. Berkeley: University of California Press, 1995.

Gómez-Quiñones, Juan. 1994. *Roots of Chicano Politics, 1600–1940*. Albuquerque: University of New Mexico Press.

Gonzales, Manuel G. *Mexicanos: A History of Mexicans in the United States*. Bloomington: Indiana University Press, 2009.

González, Deena J. *Refusing the Favor: The Spanish-Mexican Women of Santa Fe 1820–1880*. New York: Oxford University Press, 1999.

Gonzalez, Gilbert G. *Guest Workers or Colonized Labor?: Mexican Labor Migration to the United States*. Boulder, CO: Paradigm, 2013.

Gonzalez, Juan. *Harvest of Empire: A History of Latinos in America*. New York: Viking, 2000.

González, Lisa Sánchez. "Pura Bélpre: The Children's Ambassador." In *Latina Legacies: Identity, Biography, and Community, edited by* Vicki L. Ruiz and Virginia Sánchez-Korrol, 148–57. New York: Oxford University Press, 2005.

Greenberg, Amy. *A Wicked War: Polk, Clay, Lincoln, and the 1846 U.S. Invasion of Mexico*. New York: Knopf, 2012.

Gruesz, Kirsten Silva. *Ambassadors of Culture: The Transamerican Origins of Latino Writing*. Princeton, NJ: Princeton University Press, 2002.

Guerin-Gonzales, Camille. *Mexican Workers and American Dreams: Immigration, Repatriation, and California Farm Labor, 1900–1939*. New Brunswick, NJ: Rutgers University Press, 1994.

Guridy, Frank Andre. *Forging Diaspora: Afro-Cubans and African Americans in a World of Empire and Jim Crow*. Chapel Hill: University of North Carolina Press, 2010.

Gutiérrez, David G., ed. *The Columbia History of Latinos in the United States since 1960*. New York: Columbia University Press, 2004.

Gutiérrez, David G. "Globalization, Labor Migration, and the Demographic Revolution: Ethnic Mexicans in the Late Twentieth Century." In *The Columbia History of Latinos in the United States since 1960*, edited by David G. Gutiérrez, 43–86. New York: Columbia University Press, 2004.

Gutiérrez, David G. *Walls and Mirrors: Mexican Americans, Mexican Immigrants, and the Politics of Ethnicity*. Berkeley: University of California Press, 1995.

Gutiérrez, Elena R. *Fertile Matters: The Politics of Mexican-Origin Women's Reproduction*. Austin: University of Texas Press, 2008.

Gutiérrez, Rámon A. *When Jesus Came, the Corn Mothers Went Away: Marriage, Sexuality, and Power in New Mexico, 1500–1846*. Stanford, CA: Stanford University Press, 1991.

Gutiérrez, Ramón A., Genaro M. Padilla, and María Herrera-Sobek, eds. *Recovering the U.S. Hispanic Literary Heritage*. Vol. 3. Houston, TX: Arte Público Press, 1993.

Gutiérrez Nájera, Lourdes. "Hayandose: Zapotec Migrant Expressions of Membership and Belonging." In *Beyond El Barrio: Everyday Life in Latina/o America*, edited by Gina M. Pérez, Frank A. Gurdy, and Adrian Burgos Jr., 63–80. New York: New York University Press, 2010.

Harrington, George F. "The Virginians in Texas." *Harper's New Monthly Magazine* 34, no. 203 (April 1867): 621–33.

Heidenreich, Linda. *This Land Was Mexican Once: Histories of Resistance from Northern California*. Austin: University of Texas Press, 2007.

Hernández, Kelly Lytle. *Migra!: A History of the U.S. Border Patrol*. Berkeley: University of California Press, 2010.

Hernández, Ramona. *The Mobility of Workers under Advanced Capitalism: Dominican Migration to the United States*. New York: Columbia University Press, 2002.

Hewitt, Nancy A. "Luisa Capetillo: Feminist of the Working Class." In *Latina Legacies: Identity, Biography, and Community*, edited by Vicki L. Ruiz and Virginia Sánchez-Korrol, 120–34. New York: Oxford University Press, 2005.

Hoffnung-Garskof, Jesse. *A Tale of Two Cities: Santo Domingo and New York after 1950*. Princeton, NJ: Princeton University Press, 2008.

Hoganson, Kristin L. *Fighting for American Manhood: How Gender Politics Provoked the Spanish-American and Philippine-American Wars*. New Haven, CT: Yale University Press, 2000.

Ibor, Jorge, and Arnoldo De León. *Hispanics in the American West*. Santa Barbara, CA: ABC-CLIO, 2006.

Jacoby, Karl. *Shadows at Dawn: A Borderlands Massacre and the Violence of History*. New York: Penguin Press, 2008.

Kanellos, Nicolás. *Hispanic Periodicals in the United States: A Brief History and Comprehensive Bibliography*. Houston, TX: Arte Público Press, 2000.

Kanellos, Nicolás. "José Alvarez de Toledo y Dubois and the Origins of Hispanic Publishing in the Early American Republic." *Early American Literature* 43, no. 1 (2008): 83–100.

Lavrin, Asunción. "La Malinche (Malinalli Tenepal)." In *Latinas in the United States: A Historical Encyclopedia*, edited by Vicki L. Ruiz and Virginia Sánchez-Korrol, 364–66. Bloomington: Indiana University Press, 2006.

Lazo, Rodrigo. *Writing to Cuba: Filibustering and Cuban Exiles in the United States*. Chapel Hill: University of North Carolina Press, 2005.

Levitt, Peggy. "Transnational Ties and Incorporation: The Case of Dominicans in the United States." In *The Columbia History of Latinos in the United States since 1960*, edited by David G. Gutiérrez, 229–56. New York: Columbia University Press, 2004.

Limón, José Eduardo. *Dancing with the Devil: Society and Cultural Poetics in Mexican-American South Texas*. Madison: University of Wisconsin Press, 1994.

López, Ian Haney. *White by Law: The Legal Construction of Race*. New York: New York University Press, 1996.

Loza, Steven. *Tito Puente and the Making of Latin Music*. Champaign: University of Illinois Press, 1995.

Luibhéid, Eithne. *Entry Denied: Policing Sexuality at the Border*. Minneapolis: University of Minnesota Press, 2002.

Luibhéid, Eithne, and Lionel Cantú Jr., eds. 2005. *Queer Migrations: Sexuality, U.S. Citizenship, and Border Crossings*. Minneapolis: University of Minnesota Press, 2005.

Massey, Douglas S., Jorge Durand, and Nolan J. Malone. *Beyond Smoke and Mirrors: Mexican Immigration in an Era of Economic Integration.* New York: Russell Sage Foundation, 2002.

Matos-Rodríguez, Félix V. *Women and Urban Life in Nineteenth-Century San Juan, Puerto Rico.* Gainesville: University Press of Florida, 1999.

Matos-Rodríguez, Félix V., and Linda C. Delgado, eds. *Puerto Rican Women's History.* New York: M. E. Sharpe, 1998.

McKiernan González, John. *Fevered Measures: Public Health and Race at the Texas-Mexico Border, 1848–1942.* Durham, NC: Duke University Press, 2012.

Menchaca, Martha. *The Mexican Outsiders: A Community History of Marginalization and Discrimination in California.* Austin: University of Texas Press, 1995.

Menchaca, Martha. *Recovering History, Constructing Race: The Indian, Black, and White Roots of Mexican Americans.* Austin: University of Texas Press, 2001.

Mitchell, Pablo R. *West of Sex: Making Mexican America, 1900–1930.* Chicago: University of Chicago Press, 2012.

Molina, Natalia. *Fit to Be Citizens?: Public Health and Race in Los Angeles, 1879–1939.* Berkeley: University of California Press, 2006.

Montejano, David. *Anglos and Mexicans in the Making of Texas, 1836–1986.* Austin: University of Texas Press, 1987.

Montoya, María E. *Lost in Translation: The Maxwell Land Grant and the Conflict over Land in the American West, 1840–1900.* Berkeley: University of California Press, 2002.

Mora, Anthony. *Border Dilemmas: Racial and National Uncertainties in New Mexico, 1848–1912.* Durham, NC: Duke University Press, 2011.

Navia, Juan M. *An Apostle for the Immigrants: The Exile Years of Father Félix Varela y Morales, 1823–1853.* Salisbury, MD: Factor Press, 2002.

Nevins, Joseph. *Operation Gatekeeper: The Rise of the "Illegal Alien" and the Making of the U.S. Mexico Boundary.* New York: Routledge Press, 2002.

Nieto-Phillips, John M. *The Language of Blood: The Making of Spanish American Identity in New Mexico, 1880s–1930s.* Albuquerque: University of New Mexico Press, 2004.

Nostrand, Richard L. *The Hispano Homeland.* Norman: University of Oklahoma Press, 1992.

Nostrand, Richard L. "Mexican Americans Circa 1950." *Annals of the Association of American Geographers* (September 1975): 378–90.

Oboler, Suzanne. *Ethnic Labels, Latino Lives: Identity and the Politics of (Re)Presentation in the United States.* Minneapolis: University of Minnesota Press, 1995.

Oboler, Suzanne, and Deena J. González, eds. *The Oxford Encyclopedia of Latinos and Latinas in the United States.* New York: Oxford University Press, 2005.

O'Neil, Brian. "Carmen Miranda: The High Price of Fame and Bananas." In *Latina Legacies: Identity, Biography, and Community,* edited by Vicki L. Ruiz and Virginia Sánchez-Korrol, 193–208. New York: Oxford University Press, 2005.

Oropeza, Lorena. *Raza Sí!, Guerra No!: Chicano Protest and Patriotism during the Viet Nam War Era*. Berkeley: University of California Press, 2005.

Orozco, Cynthia E. *No Mexicans, Women, or Dogs Allowed: The Rise of the Mexican American Civil Rights Movement*. Austin: University of Texas Press, 2009.

Padilla, Genaro M. *My History, Not Yours: The Formation of Mexican American Autobiography*. Madison: University of Wisconsin Press, 1993.

Pascoe, Peggy. *What Comes Naturally: Miscegenation Law and the Making of Race in America*. New York: Oxford University Press, 2009.

Peña, Susana. *Oye Loca: From the Mariel Boatlift to Gay Cuban Miami*. Minneapolis: University of Minnesota Press, 2013.

Peña, Susana. "Visibility and Silence: Mariel and Cuban American Gay Male Experience and Representation." In *Queer Migrations: Sexuality, U.S. Citizenship, and Border Crossings*, edited by Eithne Luibhéid and Lionel Cantú Jr., 125–45. Minneapolis: University of Minnesota Press, 2005.

Perales, Monica. *Smeltertown: Making and Remembering a Southwest Border Community*. Chapel Hill: University of North Carolina Press, 2010.

Pérez, Emma. *The Decolonial Imaginary: Writing Chicanas into History*. Bloomington: Indiana University Press, 1999.

Pérez, Gina M. "Hispanic Value, Military Values: Gender, Culture, and the Militarization of Latina/o Youth." In *Beyond El Barrio: Everyday Life in Latina/o America*, edited by Gina M. Pérez, Frank A. Gurdy, and Adrian Burgos Jr., 168–88. New York: New York University Press, 2010.

Pérez, Gina M. *The Near Northwest Side Story: Migration, Displacement, and Puerto Rican Families*. Berkeley: University of California Press, 2004.

Pérez, Gina M., Frank A. Gurdy, and Adrian Burgos Jr., eds. *Beyond El Barrio: Everyday Life in Latina/o America*. New York: New York University Press, 2010.

Pérez, Louis A., Jr. *Cuba and the United States: Ties of Singular Intimacy*. Athens: University of Georgia Press, 2003.

Pew Research Center Hispanic Trends Project. 2014. http://www.pewhispanic.org/. Accessed February 19, 2014.

Poyo, Gerald E. *"With All, and for the Good of All": The Emergence of Popular Nationalism in the Cuban Communities of the United States, 1848–1898*. Durham, NC: Duke University Press, 1989.

Pubols, Louise. *The Father of All: The de la Guerra Family Power and Patriarchy in Mexican California*. Berkeley: University of California Press, 2010.

Quiñonez, Naomi H. "Gloria Anzaldúa." In *Latinas in the United States: A Historical Encyclopedia*, edited by Vicki L. Ruiz and Virginia Sánchez-Korrol, 51–52. Bloomington: Indiana University Press, 2006.

Ramos, Raúl A. *Beyond the Alamo: Forging Mexican Ethnicity in San Antonio, 1821–1861*. Chapel Hill: University of North Carolina Press, 2008.

Randazzo, Timothy J. "Social and Legal Barriers: Sexual Orientation and Asylum in the United States." In *Queer Migrations: Sexuality, U.S. Citizenship, and Border Crossings*, edited by Eithne Luibhéid and Lionel Cantú Jr., 30–60. Minneapolis: University of Minnesota Press, 2005.

Reid-Vazquez, Michele. *The Year of the Lash: Free People of Color in Cuba and the Nineteenth-Century Atlantic World*. Athens: University of Georgia Press, 2011.

Reséndez, Andrés. *Changing National Identities at the Frontier: Texas and New Mexico, 1800–1850*. Cambridge: Cambridge University Press, 2004.

Reséndez, Andrés. *A Land So Strange: The Epic Journey of Cabeza de Vaca*. New York: Basic Books, 2007.

Reyes, Bárbara O. "Apolinaria Lorenzana." *In Latinas in the United States: A Historical Encyclopedia*, edited by Vicki L. Ruiz and Virginia Sánchez-Korrol, 407–8. Bloomington: Indiana University Press, 2006.

Rivera, Eugenio. "La Colonia de Lorain, Ohio." In *The Puerto Rican Diaspora: Historical Perspectives*, edited by Carmen Teresa Whalen and Víctor Vázquez Hernández, 68–87. Philadelphia: Temple University Press, 2005.

Rodríguez, Clara E. *Changing Race: Latinos, the Census, and the History of Ethnicity in the United States*. New York: New York University Press, 2000.

Roque Ramírez, Horacio. " 'That's My Place!': Negotiating Racial, Sexual, and Gender Politics in San Francisco's Gay Latino Alliance, 1975–1983." *Journal of the History of Sexuality* 12 (2003): 224–58.

Rosales, Arturo F. *Pobre Raza: Violence, Justice, and Mobilization among México Lindo Immigrants, 1900–1936*. Austin: University of Texas Press, 1999.

Ruiz, Vicki L. *Cannery Women, Cannery Lives: Mexican Women, Unionization, and the California Food Processing Industry, 1930–1950*. Albuquerque: University of New Mexico Press, 1987.

Ruiz, Vicki L. *From Out of the Shadows: Mexican Women in Twentieth-Century America*. New York: Oxford University Press, 1998.

Ruiz, Vicki L. "Luisa Moreno and Latina Labor Activism." In *Latina Legacies: Identity, Biography, and Community*, edited by Vicki L. Ruiz and Virginia Sánchez-Korrol, 175–92. New York: Oxford University Press, 2005.

Ruiz, Vicki L., and Virginia Sánchez-Korrol, eds. *Latina Legacies: Identity, Biography, and Community*. New York: Oxford University Press, 2005.

Ruiz, Vicki L., and Virginia Sánchez-Korrol, eds. *Latinas in the United States: A Historical Encyclopedia*. Bloomington: Indiana University Press, 2006.

Sánchez, George J. *Becoming Mexican American: Ethnicity, Culture and Identity in Chicano Los Angeles, 1900–1945*. New York: Oxford University Press, 1993.

Sánchez-Korrol, Virginia. "Antonia Pantoja and the Power of Community Action." In *Latina Legacies: Identity, Biography, and Community*, edited by Vicki L. Ruiz and Virginia Sánchez-Korrol, 209–24. New York: Oxford University Press, 2005.

Sánchez-Korrol, Virginia. *From Colonia to Community: The History of Puerto Ricans in New York City*. Berkeley: University of California Press, 1994.

Santiago-Valles, Kelvin A., and Gladys M. Jiménez-Muñoz. "Social Polarization and Colonized Labor: Puerto Ricans in the United States, 1945–2000." In *The Columbia History of Latinos in the United States since 1960*, edited by David G. Gutiérrez, 87–145. New York: Columbia University Press, 2004.

Schmidt Camacho, Alicia. *Migrant Imaginaries: Latino Cultural Politics in the U.S. Mexico Borderlands*. New York: New York University Press, 2008.

Sheridan, Clare. " 'Another White Race': Mexican Americans and the Paradox of Whiteness in Jury Selection." *Law and History Review* 21, no. 1 (Spring 2003): 109–44.

Skwiot, Christine. *The Purposes of Paradise: U.S. Tourism and Empire in Cuba and Hawai'i*. Philadelphia: University of Pennsylvania Press, 2010.

Sotomayor, Sonia. *My Beloved World*. New York: Knopf Doubleday Publishing Group, 2013.

Spencer, George W. "The Treatment of Fracture of the Clavicle by Incision and Suture." *American Journal of the Medical Sciences* 113, no. 4 (April 1897): 445–54.

Torres-Saillant, Silvio. "Before the Diaspora: Early Dominican Literature in the United States." In *Recovering the U.S. Hispanic Literary Heritage*, Vol. 3, edited by Ramón A. Gutiérrez, Genaro M. Padilla, María Herrera-Sobek, 250–67. Houston, TX: Arte Público Press, 1993.

Valdés, Dionicio Nodin. *Barrios Norteños: St. Paul and Midwestern Mexican Communities in the Twentieth Century*. Austin: University of Texas Press, 2000.

Valerio-Jiménez, Omar S. *River of Hope: Forging Identity and Nation in the Rio Grande Borderlands*. Durham, NC: Duke University Press, 2012.

Vargas, Zaragosa. *Crucible of Struggle: A History of Mexican Americans from the Colonial Period to the Present Era*. New York: Oxford University Press.

Vargas, Zaragosa. *Proletarians of the North: A History of Mexican Industrial Workers in Detroit and the Midwest, 1917–1933*. Berkeley: University of California Press, 1993.

Wagenheim, Olga Jiménez de. *Puerto Rico: An Interpretive History from Pre-Columbian Times to 1900*. Princeton, NJ: Markus Wiener Publisher, 1997.

Weigle, Marta. *Brothers of Light, Brothers of Blood: The Penitentes of the Southwest*. Albuquerque: University of New Mexico Press, 1976.

Whalen, Carmen Teresa. "Colonialism, Citizenship, and the Making of the Puerto Rican Diaspora." In *The Puerto Rican Diaspora: Historical Perspectives*, edited by Carmen Teresa Whalen and Víctor Vázquez Hernández, 1–42. Philadelphia: Temple University Press, 2005.

Whalen, Carmen Teresa. *From Puerto Rico to Philadelphia: Puerto Rican Workers and Postwar Economics*. Philadelphia: Temple University Press, 2001.

Whalen, Carmen Teresa, and Víctor Vázquez Hernández, eds. *The Puerto Rican Diaspora: Historical Perspectives*. Philadelphia: Temple University Press, 2005.

Index

About the Author

Pablo R. Mitchell is professor of History and Comparative American Studies at Oberlin College in Oberlin, Ohio. He is the author of two books, the prize-winning *Coyote Nation: Sexuality, Race, and Conquest in Modernizing New Mexico, 1880–1920* (2005), and *West of Sex: Colonialism and the Making of Mexican America, 1900–1930* (2012). He conducts research and teaches on topics related to Latina/o history, sexuality, mixed heritage, the United States-Mexico borderlands, and the American West. Mitchell holds a doctorate in history from the University of Michigan.